British Politics, Society and the State since the Late Nineteenth Century

MALCOLM SMITH

MACMILLAN

First published 1990

Published by
MACMILLAN EDUCATION LTD
Houndmills, Basingstoke, Hampshire RG21 2XS
and London
Companies and representatives
throughout the world

Edited and typeset by Povey/Edmondson,
Okehampton and Rochdale, England

Printed in Singapore

British Library Cataloguing in Publication Data
Smith, Malcolm
British politics, society and the state since the late nineteenth
century.
1. Great Britain. Politics, history
I. Title
320.941
ISBN 0–333–45572–X (hardcover)
ISBN 0–333–45573–8 (paperback)

For Elaine, who hates politics

CONTENTS

Acknowledgements

I would like to thank all the undergraduates who have sat my course on British political history over the years, for the important feedback they provided while I sorted out my ideas. The staffs of the National Library of Wales, Aberystwyth and St David's University College, Lampeter, have always been courteous and helpful, even when the book I asked them to find for me was staring me in the face.

Martin Polley and Martin Wright deserve special thanks for reading the text in full and for making many useful comments and suggestions. Needless to say, what faults remain in the book are mine, not theirs.

Lampeter,
August 1989   Malcolm Smith

INTRODUCTION

This book is intended as a study of British political responses to the demands generated by a century of almost continuous crisis. The theme of the book is the evolution of concepts of the state to meet the inexorable consequences of economic and social change. Britain has, in fact, negotiated the twentieth century remarkably successfully. Compared with the history of most developed nations in the twentieth century, that of Britain has been comparatively uneventful. There has been nothing like the events that occurred in Russia in 1917, nor what happened in Germany and Italy between the wars, nor even what happened in the United States in the Roosevelt era or during the Vietnam war. How does one account for the fact that Britain has come relatively unscathed, remained comparatively stable, through the experiences of the last one hundred years?

It should be said immediately that the answer to such a question must be a complicated one, and personally I do not believe that one can explain it simply in terms of the 'British national character', the popular notion that 'we do things differently over here'. If the British do things differently, then there must be reasons why that is true. If there *is* a British national character then it is not God's inexplicable gift, it is rather a product of economic, social, cultural and ultimately political forces. An answer to this question in fact has a great deal to do with the process of theoretical adaptation of the notion of the state – what it is, and who it exists to serve – and also with the cultural and political processes that have translated this series of theoretical adaptations into consensual practice. The periodic problems that have occurred have been the results of failures of theoretical adaptation, and the consequent difficulty of negotiating consensus.

1

The whole question of state intervention in the workings of the economy and of the social formation is, of course, a very fashionable issue; the 'Thatcher revolution' amounts to a crusade against what are seen to be the threats to individual liberty which the contemporary Right in Britain believes are endemic to the idea of collectivism in politics. But the subject is not simply of fashionable interest, for the core political debate of the 1970s and 1980s has actually been the central issue in politics for almost one hundred years. Nor is it simply a political issue, for the proponents of the New Right put the case against collectivist intervention in similar moral terms to previous exponents of individualism. The suggestion that the fight for freedom from the state is the major element in the cultural regeneration of British society, the fight back against a decadent and weak-kneed undermining of the roots of Britain's former greatness, simply emphasises the point that politics is not, as the cynics would claim, simply a game; it is a debate about the nature of Britain.

This fundamental point about politics is disguised in periods of consensus, simply because it is in the nature of consensus that no clear alternatives are on view, and for long periods this century Britain has in fact been governed by just such a consensus. During the 1970s and the 1980s, however, consensus broke down and it seems unlikely that, if a new consensus is constructed, it will be along the lines that have dominated British political development this century. The structure of the development of twentieth-century politics, of notions of the nature of Britain, has thus been made more visible. The prime targets of the Thatcher revolution have been the politicians of the 1960s, not only because they are deemed to have taken collectivism to excess but also because those excesses are believed to have been only the most obvious elements in an overall libertarianism which put Britain on the road to ruin. Libertarianism has been opposed to freedom, and connected to the opposition between collectivism and individualism. But state intervention did not begin in the 1960s, nor even with the work of the Labour governments of 1945 to 1951. Though the superstructure of the Welfare State as we now know it is a postwar creation, its roots lay in the years of the Second World War, which in turn depended on the experience and the theorising of the interwar years, of the Great War before that and, finally, on the work of the Liberal governments of 1906 to 1914, which was itself a developing response to the perceived 'crisis of liberalism' of the late nineteenth century. Thatcherism, in other words, confronts not just the 1960s, but a hundred years of British political development.

The development of collectivism, and recent attacks on it, have not, of course, been matters fought out simply at the theoretical level. Ultimately, with the development of the mass vote, it has been a pragmatic issue. Politics has been called the art of the possible, but perhaps it would be nearer the truth to call it the art of the necessary. Politicians simply have to respond to the demands of the voters. The state, after all, is not simply an impersonal collection of institutions which owe their existence and their power to some higher and unquestionable authority. At the same time, the significance of the theoretical debate must not be underestimated, because of the way in which it frames perceptions of problems as they develop. As Margaret Thatcher once said, the most difficult task in politics is to change ideas and a measure of the success of Thatcherism in changing ideas has been the abandonment by the mainstream Left of so many of what seemed to be the central tenets of British socialism. 'Relevance' has been a key word in recent Labour party debates on policy, an attempt to come to terms with the shift in the parameters of political debate which Thatcherism has successfully engineered. Yet, clearly, Thatcherism did not come out of theoretical thin air, any more than did collectivism. New ideas emanate from the problems left behind by the implementation of previous ones. They become dominant because, in certain economic and social conditions, they make sense of the world for more people than they do not. Electors, similarly, do not vote in a theoretical vacuum; they take their choice from the options on offer, which are framed by a compromise between the ideal, the practicable and the popular.

Collectivism and individualism have represented the poles of political thought in twentieth-century Britain and, for most of the time, collectivism has been dominant. The fundamental point at issue in British politics for nearly one hundred years has been the relationship of the individual to society, insofar as it concerns the disposition of property and capital. The question has been, in fact, whether there is a social contract which decrees that property and capital belong to society as a whole and whether, in return for the right to hold property and capital, society has the right to demand that at least a proportion of surplus wealth be used for the good of that section of society most vulnerable to the vagaries of economic change. And if this is to be allowed, how great a proportion should be used, bearing in mind the need not only to retain incentive and to generate economic growth, but also to preserve the social peace? Liberal thought adapted in the late nineteenth century to accept the basis of this social contract, at a time when the mid-Victorian economic boom showed signs of faltering, and when extensions to the franchise were bringing the problems of the poorer sections of the community more fully into the political arena. The Labour party, in turn, was to accept collectivism as an evolutionary approach towards the ultimate aim of creating a socialist state. Continuing economic problems were to ensure the fuller development of collectivism right the way through the first half of the twentieth century. Minor hiccups in this process, such as that which occurred after the Great War, served only to confirm the general rule by provoking the threat of social turbulence. A series of compromise equilibria, grouped around the notion of collectivism, was thus established between the claims of unrestricted capitalism on the one hand, and those of socialism on the other – compromises which effectively controlled the consensual middle ground of politics and which, by the 1950s, seemed virtually unassailable. By the mid-century, indeed, both major parties could claim to have helped in seeing off the class war. Some in the Labour party even claimed that collectivism had actually completed a social revolution by consensus and the Conservatives were equally proud of the fact that Britain had 'never had it so good'.

This book is not supposed to be another general history of Britain. There are already many good studies of that kind, in which the changes that have taken place will be found set out in much greater detail than they are here. Nor is the book supposed to be an attack on the notion of a general history, a suggestion that what is normally set down in a large number of pages can in fact be reduced to a few. The role of a general history is to assimilate and to make available to many the research of a few. The role of a book of this kind is to take one further step back from the detailed research and to look for patterns, the larger shifts and the larger continuities that, when one puts all that research together, can be seen to have shaped recent history. It is an attempt to show, in short, the processes by which we have arrived at current political debates.

Basically, the debates that have been central to the development of twentieth-century British historical research have been threefold and it is these debates which have conditioned the organisation of this book. First, research into the first twenty years of the century has centred around the theme of the changes in the nature of British liberal thought and practice, changes variously ascribed to the development of a new class consciousness which undermined the social unity of the mid to late nineteenth century, to the failure of the Liberal party as prime repository of traditional liberal ideas to adapt to changing economic and social circumstances, to the impact of the Great War, or to some combination of these factors. It is this debate which determined the starting point of this book and the study in the first two chapters of the changes and continuities which characterised British political development from the late nineteenth century to the early 1920s. Second, the impact of the Great Depression of the interwar years has recently gone through a major historical reinterpretation, so much so that it is no longer acceptable to dismiss the period simply as 'the locust years'. The experience of the Depression, coming as it did so rapidly on the heels of the trauma of the Great War, was to have profound effects on British political development, not all of them simply negative. The evidence of consensus in interwar Britain is now as clear as the evidence of major divisions. This change in perception of the interwar years has in turn had a knock-on effect on the third major area of research, that of the significance of the Second World War, once seen as the major reaction to the interwar years that put Britain on the road to the Welfare State, but now just as often seen as only a further evolutionary step down the road to collectivism. It would still be difficult to deny the immense importance of the opportunities provided by the war years, however; it was in the 'People's War' that John Maynard Keynes and William Beveridge finally provided the blueprints that not only formalised what had been happening for the last fifty years, but also set the political agenda for the next forty.

Keynes and Beveridge did not make Britain's problems go away, however; they simply made them easier to live with. No political consensus based on compromise can last forever: in an ever-changing economic and social context, the days of the Keynes–Beveridge axis were always numbered, just as were those of the other compromise equilibria that had preceded it. But Keynes and Beveridge in fact may well have taken Britain to the end of the collectivist road. The options that were left were either to stagnate, to make the decisive move over the clear boundary that still separated collectivism from socialism, or to begin to roll back the tide of interventionism. Ultimately, the divisions between a socialist view of the world and an invididualist one are irreconcilable; collectivism only temporarily papered over the cracks. The whole debate on collectivism, from start to finish, was linked to the question of the social friction likely to result from Britain's relative economic decline. If that decline could be halted, then collectivism could cope with social friction. The Keynesian formula was the most sophisticated piece of economic engineering that collectivism produced, and its failure to stabilise the British economy virtually sealed the fate of collectivism as a whole. In what follows, we may well be dealing with how basic decisions about Britain's future were shelved for over seventy years. Yet, even if that is so, the story is by no means a wholly negative one. The problem of adapting to relative economic decline was always going to be a difficult one and the fact that, for so long, that was achieved with a minimum of social friction is a tribute to the foresight, the nerve and the resilience of three generations of British politicians.

THE CRISIS OF LIBERALISM

THE CONTEXT OF VICTORIAN LIBERALISM

Perhaps because the changes that took place were neither as dramatic nor as well-catalogued as the events of the early nineteenth century or the years between the two world wars, it is too easy to forget that the late nineteenth century was also a period of dramatic economic and social change. In the last quarter of the nineteenth century, for the first time, a British industrial economy which depended overwhelmingly on exports was faced with major competition in international markets. At the same time the huge population growth that had been accelerating throughout the century continued apace, and with it that major change in living style – the development of an overwhelmingly urban population with its changed cultural relationships – was transfiguring the British social landscape. These changes were to encourage a pragmatic political response, an adaptation to the new facts of life as they faced British society entering the twentieth century. In particular, they demanded a change in understanding of the role of the state in an increasingly complicated world, a world in which the political simplicities of an age of virtually unimpeded economic and social progress could no longer apply.

The 'Crisis of liberalism' of the late nineteenth century was not simply a crisis of the Liberal party, though arguably it affected the Liberals more than any other political grouping. The crisis was more than anything else a crisis in ways of thinking about the relationship between nation and state, a crisis which stemmed from the tensions between two streams of Victorian political thought when faced with changing contemporary problems. These two streams may broadly be thought of as the individualist and the collectivist school. Individualist ideology in Britain in the mid- to late-nineteenth century hinged around a particular conception of the term 'freedom'. The fundamental assumption was that the free interplay of individuals on the economic, the social and the political levels was the surest method of producing the greatest happiness of the greatest number. This was the concept which dominated national politics and, although in practice it was as often broken as confirmed, it remained the ideal formulation of the role of the state. As an ideal formulation, it was given added impetus by the intrusion of scientific thought into the political world. Underpinning this dominant political philosophy was an application of Darwin's theory of evolution by natural selection in the biological world to the world of politics and society as well, an application which was deemed to give that political philosophy the accolade of 'natural law'. Herbert Spencer in particular saw natural selection working as a balancing force in society, a law which should not be tampered with, for the results could be as chaotic as any tampering with biological natural law. Thus the ideal of producing the greatest possible sum of individual happiness was squared with the benefit and progress of society as a whole. The competition which would develop from the free interplay of individuals would benefit not only those individuals who were astute enough to benefit personally: society as a whole would also benefit as it evolved to meet changing economic and social conditions. The role of government was primarily to ensure that this natural law applied as far as possible, its fundamental task being to break down the power of institutions and assumptions which might stand in the way of the fullest possible application of free competition.

In economic affairs this principle was enshrined in the ideas of laissez-faire. From the repeal of the Corn Laws in 1846, through Gladstone's Free Trade budgets, to the economic crises of the last twenty years of the century, there was little organised opposition to the idea that the primary aim of government economic policy was to unshackle trade from the leftovers of Protectionism. Laissez-faire would allow, it was assumed, the free interplay of individuals at the economic level, which would both maximise profit for the individual and also create job opportunities for the rest. On an international level, too, it was argued, laissez-faire would ensure the free interplay of nations, breaking down those nationalist frictions that could lead to war; Protectionism and Imperialism, on the other hand, only fostered militarism. In social policy, the individualist conception of freedom largely meant 'self-help'; the prime function of government in this area was to allow self-help to apply by deterring idleness and by encouraging thrift. The New Poor Law of 1834, the backbone of nineteenth-century social policy, provided the workhouse as the ultimate deterrent against workshyness, thus forcing individuals to help themselves. Though the deterrent principle was offset in practice by paternalistic Poor Law Guardians, and although government was prepared to intervene to protect in major areas like public health or industrial safety, the general assumption was that any governmental intrusion in social affairs beyond the strict minimum should be rigidly scrutinised.[1]

The key to the individualist ethic, however, lay in the notion of political freedom. The extension of the franchise, to those who had proved themselves worthy of the right to vote, at least, would point a sword at the heart of Old Corruption. The opening up of the great institutions of state to the full force of competition not just by extensions of the parliamentary franchise, but also by the disestablishment of the Church of England, by the abolition of the system of purchasing commissions in the Army and by the introduction of examinations in recruiting for the Civil Service, would ensure the development of a meritocracy to replace oligarchy as the shaping force of society. It was this conception of individual freedom that was to become indelibly, though somewhat unfairly, associated with the Liberal party. Though the Conservative party as a whole accepted laissez-faire economics and most of the other central tenets of individualism by the late nineteenth century, the fact remained that it was the Liberal party which was seen to have turned this conception of 'liberalism' into nothing less than a crusade. As the mid-Victorian boom turned into the Great Price Fall, individualism began to falter as a relevant doctrine, and the Liberal party also inevitably faltered electorally.

There was also, however, a powerful tradition of collectivism, particularly at the level of local politics, which could just as legitimately be portrayed as the real face of Victorian liberalism. The 1835 Municipal Corporations Act had extended the 1832 parliamentary franchise to many of the old boroughs, some of which soon became the pioneers of an interventionist community politics. Indeed, it could be argued that while central government in the nineteenth century was not on the whole prepared to intervene, it was at least prepared to facilitate intervention by the developing system of local government. The 1848 and 1875 Public Health Acts, or the Artisans' and Labourers' Dwelling Improvement Acts of 1875 and 1879, are examples of the way in which government was frequently pushed by progressive local authorities into enabling legislation, vesting authority for nascent social services in the communities themselves. In the new urban areas, 'municipal socialism' had made significant inroads by the 1880s. In Birmingham, for example, Joseph Chamberlain's Liberal caucus had acquired municipal control over public utilities and had provided hospitals, parks, free libraries and museums. As a more democratic franchise was spread through the whole of local government, so a new breed of Liberal began to emerge from these grass roots. Chamberlain's brand of community politics was taken up by the so-called New Liberals who argued that, in the name of human dignity, laissez-faire would have to be adapted at the national as well as the local level: 'Laissez-faire . . . is not done with as a principle of rational limitation of State interference', wrote J.M. Robertson, a leading New Liberal thinker, 'but it is quite done with as a pretext for leaving uncured deadly social evils which admit of curative treatment by State action'.[2]

Collectivist liberalism owed its ideological development to the work of political philosophers such as T.H. Green and J.A. Hobson, who questioned the classical assumptions of John Stuart Mill on the relationship between individual and state. Green stressed the importance of 'positive freedom' as opposed to the merely 'negative freedom' of individualism, and pointed out that there were circumstances in which only intervention by the state and by local government could ensure the material well-being on which the ultimate realisation of full individual potential depended. Thus, the relationship between the individual and the state should be seen as basically organic rather than antagonistic. In order to intervene in social matters, however, the state needed to raise finance, and this in turn implied that some measure of redistribution of wealth was an inevitable consequence of intervention. The New Liberals, by distinguishing between 'earned' and 'unearned' income, provided the theoretical wherewithal for a differentiated tax system which could finance collectivist interventions at the national as well as the local level. Landed wealth was particularly open to scrutiny, being based – as the New Liberals saw it – on the rent increases resulting from population increases, while the amount of land available for settlement remained finite. Henry George argued that landowners should pay for the privilege of their ownership, and Hobson that the land should become the chief source of community revenue, since the money that lined landowners' pockets was the result not of their exertions but of the fact of population rise; this increase in land values should therefore revert to the community which had in effect created it.

Collectivism was quite clearly opposed to individualism, because it was a system of social engineering. But what bound the two wings of liberal thought together, and what makes it legitimate to describe it as a single rather than a diffuse body of thought in late-nineteenth century Britain, was their mutual antipathy both to revolutionism and to the concept of social class as the determining element in social and political relationships. Founded on the assumption that there existed a community of interest which bound individuals together across economic divides, the New Liberals were careful not only to distance themselves from socialist methods, but also to argue that socialist aims were actually more easily attainable by New Liberal evolutionism than by class warfare. First, however, the New Liberals had to gain control of their own party, and to fight off the challenge from a rather more flexible and adaptable Conservative party. In the interim, a real threat to both parties lay in the emergence of a working-class consciousness which sought its own mode of political expression and, eventually, a thorough reconstruction of society along socialist lines. In the complex interplay of relative economic decline and class development lay the roots of a compromise between the individualist tradition and emerging socialist ideas, a form of collectivism which would demand that the state take an active role as referee and first-aid post, rather than that it should merely observe impartially the workings of the supposedly iron and inexorable natural laws of social and economic change.

THE ECONOMIC SETTING: THE GREAT PRICE FALL

Structural changes taking place in the international and in the British economy in the last quarter of the nineteenth century were to play, in the long term, a crucial role in altering the terms of reference of British politics. The phenomenon known as the Great Price Fall was to prompt the first real challenge to the dominant principles of economic policy. Yet, during the period before 1914, only one significant radical economic idea made any kind of impact on politics – the Tariff Reform campaign which centred around Joseph Chamberlain. In fact, dominant economic thinking was to survive the first evidence of Britain's relative decline as an economic power, and the most important immediate effect of the Great Price Fall on British politics was to be indirect rather than direct, a re-emphasis of the rift along class lines in the social formation.

For most of the Victorian period, Britain's economic expansion seemed to be both effortless and inexorable. As the world's first industrial nation, and with a long tradition and well-developed organisation in international trade, British industrial production had the whole world into which to expand. With the benefit of hindsight, however, it is possible to see that there were four crucial weaknesses in the direction of the British economy. Once these weaknesses began to become apparent, then the class collaboration built upon economic success was likely to come unstuck. First, Britain's economy was abnormally reliant on exports. The Big Four in the industrial economy – textiles, heavy metal production, shipping and coal – all relied overwhelmingly on export markets. This over-reliance on exports meant that the economy as a whole was very susceptible to changing conditions of world trade over which, in the days before international collaboration on trade questions, Britain had no control. Changes in international trade would not only affect the Big Four, however, because other major sectors in the industrial economy – the transport and construction industries in particular – were ultimately reliant on the demand generated by the export industries; a fall-off in demand for Britain's staple exports would therefore create secondary depression in other areas of the economy.

The second problem was the traditionally small scale of British industrial enterprise. The coal industry, for example, was a mass of relatively small firms, competing with each other as well as on the international stage. They operated on relatively low capitalisation and found it difficult to meet the costs of re-tooling to meet any changes in international trading conditions. Over-reliance on exports was compounded by a third problem, the similarly export-oriented outlook of British financial institutions. Britain had an inherent trade gap developing through the second half of the nineteenth century, usually filled by 'invisible exports' – loans, insurance and other allied financial services – centred on the City of London, which became the financial centre of the world. The export of capital had the important secondary function of putting sterling abroad where it could be used to buy British goods. It also meant, however, that British finance was as reliant on world conditions as was the industrial economy. There developed, too, an investment complacency as a result of this large world demand for British finance, a myopia when it came to the need to finance the re-tooling of ageing British industries or 'secondary' industrialisation, in the chemicals industry for example, a major development area in late-nineteenth- and early-twentieth-century trade. The fourth problem was the long-term decline of Britain's agricultural economy. The opening-up of the North American prairies as huge food-producing areas, and of Australian and New Zealand agriculture, combined with new technological processes such as canning and refrigeration to flood the British market with cheap food. It was these developments which allowed Britain's burgeoning urban population to be fed, and fed cheaply, but it also meant that British agriculture's share of the national income was to fall from 33 per cent in 1801 to 29 per cent in 1851, and to a mere 8 per cent by 1901. Four-fifths of Britain's principal foodstuffs were imported by the turn of the century, the result being that Britain literally had to continue developing her exports in order to buy the food to survive.

None of these problems was clear through the Great Victorian Boom, when laissez-faire appeared to produce an ever-expanding trade and an ever more prosperous Britain. The class warfare of the earlier stage of industrialisation disappeared as the monetary benefits of expanding trade filtered down through the social classes; a steadily-improving standard of living proved to be the best recipe for social and political tranquility. From the 1870s through to the 1890s, however, a profound unease among the industrial community was caused by a long-term fall in trade prices. Over the century as a whole, prices had followed a cyclical pattern of peaks and troughs but, after the peak of the early 1870s, the troughs were noticeably more prolonged and the peaks too short-term to compensate. Part of the reason for this price fall was a change in the terms of trade. The voracious demand for coal on the one hand, and the sagging world wheat price on the other – caused by over-production in the Steppes and the prairies – impaired the ability of the primary producing countries to import industrial goods. The terms of trade, however, perceptibly improved after the mid-1880s, while prices continued to remain low for another decade, so that this reason cannot in itself provide a full answer. Monetarists have further explained the Great Price Fall by emphasising the significance of changes in international money supply in this period. The shortage of gold which resulted from the general rush to adopt the Gold Standard – which involved nations linking the supply of money to the amount of gold they held in reserve – meant that the supply of money failed to keep pace with the growth of industrial activity, and prices inevitably fell. Though this may go some way towards explaining why all industrial countries felt the effects of low prices in this period, it does not in itself fully explain why Britain went on feeling these effects for rather longer than many other countries.[3]

More significant in the British case was the development of international competition. The eruption of new industrial economies into world trade, having developed firstly on a sound home demand, had an immediate and telling effect on a nation which had had world trade virtually to itself for so long. By the 1890s Britain had been overtaken in the crucial field of steel production – crucial because Britain relied on exports to sell 80 per cent of her annual production – by both Germany and the United States. Organised into large combines like US Steel and Krupps, using both mass production techniques and hard-sell marketing philosophies, the new industrial economies proved quickly to be extremely powerful. In 1905 the biggest British steel firm was Vickers, with a capitalisation of some £7440 million, whereas the biggest American steel firm, US Steel, had a capitalisation of £282 474 million. There were, in fact, already eight American firms with a bigger capitalisation than the biggest British firm (Imperial Tobacco, at £17 545 million). In the developing fields of engineering and chemicals, moreover, the situation was if anything actually worse. Britain had hardly begun to gear herself to the new industries. In 1913 British universities produced only 9000 undergraduates against Germany's 60 000; Britain was educating only 350 pure and applied scientists per annum against Germany's 3000 graduate engineers alone.[4]

The long-term significance of the development of international competition was to be disguised, however, as prices began to pick up at the turn of the century. This upturn had little to do with a successful response to international competition as such; it had much more to do with the exploitation of the captive market of the Empire and the rearmament boom. In a sense, Britain ducked out of the full implications of meeting international competition head-on, relying instead on the short-term benefits that could be gathered from consolidating Imperial expansion. With the developing military threats, too, Britain found herself with a new area of demand for coal and steel. In these ways, Britain's economic recuperation actually involved a reinforcement of international frictions, taking Britain directly down the road that was to lead to the Great War. The war itself was to create even greater demands for all that British industry could produce. But when the bubble burst in 1918, the consequences of Britain's vulnerability to competition – consequences offset and disguised by the short-term demand of the previous twenty years – were to come to the fore with a vengeance, in the context of a worldwide depression of unprecedented severity and duration. The implications of the structural weaknesses in the British economy were then to occupy the centre stage of British politics until the present day.

THE SOCIAL SETTING: CLASS AND URBANISATION

While the economic historians argue that the Great Price Fall was a consequence of changes in the terms of trade, changes in the money supply, the development of international competition, or a combination of these factors, there was a fourth, contemporary explanation, significant for its effect on the relationship between the social classes. This was the argument that prices were falling because the cost of production, wages in particular, had risen. The development of legal trade unionism was seen by many contemporary industrialists to be a major cause of the deceleration in economic growth. This argument, followed up by a counter-attack by employers against the demands of organised labour, was to be the most important of the indirect ways in which the Great Price Fall was to effect the British social formation and, ultimately, British politics, by challenging one of the most basic assumptions of the class alliance of the mid-century.

In the 1840s, and again in the 1860s, the cartoonist George Cruikshank had captured the essentials of the ideology of the classless society in his famous cartoon, 'The British Beehive'. He pictured the British national family as a product of the interrelationship of craftsman with employer, free trade with freedom of the press and of religion, underpinned by the Bank of England, the Royal Navy, Army and Mercantile Marine, and overseen by the Queen and the British constitution. The dominant ideology of the mid-century pictured the industrial economy as the product of an historic partnership between the capital of the landed aristocracy, the managerial enterprise and expertise of the newly-emerging bourgeoisie, and the skill of the British artisan and craftsman – a cross-class alliance which benefited all its participants, and which was directly opposed to the socialist concept of an essential difference of interests between the landed, the middle and the working classes. It was this central idea of a mutually beneficial class collaboration which underpinned the domination of Victorian politics by the 'classless' ideals of liberalism in general, and by the Liberal party in particular. As the economy began to show signs of faltering in the last quarter of the nineteenth century, however, sustaining this construction of national integration and social interdependence became increasingly problematic.

By the end of the century British society had gone through further dramatic change since Cruikshank's time. In the 1840s, as many still lived on the land as in the towns. By 1911, not only had the population of the country as a whole nearly doubled, but no less than 80 per cent of this much-enlarged population now lived in large towns and cities. Particularly significant had been the development of the great conurbations: Greater London, for example, was already home for three and half million in 1861, but for double that number by 1911. In local government as well as in national politics, the new large towns came to predominate. The 1888 and 1894 Local Government Acts were founded on the assumption that urban Britain was now profoundly different from rural Britain. The problems of the new urban areas, it was also believed, should not be resolved at the expense of the old village communities. The Counties were therefore separated from the County Boroughs, while London was made an administrative County in its own right. The pressures from the urban areas themselves for independence from the deferential world of county politics was such that government was prepared to lower the minimum population of the County Boroughs from 150 000 to 50 000. The 57 original County Boroughs had become 82 by 1925, while the extension of existing county boroughs was also to bite deeply into County political territory.

The second half of the nineteenth century thus saw the consolidation of a separate urban politics. It also saw the development, within that urban society, of separate class cultures. The propagation of the first generation in history to grow up entirely in an industrial/urban environment, cut off from the slow-moving and deferential world of the countryside, produced in its train a series of momentous social consequences. Within the new urban environment, and particularly in the conurban environment, the up-tempo life of a big city and the cash nexus of factory work began to alter substantially assumptions about the national family. In the rural environment the master was always proximate, and the rhythms of the working year mingled almost inextricably with the rhythms of spare time. Not that this had always prevented eruptions of class feeling: the notion that pre-industrial society was a classless idyll was in fact the invention of the industrial age. Rural society was founded upon an implicit under-standing not only of what servant owed to master but also of what master owed to servant. This symbiosis went beyond work-time to cover the whole range of social relationships. Attempts to interfere with the traditional rights and customs of the rural working class – the banning of fairs or of certain bloodsports, for example – could be met with the most fierce resistance.[5] The urban and industrial environment, however, produced a very different relationship between master and servant. Work-time and leisure-time were not so closely interlinked as they were in the archetypal village community. Beyond the ability of the wage-earner to complete the working day efficiently in return for a wage, the employer was not, typically, directly concerned with the life of the labourer. Though there were concerted attempts to police the attitudes and assumptions of the working class as they displayed themselves in leisure activities, the wage-labour system in fact marked a decisive break from the notion of the organic community with a common culture, the disappearance of which was to be mourned so deeply by Victorian nostalgists.

There can be no question that the working class was doing relatively well out of the transition to urban society. Real wages rose by something like 60 per cent between 1860 and 1900. Cheap food from abroad lessened the traditionally heavy proportion of the working-class income spent on simply keeping body and soul together, though this was somewhat offset by the rise in rents, a consequence of the pressure of urban population increases on the available housing stock. Most working people had more money in their pockets than their parents had done, and with union campaigns for a shorter working day and annual holidays, they had more spare time to spend it. The fastest-growing town in the 1890s was in fact Blackpool. The working class was enjoying its first consumer boom. But this increased standard of living played itself out in the social sphere in leisure patterns which displayed a distinctly class-based leisure routine. The development of football is just one significant case in point. The game became a truly mass sport when professionalisation ensured that the development of the game was to be dominated by working-class players and spectators. The game became an important emblematic element in the development of working-class civic pride in otherwise dingy cities, especially those in the North such as Preston whose team, Preston North End, dominated the Football League in the 1890s. The development of the national football sides as in turn to be significant in the development of a new national identity for the working class in Scotland, Wales and Northern Ireland as well as in urban England. Football was only one of the many avenues through which a distinctly working-class culture began to emerge as a very significant element in a new national make-up, inaugurating a quiet struggle for control of the future of the national family.[6]

The leisure pursuits of the urban working class were richly diverse, from male-voice choirs through whippet racing, self-improving education and gardening to music halls. During the late nineteenth century it is possible to discern the complex pattern of what soon came to be thought of as a typical and discrete urban working-class lifestyle. There were some clear signs of successful permeation of middle-class values into the urban working class; the respectability, thrift and temperance of the better-off working class is often seen as major evidence of a deferential class relationship. But these permeations became part of a self-defensive working-class culture.[7] There were good reasons for maintaining respectability, thrift and temperance, after all − to maintain personal dignity and to avoid the voluminous pitfall of unemployment − and there is no reason to assume that these characteristics necessarily meant the same thing to the working class as they did to the middle class. Working-class respectability could be read as a sign of collective dignity, self-respect and pride, just as easily as it could be read as a sign of deference to the middle class.

Even the revolution in shopping mirrored a distinctive culture in the urban working class. While the development of up-market stores in the West End of London, for instance, catered specifically for a middle-class clientele, the Co-operative Movement developed in particular for the working class, its organising principles centring on the mutually-reinforcing collectivism of a defensive socio-economic group. The point that must be made here is that the urban way of life transformed social relationships in a variety of different ways. It would be simplistic in the extreme to assume that working-class consciousness can only be measured in terms of industrial and political anatagonisms. Collective negotiation and self-defence are equally legitimate measures to adopt; these are, in fact, simply different forms of struggle. It was in the subtlety of the negotiating and self-defensive stance of working-class consciousness in late-nineteenth-century Britain that the complexities of labour politics began.

Not only were employers and employees drifting apart culturally, they were also being forced apart by the emergence of a new social grouping, the lower-middle class. With the development of industrialisation there had occurred a division of labour within the middle class analogous to that which had already occurred within the working class. The growth of companies demanded larger capitalisation than was available within the old notions of the owner-manager. The development of boards of directors, as representatives of the shareholders, controlling an enterprise through a managing director, was a result of the growth of companies and the consequent need to pool capital. In effect, this division between ownership and management created a new super-class, a plutocracy, whose major interest was financial, and whose relationship to industrial production as such was indirect.[8] At the same time the development of the workload upon management demanded the increasing delegation of minor duties to clerical staff. White-collar workers were the fastest-growing social group of all, already 20 per cent of all families by the 1860s. This grouping emerged from the large increase in consumer industries, the increase in banking, commerce and transport, and the development of larger conglomerate firms in response to foreign competition. A vulnerable group economically, since they had neither the capital of the true middle class nor the indispensable production skills of the manual labourer, they developed in fact as a service group for management, and proved to be inextricably tied to management in their outlook. Though virtually indistinguishable, in terms of wages, from the working class, they developed a strong conformism. Respectability was the hallmark of the lower-middle class, both the tool of their trade and the only sure way to preserve their social status. Significantly, the interposition of the clerical workforce between management and the factory floor – quite literally in the workplace, as well as metaphorically in the social sphere – cut off a most important line of communication between the social classes. In the long term, the lower-middle class was to act as an important social buffer in its own right – the ultimate source of the popular appeal of Conservatism as a political philosophy – but at the price of widening the gap between the owners of the means of production and the people who did the producing.[9]

The classes were also moving apart in a geographical sense. The development of urban transport gave the middle class the chance to move out of the increasingly squalid urban centres into the new suburbs. Greater London doubled in population between 1861 and 1911, while Inner London only increased by 50 per cent over the same period. Competition between the forms of urban transport helped to create the demand for this middle-class emigration. The underground began to take over the short-haul commuter traffic from motor-bus transport, motor-bus transport in turn began challenging for the medium-haul commuter traffic of the railways, and the railways reached further out from the old city limits to create new demand. The result was the creation of the concentric rings of middle-class outer suburbia, lower-middle class inner suburbia and the working-class inner-city areas which were to become typical of the classic social shape of the fully-developed city.[10] In the earlier period of industrialisation, the owner-manager of the archetypal small firm in the archetypal small industrial town had lived near the factory and had been literally visible to the workforce in the factory. The increasingly typical managing-director of the late nineteenth century and Edwardian period, however, lived in outer suburbia, worried about his board of directors, and sat surrounded at work not by the hum of industrial production but by the scratching of pens and, later, the clatter of typewriters. By 1909, the radical Charles Masterman could melodramatically picture the only contact the typical middle-class manager might have with the working class as a glimpse through the commuter train window:

> Every day, swung high upon embankments or buried deep in tubes underground, he hurries through the region where the creature lives. He gazes darkly from his pleasant hill villa upon the huge and smoky area of tumbled tenements which stretches at his feet. He is dimly distrustful of the forces fermenting in this uncouth laboratory.[11]

With these developments, the myths of the possibility of social mobility and of the reality of social cohesion were being severely tested. By the end of the nineteenth century social class was at least as important as the idea of the national family in British self-perception. Nevertheless, these two opposed ideas were not to be allowed to develop into overt antagonisms. Political transformation was to maintain a viable class society.

DISCOVERING THE WORKING CLASS: THE ANALYSIS OF POVERTY

The aims and aspirations of the lower rungs of the social hierarchy were brought firmly into the political arena by the extensions of the franchise of 1867 and 1884. Almost as significant was the effect of the Redistribution Act of 1885, which produced the modern, small single-member electoral constituency, the boundaries of which so often coincided with the class ghettoes emerging from the suburbanisation process.

From this point on, with urban constituencies often being dominated by one or other of the social classes, the potential was there for the development of class politics. Five and three-quarter million had the right to vote under the Third Reform Act, more than twice as many as under the 1867 Act, which in turn had more than doubled the electorate of 1832. But franchise reform still left 41 per cent of the adult male population in Britain without the vote. Franchise extensions were not designed, after all, as steps on the road to democracy, an alien concept which flew in the face of prevailing meritocratic ideas. The effects of 1867 and 1884 were to bring into play the largely conservative values of the lower-middle class and the so-called 'Labour Aristocrats', those at the top of the wages tree. But the facts of life as they stood for those still excluded from the political club also assumed new importance, because the respectability of the members of the lower-middle class and the Labour Aristocrats depended on them remaining in employment, the only thing that distinguished them as economic groups from the 'submerged one-tenth' of the population which had never really benefited from the process of industrialisation. Just beyond the possibility of unemployment for these new electors lay the workhouses – the 'Bastilles' as they were popularly known – and the ultimate humiliation of a pauper's funeral. While their aspirations to respectability may have governed the decision to extend the franchise to these groups, it was to be the new electors' need for security which was to condition their development as politically-significant areas within the electorate.[12]

Investigation of social conditions brought a new awareness of the plight of those left out from voting rights, and which awaited anyone with the vote unlucky enough to fall into the poverty trap. The result of the new empiricism was to centre attention as much on the dereliction of responsibility by middle-class liberalism as on the supposed explosive potential of the working class. The Hyde Park riots of 1866 were, after all, simply isolated affairs. As the social investigators dared to enter the working-class lair, startling revelations began to undercut the notion that self-help and deterrence, as principles of social policy, were even relevant to the social problems and social fears of many in the population. The sensationalist approach of books such as Andrew Mearns' *The Bitter Cry of Outcast London*, or General Booth's *In Darkest England*, made poverty an issue of popular politics.[13] They also paved the way for a more scientific approach to the problems of contemporary poverty. Like General Booth, Seebohm Rowntree was brought to the study of urban poverty through a Christian conscience. A Quaker, and a member of the York-based chocolate-manufacturing family, Rowntree's study of his native city demonstrated that 30 per cent of the working class there were living on or below subsistence level. Charles Booth found an almost exactly proportionate problem in London. But it was not simply the extent of the problem that social investigators such as Rowntree and Booth revealed which proved so worrying; it was the analysis of the causes of poverty which they put forward, and the fact that so many of these causes were entirely blameless, that required careful rethinking of individualist liberal tenets. Though Rowntree adopted the moralising attitude typical of his generation and his class – blaming the demon drink and other supposedly typical working-class vices for consolidating the problem of poverty – he argued that most poverty could not be avoided by those who became its victims. In particular, there were specific periods in the life cycle when poverty was difficult to avoid, especially during childhood and old age. The typical inmates of the York workhouse were not in fact lazy, able-bodied layabouts, but children, the old and the infirm, groups who by definition were simply not able to help themselves.[14]

It was evidence such as this which produced the argument that the state could intervene – without disrupting the laws of labour supply and demand – to help such people, by the introduction of health-care plans, old age pensions and, perhaps, family benefits. Governments could, in other words, help those sections of the impoverished to whom the principle of deterrence was simply inappropriate, by creating a social safety net. Rowntree and Booth also centred attention on the extent of the problem of unemployment as a cause of poverty, a factor underlined by others' analysis of the effects of the Great Price Fall. In 1894, for example, came the first official recognition of the existence of cyclical unemployment caused by the natural and inevitable downswings in the trade cycle.

With trade in depression, it could not be the case that all able-bodied men could find work if they simply looked for it. Such unemployment would not only be blameless, it would also be merely short-term until the trade cycle picked up. From the recognition of this problem sprang the idea of a nationally-organised unemployment insurance scheme to protect against this temporary unemployment, giving out benefits only for the short period before trade revived and jobs were again available. By 1911, William Beveridge could produce a pamphlet with a title which would have made little sense a generation earlier, *Unemployment, A Problem of Industry*. The pamphlet was recognition that what had previously been considered a problem of personal morality was now seen to be an objective problem of the economy.[15] Not only among social investigators were the tenets of liberal individualism being subjected to investigation: among many Imperialists, too, the notion of National Efficiency favoured some measure of state intervention to offset the waste and inefficiency involved in poverty. The argument was that to meet the challenge of international competition on both the economic and military levels, it was necessary to maintain the racial standards of the British people. Poverty must be tackled because it was nationally debilitating. This argument did have its seamier side, however; eugenicists also used it to argue that the point of helping the 'respectable' poor was to separate them from those in the social sump tank, such as the mentally handicapped, who could then be dealt with more radically to purify the genetic stock.

By the turn of the century the notion had gained wide respectability that poverty could be widely alleviated – and the everyday fears of the new electors largely assuaged – without destroying the moral fabric of society, by providing succour in specific and blameless contexts such as sickness, old age, temporary unemployment and childhood.[16] The New Liberals argued urgently within the Liberal party that liberalism must change with the times, must identify and meet new challenges, redefining liberalism in the process. In current conditions, as the Minority Report of the Poor Law Commission commented in 1909, freedom was 'a mockery and a farce'. Traditionalist elements could not even claim any longer that existing social policy did at least have the saving grace of being cheap. The Poor Law was costing £5 million annually in the 1880s, £10 million in the 1890s, and £14 million by the time the Royal Commission was set up in 1905. The New Liberals planned to use differential taxation to pay for new schemes. Progressive Conservatives were equally concerned, however, that social policy must become a priority in the Tory programme. Though indirect taxation was to be their favoured means of raising the revenue, Joseph Chamberlain was to argue that the introduction of tariffs would provide revenue for social reform and simultaneously protect British trade from the new foreign competition.

Rowntree had also detected other but more insidious causes of poverty than those upon which the major political parties could broadly agree. Underemployment, as well as inadequate wages for many of those in employment, were factors left to labour thinkers to analyse as incapable of solution without fundamental change in the economic fabric. Marx's notion of the capitalist norm wage – the idea that capitalist accumulation inevitably meant pressure on wages to the point at which the wage-earner would be paid just enough, all other things being equal, to keep him going as a productive unit – had its British counterpart in H.G. Wells' notion of 'marginal man'. Trade unions campaigned for legislation on those causes of poverty more deeply structured into the economy, arguing that the regulation of working hours and the introduction of minimum wages would not only end the exploitation involved in making working people work overlong hours to compensate for low wages, but would also spread employment more evenly around the available pool of labour. These measures, however, would involve a more radical rethink of the role of the state than anything yet proposed within the major parties, because they would take the government into the core of the relationship between labour supply and demand. The socialists believed that both the New Liberal 'progressives' and the reforming Tories were simply toying with the real problem, treating the symptoms of the disease of poverty rather than seeking to prevent the disease itself, which ultimately could only be achieved by changes in the basic organisation of the means of production. From these different standpoints, New Liberals, Tory reformers and socialists set about the task of organising their own parties and of winning the hearts and minds of a socially and ideologically complicated electorate.

LIBERALS, CONSERVATIVES AND THE ELECTORATE

The Liberal party had been formed as an alliance between the anti-centralist tendencies of the Whigs and the free enterprise ideologues of the Manchester school of economic radicals. What the two sides of the alliance originally shared was a common distaste for state intervention but, in the longer term, what separated them was to be just as decisive in shaping the fortunes of the Liberal party. The alliance had always been uneasy, given that the Whig landowners were in fact one of the prime targets of the economic radicals' campaign against restrictive oligarchy, but the common antipathy of the two groups to intervention by any state machinery was enough to bind them together through the easy years of the mid-Victorian boom. The conversion of the Peelites in the Conservative party to free trade in the 1840s split the opposition disastrously, virtually guaranteeing the political ascendancy of the Liberals. With Palmerston playing the patriotic card abroad, and with Gladstone organising the free trade economy, the Liberals were able to dominate both Left and Right in a wide consensus.

But voting Liberal in the third quarter of the nineteenth century denoted much more than simply acceptance of the principles of free trade and self-help, for the Conservatives gradually came round to accept the same ideas after the debacle of the Peelite desertion. Voting Liberal denoted in fact a fully-fledged outlook on life. The Liberal party, especially for the non-conformists, was Christianity in politics: 'We stand immovably on this eternal rock', proclaimed the radical preacher Hugh Price Hughes, 'whatever is morally wrong can never be politically right'. Not that the Liberal party was ever simply the party of the non-conformists. Indeed it was the High Anglican William Gladstone who abrogated to himself the right to speak for the Almighty in the House of Commons.

The Liberals were not the party of any single denomination, but of Victorian religious fervour in general. Gladstone turned free trade, the Bulgarian atrocities, and Ireland from complicated political issues into simple moral crusades: 'The Almighty seems to sustain me for some purpose of his own', he confided to his diary in 1868, 'deeply unworthy though I know myself to be. Glory be to His name'.[17] To be continually on a divine mission was no doubt uplifting, and the fervour no doubt accounts in large part for the particular appeal of Gladstonian Liberalism in the third quarter of the nineteenth century; but fervour could also be extremely wearing in an increasingly secular society, such as Britain was rapidly becoming as the new conurbations grew convulsively in the last quarter of the century. Already by the 1880s there were some murmurs within the party about the style of Gladstone's leadership, mutterings about the political strain of being 'constantly dragged around the country by an old lunatic'.[18] The problem was that the very fervour of Gladstonian Liberalism made it less likely that the party would be able to respond flexibly when some of the tenets of classic individualist liberalism clearly needed adaptation in the late nineteenth century. If Gladstone in effect made the Liberal party the dominant force of British politics, it must also be said that his longevity was also a factor in threatening that dominance.

The Conservative party in the generation after 1846 was composed of a set of virtually unknown backbenchers. All the great seers of political thought – Adam Smith, David Ricardo, Richard Cobden, John Bright, Jeremy Bentham, J.S. Mill, Herbert Spencer – were claimed to a man by the Liberals as part of their particular intellectual inheritance. Benjamin Disraeli owed his emergence into prominence among the Conservatives to the fact that he was virtually the only Tory who could give as good as he got in parliamentary exchanges. Disliked by many High Tories as a superficial charmer with a butterfly mind, Disraeli nevertheless managed to generate in 'Young England' some hopes for a Tory revival. 'Young England' may have been a vague and unspecific concept, and Disraeli was perhaps only vaguely responsive to the problems of the urban areas of Britain, yet he was to form a new image for Conservatism, the basis for a later populist revival in 'Tory

Democracy' under Lord Randolph Churchill. The death of
Palmerston, and the succession of Gladstone and the 'Little
Englanders' to the leadership of the Liberal party, gave
Disraeli the chance to don Palmerston's patriotic mantle, to
seize the initiative in an area which the Liberal party had now
vacated. Disraeli's extension of the franchise in 1867,
moreover, not only proved that the Conservatives could be
just as liberal as the Liberals (the measure in fact went even
further than Gladstone's contemporary plans for franchise
extension), it also opened up the electoral potential of lower-
middle class 'Tory villadom', of making a very significant
capture of a major element in the new electorate.

The Conservatives' gradual acceptance of free trade was
offset by lingering protectionist as well as paternalist
sympathies, both hangovers from pre-1846, in some corners
of the party. These older ideas were to allow the party to adopt
a more flexible and adaptable attitude in the changing
conditions of the late century. Lord Randolph Churchill
proved capable not only of stumping the country like the best
Liberal radical, but also of hinting at the possibility of reforms
in social policy, of hinting at the possibility of economic
protection, of hinting in particular at the defence of the
Church of England. The last was particularly important in the
context of the aspirations of the lower-middle class. In his
famous pronouncement that 'Ulster will fight and Ulster will
be right', moreover, Churchill promised a defence of the unity
of the kingdom which may well have made significant inroads
into the lower-middle- as well as the working-class anti-Irish
and anti-Catholic vote, particularly in Cheshire and
Lancashire. Churchill's political career was almost as flashy
as Disraeli's, though much shorter, and their iconoclastic
attitude towards some of the more stolid tenets of Victorian
liberalism provided a vitality and levity to contrast with
octogenarian Gladstonism. Churchill was perfectly frank in his
opportunism and in his populism: 'the aristocracy and the
working class are bound together', he calculated, 'by the
indissoluble bonds of a common immorality'.[19] From 1867
there were signs from the Conservative party that they could
well appeal to the bulk of the new electorate, just as easily as
could the Liberals. The Whiggish landed class was already

switching allegiance to Conservatism as the economic crisis deepened, and as the attacks upon them from the Liberal radicals continued. Managers and financiers were also being attracted by the Imperialist stance of the party, and their hints of protection. As early as 1869 there were straws blowing in the wind when W.H. Smith, the typical self-made man who a generation earlier would have gone almost automatically into the Liberal party, fought and won for the Tories the Westminster by-election against John Stuart Mill himself. Though patricians, Churchill included, might look down their noses at the increasing number of 'new men' in the party, the increasing appeal of Conservatism to the entrepreneurial middle class was to be critical in the realignment of the electorate. The Conservatives were soon to attract Joseph Chamberlain himself, the self-styled spokesman of the provincial middle class. For the working-class electorate, too, it was by no means clear that a continuation of the Liberals' grim self-help doctrine could command their respect for very long. As Britain threatened to split more clearly along class lines in response to the Great Price Fall, and as the social dynamics of the developing urban areas began to pattern class relationships into the political geography of the nation, it was not self-evident that a Liberal party which still professed to speak for both employer and employee against the landlords was even relevant.

Though the New Liberals were prepared to change front to save the party from an electoral slide, they were thrown into political impotence for a critical twenty years by the emergence of the Irish problem. By the time they were left free to introduce radical social reform by the landslide to the Liberals in the general election of 1906, key captures of strategic sections of the new electorate had been made by the Conservatives and by the new Labour party. This was not to lead in any automatic sense to the downfall of the Liberal party, but it was to place the party in an acute tactical bind. The Third Reform Act of 1884, enfranchising rural house-holders, had tipped the balance in predominantly rural Ireland, which had been a major traditional area of Liberal support. The extension of the franchise gave the Irish Nationalists a landslide. They won all the 77 seats in Southern

Ireland, and they split the Ulster vote with the Conservatives. This new factor was compounded by the electoral weakness of the Liberals in all-powerful England, which accounted for 456 of the 670 seats in parliament after the 1885 redistribution. The Liberals only attained a majority of 19 in the English seats in 1885, while their majority of 71 over the Conservatives rested on their preponderance in Scotland and Wales. This reliance on the 'Celtic fringe' was to continue in subsequent elections. The problem was that not even the full power of the Scottish and Welsh radical vote could hope to offset the inreasing Conservative preponderance in England. No doubt the Nationalists' injunction to their supporters to vote Conservative in constituencies where there was no Nationalist candidate cost the Liberals dearly in England, perhaps as many as 27 seats, but the relatively poor showing of the Liberals in England also reflected a failure to make any decisive and long-lasting capture of the new urban electorate of post-1867.[20] The Liberals were only deprived of a working majority in the new House by two seats (justifiably assuming that the Independents in the new parliament would have voted with the Liberals on matters of confidence), but those two seats were to cost them dearly.

Having bound themselves to Irish Home Rule in 1885 – a simple political necessity as much as a new moral crusade, given the outcome of the election – the inherent electoral problem was to be compounded. The Irish Nationalists retained a firm grip on Ireland, winning more than eighty seats in every election up to the Great War, while the split in the Liberals which resulted from the First Home Rule Bill caused them electoral disaster in England in 1886. Though they retained the large majority of their seats in Scotland and Wales, the Liberals were reduced to just 123 seats in England. The defecting Liberal Unionists, on the other hand, won 55 of their 79 seats in the 1886 election in England. It was a disaster from which the Liberals were never fully to recover. The Liberal government of 1892–5 was again to be reliant on the Nationalists, and the long fight over the Second Home Rule Bill stymied New Liberal attempts to push through the social reforms that just might have eased their electoral problems. Indeed, they were only ever to win one more overall majority;

and the landslide to the Liberals in the election of 1906 proved to be simply a hiccup in this pattern, an Indian summer. In the two elections of 1910, the Liberals were once again reliant on the Irish Nationalists, simply because they could not win enough seats in England.

The Irish problem, then, was both cause and symptom of Liberal difficulties. Irish nationalism became a problem because the Liberals could not win an overall majority without the Nationalists' support, but the Home Rule issue only lost the Liberals further support in England. Quite apart from its innate controversies, moreover, the passions roused by Ireland effectively denied the parliamentary time to the New Liberals to put a new face on the party for the electorate. In this sense, the split over Home Rule was much more significant than the mere number of deserters from the parliamentary party would suggest. It is true that the desertion of the Whigs on the issue made the party ideologically more coherent: the radicals were now in firm control and had to make no more concessions to landed property power.[21] It is true, too, that Joseph Chamberlain may have been a spent force within Liberal radicalism by the time of his desertion over Ireland, and that his allegiance to Unionism was in turn almost to break Conservatism in two, on the question of tariff reform. But with the Whigs among the Liberal Unionists also went a considerable source of party funds, as well as the major element in Liberal support in the House of Lords. Gladstone had to resort to the questionable expedient of selling peerages in order to try to offset both these problems. The House of Lords proved to be a particularly acute problem, nevertheless, blocking Home Rule Bills which the Liberals could only just get through the House of Commons with Irish Nationalist support. Inevitably, therefore, Home Rule became inextricably tied to the question of reform of the House of Lords. 'Respectable' political opinion found it difficult to stomach a party that carried dissolution of the United Kingdom as its apparently major commitment, and was prepared to overthrow the constitution in order to secure it. The Liberals could not escape Home Rule, and the long struggle to secure Home Rule in turn dented the Liberals' credibility as a major engine of social reform. Meanwhile, the social grievances of urban Britain sought a new voice.

THE EMERGENCE OF THREE PARTY POLITICS: THE ORIGINS OF THE LABOUR PARTY

The development of the Labour party ultimately depended on a switch of political allegiance among that portion of the better-off working class which had been enfranchised in 1867, which traditionally saw Liberal Radicalism rather than socialism as the best means of improving the working-class lot. These were the so-called 'Lib-Labs', working-class in interest but moderate in their politics. The Lib-Labs, however, were to prove difficult to convert, especially after the departure of the Whigs from the Liberal party seemed to suggest that a radical rejigging of the political landscape to defend working-class interests would be unnecessary. Founded in the 1890s, it was to take the Labour party more than a decade to secure any significant parliamentary representation. Even then, it seemed possible that the Liberal party could confine and control the development of separatist working-class politics. In its attempt to woo traditionalist Lib-Lab support, the Labour party was to abandon much of its specifically socialist programme in favour of something that looked very like New Liberalism.

On the one hand, this very conscious ideological moderation made it difficult for the Labour party to clear political ground for itself. Labour MPs could be dismissed by Joseph Chamberlain as 'mere fetchers and carriers for Liberalism'. On the other hand, their ability to erode working-class support for the Liberal party was deeply worrying to the Liberal leadership. The paradox was that the Labour party emerged as a class-based party, but without offering a fully-blown alternative ideology. The Labour party agreed with virtually everything that the New Liberals had to say, yet still retained its independence. This was a reflection of the fact that social class had now become a primary determinant in political affiliation, but it was also a reflection of the fact that the emergence of social class did not necessarily have to mean direct confrontation for control of the state. The Labour party's reliance on converting the Trades Union Congress, the bastion of Lib-Labism, to the ideas of an independent party, involved a mobilisation of class consciousness on issues like the need for working-class parliamentary candidates and securing the threatened rights of trade unions, the strike weapon in particular, but it also involved a specific rejection of a radically socialist alternative. Instead, it channelled working-class grievances along traditionalist, progressivist lines. Nevertheless, the Labour party certainly contained socialists, even if it was not a socialist party as such. This blend of inherent moderation and implied radicalism was to prove a source of both strength and weakness; it broadened the party's appeal, but it often left it ideologically opaque. On specifics such as unemployment and housing conditions, however, Labour could rely on a gut class reaction.

Unemployment always held a particular dread for Victorian working men and women, not only for the obvious financial stress that it caused but also for the social stigma that was associated with the Poor Law regime. But in the period of the Great Price Fall, rising living standards for the working class in employment were also threatened by the argument that a major reason for Britain's relatively poor economic performance was the cost of labour. Money wages had climbed during the classic period of the Great Price Fall, and real wages climbed even more freely as prices fell, but at the turn of the century money wages took a rapid dive as the employers' counter-attack began to take effect, and real wages fell even more steeply as prices began to recover. The steadily-increasing standard of living enjoyed by the late-Victorian working class was in jeopardy. In classic liberal economic thinking, nothing very much could be done to alleviate the situation. Supply and demand worked through the highly responsive price mechanism, while mobile capital resources were directed by a sensitive interest rate. Wages could not deviate from a natural equilibrium. If they did, then the only result would be changes in either profits or prices, either of which was bound to effect labour demand, causing unemployment which would continue until wages fell to the point at which prices and profits began to rise again. This was the rationale behind the employers' counter-attacks against the unions in the 1890s, the belief that union pressure was artificially bolstering wages. The nasty question that arose from this logic was to determine at what level this wage equilibrium would be established, in a period when British profits were being adversely affected by world competition.

The specifics of social conditions among the poorer sections of society also began to make themselves felt. Pressure on housing led to chronic overcrowding; in 1891 one-tenth of the British population lived more than one to a room; in London the figure was one-fifth and in the North-East one-third. Even with such overcrowding, the cost of rents was immense, amounting to 23.5 per cent of income in some areas.[22] The long-term worries that came with the Great Price Fall made it conceivable that 'marginal man' might become reality rather than simply a socialist chimera: workers might be forced to accept wages and conditions which would just about maintain them as viable economic units, unless industrial labour organised to confront the classic liberal economic case. Laissez-faire and self-help had always implied the freedom to starve as well as the freedom to prosper, but with the vote there existed the wherewithal to do something about it. With the organised working class caught in the employers' counter-attack, and constantly mindful of the consequences of falling into the poverty trap, the appeal of the socialist minimum demands – for the collective regulation of the labour market, for the regulation of working hours and minimum-wage legislation – met an increasingly positive response. In the relatively easy times of the mid-Victorian boom, the fundamental difference of interest of employer and employee could be disguised, but in a period of prolonged low prices and profitability the cross-class partnership came under intense pressure. Though Labour Aristocrats – artisans and other skilled workers used to commanding high wages – might remain wedded overall to liberalism, it was the collective strength of trade unionism which allowed their 'respectability', which underpinned their self-reliance, and the case for intervention in the workings of the labour economy was insurmountable if the economic and social status they enjoyed at the top of the labour tree was to continue. How much more appealing were the arguments of labour politicians to those who had never enjoyed that relative security of employment and income.

The most committed of the socialist groups in Britain at this time in fact hoped to create a mass movement by bypassing the traditionalists in the craft unions. The Social Democratic Federation (SDF), dominated by the ex-Conservative Marxist H.M. Hyndman, proposed instead the development of a 'new unionism' of the semi-skilled and the unskilled workforce to replace the Labour Aristocrats as the dominant force in working-class organisation. It was perhaps for this very reason that the SDF remained largely London-based, for among the large casual labour force in the capital trade unionism had never been strong, yet there remained that centuries-old radical tradition, especially in the East End. The success of the SDF in helping to organise the casual labour force proved to be considerable. The Match Girls' Strike of 1888 was followed by the dockers' strike of 1889, and the gas-workers' strike of 1889/90. By 1890, in fact, the membership of the new unions was estimated at one and a half million.[23] During the ensuing decade, however, the bubble burst. The main problem proved to be that, as unskilled or semi-skilled workers, they were much more susceptible to blacklegging than the craft unions, particularly in areas of high unemployment. This very weakness encouraged the notion that the only remedy lay in parliamentary action. Votes for independent working-class candidates might secure in law what action on the picket line could not. The SDF had considerable political success in local elections in London. In 1898 the SDF became the biggest single party on the West Ham council, and only an alliance between the Liberals and the Tories kept them out of power. Two years later, in fact, the Liberals were so reduced in both West Ham and in Bow and Bromley that they withdrew to allow the SDF a straight fight with the Conservatives.[24] In small areas of London, then, if not in the country as a whole, the SDF was able to put the Liberals into contortions, unable to make up their mind whether to oppose or to accept alternative politics on the left. In their work in organising new unionism, the SDF had demonstrated both the potential and the weaknesses of a mass movement at this particular point in Britain's history. In their educational work, though, they were to inject just a little Marxist intellectual rigour into the mainstream of British labour thinking, even though former members of the SDF like Ramsay MacDonald were finally to be most conspicuous precisely for their rejection of Marxism.

At the other end of the socialist spectrum, and with an opposing strategy, stood the Fabians. It was to be the Fabians' claim that they saved the Labour party from the potentially disastrous revolutionary path by winning the party for a policy of gradualism. In fact, the history of the early connection of the Fabians with the Labour party points clearly to the conclusion that their influence on the emergence of the party was negligible, though they certainly exercised an overweening influence once the party had become a serious contender for political power. Indeed, the Fabians originally believed that there was no need for a separate party at all, that new Liberals like David Lloyd George and Winston Churchill could be worked upon to produce socialist results within the existing political configuration. The Fabian view was that it was much more important to make thinking people socialistic than to convert what they tended to see as the unthinking masses to socialism. The creation of a spearhead group within the existing political parties, the Liberals in particular, could produce revolution from the top. The training of a new socially-conscious elite, through institutions like the London School of Economics, was a prime strategy. Undoubtedly, the Fabians were immensely articulate. They had the ability to make good arguments and to make them stick in high places, but the social exclusiveness of the Webbs, George Bernard Shaw and their ilk cut them off from the labour mainstream in the early days.[25] Indeed, the social origins of so many Fabians were to institutionalise a class breach for much of Labour party history between 'intellectuals', on the one hand and, on the other hand, the industrial wing of the labour movement. But the Fabians were later to represent the 'respectable face of Labour' to the traditional political elite, thereby playing an important part in easing Labour's way into the British political establishment.

Though both SDF and Fabians were to have educational influences on the party, it was the Independent Labour party which provided both the strategy and the tactical resources.

Alone among the socialist groups, the ILP saw the conversion of the TUC from Lib-Labism as both the quickest and the most effective way of securing a labour voice in parliament. With two million members by the turn of the century, it was the TUC which provided the only possible electoral machine which could compete with the party organisations which had been built up by the Liberals and the Conservatives. Infiltration of the TUC proved, however, an arduous business. On one level, the early opposition of the craft-based unions to the aims of the ILP is understandable enough. They were, after all, defending an entrenched position as artisans, economically indistinguishable from the lower-middle class. The liaison with the Liberal party had proved extremely fruitful; they had won from the Liberals legislation giving trade unions legal status, equality of treatment between employer and employee in cases of breach of contract, safety acts covering factories, mines and merchant shipping, as well as legislation making employers liable for avoidable accidents in the workplace. Keir Hardie himself had fully supported the Liberals' Newcastle Programme and had campaigned for Gladstone in the Mid-Lanark election of 1892. The conversion of just these moderate-minded men – the men whom the 1870 Education Act had given the power to read the Holy Bible, John Stuart Mill, Carlyle and Ruskin rather than Karl Marx – was to be an essentially reactionary rather than progressive process. As their status and their standard of living came under attack from mechanisation and from anti-union employers during the Great Price Fall, they channelled their grievances into the available form of political protest, in this case the Labour party, just as the handloom weavers before them had channelled their grievances into Chartism.

The Lib-Labs had always campaigned within the Liberal party for working-class candidatures. In this they had had little success. Though the Lib-Labs won eleven seats with Liberal backing in 1895, they were reduced to eight in 1900, in spite of their two million members. In fact, the return of working-class candidates tended to occur only in constituencies with a well-organised and large working-class vote, but this tended to mean those single-industry areas which were dominated by the most moderate of the unions, the miners and the textile workers. Bolton, for example, only went Lib-Lab in 1906. The need to find finance for election and living expenses for working-class MPs again favoured the larger, richer and more moderate unions; in other constituencies it was more likely that working-class candidates would give way to well-off Liberal radicals. Though the national leadership of the Liberal party was willing, indeed anxious, to put up working-class candidates, it was the local Liberal Associations which proved reluctant. As a result of these difficulties, Lib-Lab MPs remained a small and relatively insignificant band on Liberal backbenches. This would not have mattered had it not been for the increasingly vicious industrial issues of the 1890s. The engineers, for example, found themselves locked out and faced with their employers' attempt to form a blackleg labour association to break their power in the industry, and the miners faced almost unprecedented difficulties in their fights for wage rises.

The ILP was anxious, too, to tone down the content of its programme to suit the outlook of the Labour Aristocrats. MacDonald made it clear that the ILP believed Marxism to be an alien creed, and by the mid-1890s the ILP programme was to be virtually indistinguishable, in its major components, from that of the Liberal radicals. The major ILP proposals for immediate implementation were either already in the Liberal manifesto or extensions of existing principle. They even included measures to allow the public control of drink, a concession to the most famous of the Liberal radical pressure groups, the temperance lobby. The TUC responded. In 1890 and in 1891, the TUC rejected ILP-sponsored resolutions in favour of nationalisation, passed them in 1893, again in 1894 and again, this time overwhelmingly when the miners abstained, in 1897. Yet, on the issue of establishing a separate political party, little progress was made until 1900. In that year the Labour Representation Committee was formed by the TUC, but the response to calls for affiliation was still unenthusiastic. The ILP fielded only ten candidates in the general election of that year, all of whom came bottom of the poll, though two LRC candidates were elected along with eight Lib-Labs. This situation changed dramatically, however, in 1901 when the Law Lords upheld the case of the Taff Vale

Railway Company that the railway union was responsible for the actions of its members during a strike. This challenged the whole basis of the contemporary legal standing of trades unionism in Britain. Within a year, only the miners among the big unions still were not affiliated to the LRC. The trades unions, in other words, with their legal status threatened, were not prepared to leave that issue to the Liberals. When the crunch came, they were prepared to put their case in the hands of a new political grouping, a grouping near enough to their own Liberal inclinations not to disturb them unduly, but a grouping which was also, most importantly, avowedly working-class.[26]

The rush to affiliate to the LRC, and the rash of by-election successes enjoyed by Labour candidates in the run-up to the general election of 1906, put the party in a strong position to negotiate with the Liberals for an electoral pact which would give them a reasonable showing in the next parliament. The Liberal leadership was equally anxious to avoid splitting the left vote, as well as to remain on good terms with the new grouping. The result was that 35 seats were left without a Liberal challenge in the 1906 election: in the event, Labour won 29 seats and the Lib-Labs 24. During the parliament that followed the Lib-Labs came over to the Labour whip. With over fifty seats, in effect, the Labour party was a force to be reckoned with numerically but not, it seemed, a distinct political alternative. The Taff Vale decision was duly rescinded by the Liberal government, and the Liberals could assume that, with the unions' position now secured, Labour would simply wither on the vine. But, though the Labour party failed to make any significant new inroads into traditional Liberal support, it obstinately refused to go away. Labour held forty seats in January 1910 and picked up two more in December, though with only 8 per cent of the popular vote. It can legitimately be assumed that the Liberals would have lost a general election had there been one in 1914 or 1915, and that Labour would certainly have lost seats with them. This does not mean, on the other hand, that Labour's historic role depended solely on the opportunities provided by the Great War. The point that should be made is that 1906 proved what the success of the SDF and the by-elections before 1906 had hinted, that Labour had potential appeal in inner-city areas where the Liberals had looked a little vulnerable for a generation. It is for this reason that the supposed client relationship between Labour and Liberal in this period can easily be overstated: the Liberals needed Labour for strategic reasons, whereas Labour needed the Liberals only for tactical reasons, to effect an electoral breakthrough. Undoubtedly, the trials and tribulations of the Liberals in the Great War greatly eased Labour's progress, and the large extension of the franchise in 1918 was to make Labour a contender for government within a matter of years, but even the limited franchise of pre-1914 made it clear that a Labour presence was irreversible.

The lack of substantial differences between the immediate programme of the Labour party and the Liberals, moreover, proved as much a source of strength as it was a weakness for the new party in these early years. What Labour offered was not a distinct alternative to the Liberals but a simple replacement, and this was in a sense much more dangerous to the Liberals. A straightforwardly socialist party could have been attacked directly by Liberals, whereas a liberal Labour party presented a difficult target. In fact, Labour was involved not so much in the demolition of liberalism but, rather, in a takeover bid for that ideological tradition at a time when the Liberal party, intellectually and politically, was vulnerable to this appeal to many of its shareholders. Fundamentally, class politics was a state of mind rather than a distinct set of alternative policies in late-Victorian and Edwardian Britain. The Labour party, founded in the unions and in the workplace, was an extension of the new way of life that had developed in the Victorian urban working class, neither revolutionary nor deferential, aware of the apparent inviolability of the economic structure in the short term, but aware too of the possibilities both of self-defence within that structure and of fundamental change in the long term. In short, the Labour party was a reflection of the stable class culture that had developed in the late nineteenth century, a culture in which the mythical vision of the economic and social interdependence of the social classes that had underpinned the

Liberal party in its heyday had been exposed, but a culture in which, too, negotiation and consensus were still possible.

LIBERALISM, CONSERVATISM AND THE EMPIRE

While the Liberal party was threatened by this insidious appeal from the Left, the Right had also reorganised, building in the political space that the Liberals had left vacant on the death of Palmerston. The Liberals were in fact placed in just as difficult a political quandary by the appeal of Imperialism at the turn of the century as they were by the development of separatist working-class politics, and by the longevity of the Irish problem. Indeed if the Irish problem made it difficult for the Liberals to govern effectively – to meet the growing demand for the party to be seen as an effective engine of social reform – and if the potential erosion of working-class support to Labour threatened their future electoral position, then it could also be said that Imperial issues denied them even effective opposition. Too often the Liberals were caught paralysed not simply by the contemporary appeal of jingoism, but also by the apparently impeccable logic by which the Right could conjure up Imperialism as the inevitable consequence of laissez-faire in a more competitive world.

The fact was that, in the prevailing economic conditions of the late nineteenth century, Imperialism seemed an economic imperative, however much the Little Englanders attempted to dismiss it as simply a manifestation of a long-obsolete military-aristocratic caste system. Though statesmen at the end of the nineteenth century were no more willing to extend the boundaries of formal Empire than they had been previously, the threat of foreign competition and the inexorable tendency of British trade to move beyond the bounds of Empire dragged governments, as the most famous historians of the phenomenon have put it, 'into new and irksome commitments'.[27] When faced with the new expanding economies of countries like France, Russia and Germany, Britain was, in other words, forced to formalise Empire for both economic and strategic reasons, though she would have preferred to maintain the informal hegemony over trading areas that had been typical of the earlier part of the century. The argument is, then, not that pressure groups wanted Empire but that trade expansion decreed it. Even Gladstone, the archetypal Little Englander, had to accept the commitment. The occupation of Egypt, to protect British interests in the Suez Canal, triggered a race with the French to formalise responsibility in the area which led, indirectly and incrementally, to the partition of the entire African continent. The formalisation of Empire was, then, an inevitable consequence of the expansion of British trade once it was faced with competition; either Britain accepted military and political commitments in areas which were important for trading or strategic reasons, or British trade would be forced out by other industrialising nations less imbued with the free trade spirit. The problem was caused not only by the threat to British trading patterns, however, but also by the demands of Britain's capital export market. As Europe and the United States began to generate their own capital and squeeze British investments in these traditional areas, British capital began to find new outlets in the still-undeveloped world. This 'invisible Imperialism' could sometimes become very visible indeed: British loans to Egypt did much to destabilise the country, and then to prompt the British occupation. Lord Cromer, a Little Englander by inclination, summed up the Liberal quandary exactly when surveying his own actions in Egypt:

> It is a cruel fate which drives me, with all my strong opinions against the extension of territory and the assumption of fresh responsibilities, and with strong anti-Jingo convictions that deepen each year I live, to be constantly pushing proposals which, at all events at first sight, have a strong Jingo flavour.[28]

There can be no question either that the appeal of the 'White Man's Burden' was one that Liberal radicals found hard to resist; many of the great idealists of Empire were Liberal in origin – Milner, Cromer and Curzon, for example. It has been pointed out, too, that Joseph Chamberlain tended to see Africa as one great big Birmingham whose slums needed to be cleared.[29] But the distinction between the idea of Empire-as-mission which so appealed to Liberal radicals, and the seamier appeal of jingoism, could often be a nice one. The popular culture of Empire – from the stories of G.A. Henty or Rider Haggard to quasi-mystical texts such as J.A. Crambe's *The Origins and Destiny of Imperial Britain* – were full of the concept of 'England's Mission'. The public schools, developing rapidly through the 1870s to cater for the increased demand for military and administrative recruits that stemmed from Imperial development, imbued the sons of the middle class with diluted aristocratic ideals of service to the state. They produced their own self-reliant and unique culture; Sir Henry Newbolt's extraordinary poem from the period, 'Vitae Lampada', drawing its famous analogy between a public-school cricket match and a broken British square in the desert, and with its refrain 'Play up, play up and play the game!', encapsulates quintessentially the remarkable confidence and unquestioned loyalties of the public-school ideology.[30]

Jingoism undoubtedly made an impressive political impact lower down the scale as well, especially among the lower-middle class in reaction to the Boer War, as the 'khaki election' of 1900 proved. It was the Boer War which in fact highlighted the Liberal dilemma over Imperialism most acutely. Political freedom, after all, was a Liberal essential, yet it was precisely this freedom that was being denied the Uitlanders by Kruger, who was fearful that his nascent state would be swamped by the immigration. Liberals could hardly avoid the conclusion that the freedoms that encouraged expansionism were bound to bring with them political difficulties in an increasingly crowded world, and that those difficulties must either be stoically borne or overcome, by force if necessary. The Liberal Imperialist group was convinced that continued Little Englander sympathies were both illogical and electorally damaging, and harsh words were exchanged beween Liberal Imperialists and Little Englanders after the crushing defeat in the 1900 general election. The issues that emerged in the wake of the South African war, however, did at least create a platform on which the Liberals could reunite. The sheer cost of the war, the barbarity of the methods employed by Kitchener to win it, as well as the large commitment that would be required by Britain to put South Africa back on its feet, provided one focus for the Liberal revival of 1906.

It is fair to say, too, that if Imperialism put the Liberals in an intellectual and political fix which cost them dearly in the short term, the Boer War also tarnished the Imperial idea before Joseph Chamberlain had time to transform it into the dynamic of a new Conservatism, as he tried to do after 1903. Chamberlain's plan was to raise tariff walls around the Empire with a three-fold objective: to protect British trade, to foster Imperial integration and to raise the revenue to pay for social reform at home. His grand-slam solution to Britain's difficulties, however, was vulnerable on all points. First, it is clear that the Empire – large though it was – was nowhere near developed enough to serve as a dumping ground for British manufactured goods. Only one third of contemporary British trade was with the Empire, and no trade preference that the Empire could offer could possibly make up for the potential loss of trade with the rest of the world that the scheme potentially implied. Neither was it clear that the Empire itself would be content in a role of continued underdevelopment, consigning itself to the role of kitchen garden for the 'workshop of the world'. Further, tariffs implied dear food, and the Liberals could argue that the social reform proposed by Chamberlain and his cronies would be paid for in a dearer working-class loaf; the Conservatives would be taking away with one hand what they offered with the other. Finally, though some aspects of traditional liberalism might appear decrepit, the large majority of the Conservative party – and particularly the Unionists with whom Chamberlain had seceded from the Liberals – was not prepared to take the awesome step of abandoning free trade and moving into a world of trade wars in which Britain, as an export-led economy, might well be seriously disadvantaged.

The Tory hierarchy had no doubt hoped and assumed that, in time, Joseph Chamberlain would simply be subsumed into Conservatism, bringing his political magnetism to bear on the provincial middle class. The immediate effect of the Tariff Reform campaign, however, was to split the Tories open almost as wide as the First Home Rule bill had split the Liberals, a split which contributed substantially to the defeat of the Conservatives in the 1906 general election. Andrew Bonar Law, succeeding Balfour to the Tory leadership after the election fiasco, sought to reunite the Conservative Unionists on the one issue which had brought them together in the first place – Irish Home Rule. Much of the fury of the Conservative campaign against the Third Home Rule bill, and against the reform of the House of Lords after 1910, must be read as a concerted effort on the part of the Conservative leadership to re-establish that party unity which was so intrinsic a part of the Conservatives' tradition, and so powerful an element in their electoral appeal, as the party of stability and of efficiency in government.[31]

In retrospect, it is possible to see that the scheme of Imperial integration was not a sign of Britain's world power at its zenith. On the contrary, it was a manifestation of British power on the decline, an attempt to duck out of the international economic race by relying on consolidating what was already held in the face of an inexorable and irreversible competition. Because it did not provide a credible basis for the economic and social future, it could not provide the basis for a Tory-led electoral consensus. In the short term, moreover, Conservative electoral defeat over the issue provided the Liberals with one more chance to prove themselves. With a parliamentary majority large enough to leave them unfettered from the Irish Nationalists for the first time in twenty years, the Liberals were to set about the attempt to construct their own new consensus, before the other parties effectively divided the electorate between them.

NEW LIBERALISM IN PRACTICE

Any historian seeking to put the case that the Liberal party was in decline in the years before 1914 has to explain away the landslide victory that the Liberals won in the general election of January 1906. Certainly, the victory was impressive. The Liberals had an overall majority of 130 and the anti-Conservative majority was 354. Yet it would be difficult to conclude from the result alone that the electorate had placed a resounding vote of confidence in New Liberalism as such.

Social reform had not in fact figured very prominently in their campaign; of a total of nineteen and a half million election pamphlets issued, only two million had addressed the issues of social reform; most of the remainder were attacks on Tarriff Reform and on the Conservatives' record in office. In other words, the Liberals campaigned as the party of economic orthodoxy at least as much as they campaigned as social progressives. Indeed, it was to be two years before the most important social reforms began to occupy the centre-stage in the government, after a series of by-election reverses.[32]

If it is important to contextualise the Liberals' victory in 1906, it is equally important not to overstate the extent of the radicals' control of the party. The cabinet line-up was extremely impressive; in January 1906 Campbell-Bannerman had three future Prime Ministers working with him – Asquith, Lloyd George and Churchill. It was to be equally notable, on the other hand, that it was these three who were to dominate entirely the social reform programme of the government, whereas others in the cabinet in control of areas which were ripe for reform (John Burns at the Local Government Board in particular, with responsibility for the Poor Law) made little attempt to use their new authority to force change. Though the 1906–14 Liberal governments are famed as the triumph of the New Liberals, the bulk of the parliamentary party was in fact composed of backwoods Gladstonians who had fought their constituencies for a generation without hope of securing a seat until this unprecedented landslide: 'demagogues' like Lloyd George and 'party turncoats' like Winston Churchill did not necessarily earn their wholly unstinting respect. Perhaps the Liberals were right to distrust the two men. After all, both of them were subsequently to follow careers which seriously jeopardised their entitlement to be called Liberals at all.

It would equally be a mistake to see the work of the ensuing government as the beginnings of the Welfare State. The reforms were never intended to be either comprehensive or universal in application. Nevertheless, the achievements of the government were substantial. If they were not a radical break from the Poor Law tradition, then they certainly marked a change in the relationship between nation and state, the first major foray into what Churchill called 'the untrodden fields' of health and employment politics. The New Liberals, perceiving a threat from Labour, were determined to offset the challenge. Lord Crewe remarked in 1905: 'More than ever before, the Liberal party is on trial as an engine for securing social reform – taxation, land, housing, etc. It has to resist the ILP claim to be the only friend of the workers'.[33] Labour by-election triumphs at Colne Valley and Jarrow in 1907 only reinforced the point, pushing the government into decisive action in 1908. Their right-wing opponents were equally well aware of the significance of what the Liberals were doing, and understood the clear alternatives that they were delineating: 'social legislation is not merely to be distinguished from socialist legislation', declared A.J. Balfour, 'but it is its most direct opposite and its most effective antidote'.[34] Certainly, the Liberals were anxious to distance their social reform programme from socialism, to create a clear distinction between themselves and Labour in their appeal to the working-class electorate. Churchill and Lloyd George liked to describe the work of the Liberals as an attempt to raise the standard of living of the working class, while socialism they described as an attempt to bring everybody down to the same level.

The young persons' legislation of 1906 and 1907 extended previous social legislation, providing for school meals, for medical inspections and treatment. It also established criteria for dealing with parental neglect and cruelty, and replaced adult law and punishment with special juvenile courts and remand homes for young offenders. The problem of child poverty that had been identified by the social investigators had thus come into range, and there was in this legislation at least the germ of the concept that children should be wards of society as a whole, that they needed special provision and special engineering as the next generation. In this sense, the new legislation broke important new ideological ground. Education had already been reformed by the Conservatives in 1902, when the School Boards had been replaced by Local Education Authorities. This reform allowed great improvements in primary education, but it also stopped the experiments in secondary education that some School Boards had been attempting. In effect, the role of the fee-paying grammar schools had thus been protected. The Liberals' scholarship scheme, by which grammar schools in receipt of state aid were required to take at least 25 per cent of their intake from the state primary schools, was designed to allow social mobility in education. Many working-class families were still unable to afford to send children to grammar schools, however, even with a scholarship. The assimilation of the 'scholarship boy' into the values of the middle class at grammar schools, moreover, probably made the scheme an effective exercise in cultural hegemony.

Old age pensions were another important breakthrough in principle though, practically, the initial results may only have been meagre. The introduction of pensions in 1908 was confined only to the very poor and the very old; though it took many elderly people off the system of 'outdoor relief' organised by the Poor Law Guardians, it did very little to help those who were actually in workhouses, who were often simply too infirm to look after themselves, with or without the small sum made available.[35]

Lloyd George's budget of 1909, the so-called 'People's Budget', was the first clear sign of the major changes which New Liberals sought to make permanent in their party's attitude to wealth. Whereas John Stuart Mill had classically described the use of taxation to redress the balance of wealth as a 'relief of the prodigal at the expense of the prudent', and had believed that a tax on capital in private hands would be counterproductive, the New Liberals were fully prepared to use the power of the state to tackle the rich landowners. While the Conservatives had moved increasingly towards indirect taxation as a way of meeting the increasing cost of government, Lloyd George proposed acquiring new revenue from taxes on the increased value of land, raising taxes on unearned income, doubling death duties for millionaires, and introducing supertax for those on more than £5000 a year. At the same time, those on incomes below £500 were given an annual £10 children's tax allowance. The Conservatives attacked the principle of discrimination between 'earned' and 'unearned' income, and complained that to soak the rich was to rob the nation of productive capital, but many Liberals were also vehemently opposed to the measures. This was in spite of the

fact that the genesis of these ideas went back at least as far as
T.H. Green, and could even claim parentage in David Ricardo
and Adam Smith themselves. In the event, the House of Lords
took the unprecedented step of throwing out the budget, on the
grounds that it contained new policy, which should be debated
separately. Lloyd George saw the opportunity to conjure a
conspiracy of tariff reformers and big landlords defending their
wide acres, and using their privileges to deny the national will
– a populist campaign that should have proved irresistible to
middle-class radicals and working class alike.

It was the National Insurance Act of 1911, however, that
was to be the flagship of New Liberal reform. Covering some
fourteen million people, health insurance provided six months
monetary benefit in the case of illness, and free medical
treatment, excluding specialist care or hospitalisation. Implicit
in the legislation, however, was the assumption that this
scheme was not intended as a complete safety net. The
monetary benefit was less than half that which Rowntree
reckoned was necessary for a typical family of five. Faced with
prolonged sickness, most working men would still have to claim
from the friendly societies or look for charity. An even more
important limitation was that health insurance did not cover
dependents, so that little was done to offset ill-health among
married women. Employment insurance at first covered only a
few of the skilled trades – about two million people – those in
fact who were least likely to fall into unemployment; the casual
labour force that particularly needed this kind of protection
was for the moment ignored. The distinction between what
was thought to be the 'respectable' poor and the remainder,
the social sump tank, was never more clear in legislation than
here. Employment insurance, as it was originally conceived,
was designed primarily to prevent the 'respectable' poor falling
into the 'submerged one-tenth', to provide them with a lifeline.
The legislation thus had very little to do with treating the
problem of poverty as such. The benefit to which the
unemployed were entitled, for fifteen weeks, was even less
than that available through the health scheme.

Basic to the legislation was a continuation, in adapted form,
of the self-help principle. The benefit that was given out was
designed simply as a small supplement to ease the burden that

would still have to be borne by voluntary savings, by private insurance schemes or by charity. The national insurance principle itself, with contributions from employee as well as employer and state, was a kind of compulsory self-help. The Poor Law, moreover, continued as the ultimate deterrent. Though the Royal Commission on the Poor Law recommended major changes in its organisation, the vociferous row that developed between those who signed the Majority Report and those who signed the more radical Minority Report provided the opportunity for conservatives in the Local Government Board to drop the idea of reform altogether. Though it is fair to say that the legislation enhanced the power of local government, spending on which from rates and government support grew from £18 millions in 1889/90 to nearly £55 millions in 1911/12, the continuation of the Poor Law system confirmed the distinction between deserving and undeserving poor. For those who fell through the safety net that the legislation provided, or for those who had used up their statutory entitlement and still remained either sick or unemployed, and for the large section of the working class who were simply not touched by the legislation, the workhouse still remained the very relevant symbol of the humiliation of poverty. In short, the National Insurance Act was the very opposite of socialist both in intention and in effect. It divided the poor and it hardly treated the symptoms of poverty. In this sense, the Liberals had certainly distanced themselves from Labour in terms of defining the attitude of the state in social matters, now that intervention itself was a matter of common political agreement.

Labour broadly supported the Liberal proposals, because their immediate programme did not differ substantially from that of the progressives within the governing party. Yet the distinctions involved here, though apparently minor, had far-reaching implications. Labour support was on the somewhat negative grounds that something was better than nothing. They argued, for example, for a non-contributory scheme rather than an insurance scheme, to pay for health and unemployment. They were also more interested in schemes which would prevent poverty, rather than simply deal with some of its consequences. This was the point behind campaigns such as Labour's Right to Work Bill of 1908, which would have established a statutory right to a job as a fundamental element in social planning. Churchill did set up Labour Exchanges, to provide a nationwide network of information about job availability, but a suspicious TUC was worried that the Exchanges might be used as agencies for blackleg labour, an example of the accelerating deterioration of trust between Liberals and organised labour. In their trades and labour legislation, however, the Liberals were in fact delving into deeper and rather more signficant waters than in their social legislation, because they were here intruding into the heart of the labour market, into the hitherto sacrosanct laws of labour supply and demand. Trade Boards were set up to establish minimum wages in certain sweated trades. The miners' claim for an eight-hour day won statutory recognition, and a Shops Act provided for weekly half-holidays in the retailing industry.

The industrial unrest of the period 1910–14, moreover, was met by the Liberals with compromise as well as coercion, a partially successful attempt to show that they were still concerned to appear the friends of organised labour. The Board of Trade showed itself prepared to intervene and to arbitrate.[36] In fact, the unrest was probably more of a threat to Labour than it was to the Liberals. The development of syndicalist ideas, insignficant though they might have been overall, was symptomatic of a wider disenchantment with the achievements of the first years of Labour. Yet the securing of the financial position of the party with the Osborne Judgement (which legalised the TUC's political funds), and the beginning of payment for MPs (the lack of which had made working-class parliamentary candidature so problematic), made life a great deal easier for the new party. The argument from then on was not whether the traditional parties would be able to crush Labour, but whether the new party would remain as moderate as it had been until this time. The leadership of the party was being increasingly pressurised to give up the electoral pact with the Liberals and confront the government more directly. Indeed, while the relationship between Liberal and Labour at parliamentary level was still a relatively co-operative affair, at the grass roots, in local politics, it had taken on all the

attributes of cut-throat competition, even producing Liberal–
Tory municipal alliances to keep Labour out of office.[37]

The Liberal problem in parliament still remained their
inability to hold an overall majority. The two elections of 1910
proved to be the failure of Lloyd George's plan to turn the
People's Budget into another great Liberal crusade. Though
they could still poll well over 40 per cent of the popular vote,
the Liberals were once again unable to turn these votes into
majorities in enough of the English constituencies, particularly
in the South-East. Once again, they were reliant on the Irish.
The question of reform of the House of Lords, which Lloyd
George had hoped to tie to the upper house's refusal to pass the
People's Budget, became tied instead to the issue of Home
Rule. After the election of January, the House of Lords passed
the People's Budget in just one sitting, and steadied itself for
what everyone knew was the real issue. The Tories' head-on
assault on both Home Rule and House of Lords reform,
coupled with the feminist revolt in the streets, the industrial
unrest and, finally, the apparent near-mutiny in the British
Army in Northern Ireland, faced the government in the last
few years of the peace with the prospect of a complete
breakdown of control.

THE STATE OF THE PARTIES, 1914

With the break-up of the Liberal consensus in the late
nineteenth century, three alternatives presented themselves: a
dynamic imperialism represented by the Conservative party;
the progressivism of the New Liberals; and an independent
Labour party committed to overturning the traditional
polarity of British party politics by winning an independent
voice for the organised working class. All three of these options
involved some measure of state intervention in social matters,
with consequent important fiscal rearrangements, to meet the
needs of the enlarged electorate of post-1867 and post-1884, to
cope with the fears of large sections of that electorate as they
had been outlined by the social investigators. None of these
options can be said to have won the day before 1914.
Conservatism had been nearly ripped apart by tariff reform,

though it had been pulled back together by the constitutional issues of 1910–14, the natural political ground of Toryism. Labour had arrived in parliament, but was still fighting for full recognition both in national and in local politics. The Liberals had, in 1906, apparently recovered from the problems of the 1880s and 1890s, though the election results of 1910 left a very big question mark over the extent of this recovery. In this important transitional period, as the British political system adjusted both to a larger electorate and to continuing economic and social pressures, the only certainty was that the terms of reference of the political debate had switched from a general assumption that the state which governed least governed best to the question of how far, and in what areas, the state should intervene.

Lloyd George had hoped to be able to bring the Liberal party swinging into the twentieth century, forgetting the trials and tribulations of the previous twenty years. In retrospect, however, it is possible to see that he arrived too late to complete the transition of the Liberals from a basically middle-class party to a basically working-class party. Indeed, Lloyd George was as convinced as anyone in the Liberal tradition that sectionalism, class interest, was anathema. He had hoped to overlay class differences, to rebuild belief in the central tenet of the Victorian Liberals that freedom transcended class boundaries. To the propertied classes, Lloyd George was a dangerous populist, further alienating the well-off in the Liberal ranks, and there was no clear sign that there had been any compensating claw-back in the working-class vote. In this sense, Lloyd George as radical may have destabilised the Liberals still further, setting them up for the even more telling blows that he was soon to deal them as war leader. Fundamentally, however, the crisis that faced the Liberal party was really nothing to do with personalities at all. The development of alternative political ideas, such as those championed by the New Liberals, was a reaction to the changed economic and social climate of the late nineteenth century, a hegemonic adaptation designed to negotiate the growing gulf between the social classes and to maintain some relevance for the Liberal party as Gladstonianism came to the end of its credible life. The problem was finally one of riding two horses. It was a political fix which could just as easily have affected the Conservative party. Indeed, the political problem that the Tories suffered over the intrusion of Joseph Chamberlain and Tariff Reform was similar in type though not in scale to the problem of the Liberals. In fact, the Conservatives had reacted much earlier than the Liberals to the change in the terms of reference of politics, adopting the lower-middle class as their ultimate in-the-bank support, their natural electoral constituency. The emergence of Labour, however, was likely to rob the Liberals of any similarly reliable long-term support, in the trade unions, if left unchecked. The Conservatives' support of Imperialism had found the Liberals incoherent and divided. They had recovered from this, but major constitutional problems like Ireland and the House of Lords continued to eat into their political reserves. By 1914, in spite of the successes of New Liberalism, the Liberal party remained an unstable political grouping, lurching from one crisis to another. The tensions in the party in the ensuing war years were to create new opportunities for Labour to exploit.

Yet it was also true that the Liberals had proved to be the most courageous and the most exciting politicians of the decades before the Great War. The party that had been most famous for the dominant individualist ideology of the Victorian period, was also the party which took the first major steps along the road to state intervention. Tentative though these first steps may have been, with the benefit of hindsight they had broken new ideological ground and opened new horizons. It is also fair to say that, though the Liberal party itself was to cease to have any real prospect of political power within a decade, the contradictions, paradoxes and compromises of Victorian and Edwardian Liberalism were to continue to provide the central questions in the development of political ideas in Britain in the ensuing decades. The problems of the Liberal party before 1914 were in fact the problems of Britain as a whole, and the collapse of the Liberals did not make those problems go away.

2

THE IMPACT OF THE GREAT WAR

THE TEST OF TOTAL WAR

Many in Europe believed that the war which broke out in Europe in August 1914 would be over by Christmas. This view was not, on the whole, born out of any complacency, rather out of the assumption that contemporary military organisation and weaponry would prove to be so powerful and so expensive that no nation would be able to maintain a war effort for more than a matter of months. In fact, most of the nations which became involved in the conflict proved to have enormous reserves of industrial potential, available manpower and political commitment to the fight. The strength of defensive weaponry soon bogged down the military effort, on the Western Front at least, to a stalemated battle of attrition. Once it became clear, after repeated attempts to achieve a military breakthrough, that the war would ultimately be decided not so much by the generals but by the ability of the combatant nations to pour continuing supplies of *materiel* and manpower into the battle, then the home fronts were to become at least as important as the battle fronts in the war effort. In the last resort, victory was to go to the side which was best able to organise its industrial production and to maintain political stability at home in so doing. Czarist Russia was to crack as a political system in 1917, and Germany and Austria-Hungary were to follow suit in 1918. Britain and France ended up on the winning side not, finally, because their generals were better, but because they were able to maintain their war efforts (though only just in France's case) until the entry of the Americans into the war tipped the balance of attrition firmly in favour of the Allies.

The political strains of mobilising and maintaining a total war effort were immense. The First World War was to test both political assumptions and the efficiency of governmental organisations to the limit. In all combatant nations it was clear that government, as an institution, had simply to adapt to the new conditions or lose the war. But adaptation was no easy process. For an autocratic government like that in Czarist Russia or a semi-autocratic government like that of Imperial Germany, it was not simply the development of a new bureaucratic efficiency to deal with problems like food distribution and manpower supply that was needed, but a new credibility for the ruling elite among those who had to bear the direct strain of the war itself, either as members of the armed forces or as industrial workers. It soon became clear, in other words, that political adaptation to the needs of total war also demanded some recognition of the consequences of mass participation in the defence of the state. Mass mobilisation altered the relationship between leaders and led because it demanded an organic link between nation and state. Put simply, only with such a link was it conceivable that soldiers in a mass army would go on exposing themselves to the ultimate self-sacrifice without turning their arms on their own officers and politicians, and only if it were perceived that the national good was also the good of the working class would organised labour use its influence to maintain the industrial output without which the soldiers would be literally disarmed.

The sheer destructive potential of total war, moreover, tested concepts of the future; peace aims were to expand as the war grew more prolonged and more devastating. In the same way that German casualties fed the demand for an annexationist peace, so the rise in British casualties led to an escalation in war aims. British soldiers died for 'gallant little Belgium' in 1914, for the 'destruction of Prussian militarism' in 1916, and then in a bid to make the conflict 'the war to end wars' by 1918. The sheer scale of the casualties took over, becoming in itself a rationale both for continuing the war and for seeing it in apocalyptic terms. This was to have important consequences when it came to signing the peace. Having gone to the peace conference in Paris to secure what he hoped would be a just and lasting peace, Lloyd George reacted to public pressure to 'squeeze Germany until the pips squeaked' once discussions got under way. Above all, this was a direct consequence of the 'hate-the-hun' message that had been developed to meet the possibility that the public would tire of the appalling demands that the war generated. For the first time, the development of the means of mass communication had made it possible so to construct the national mood that the conflict would be continued until the process of total war worked its way to its ultimate conclusion, at virtually whatever cost it demanded. At the same time, the need to maintain psychological commitment to the war bred popular expectations as to its outcome which were often at variance with politicians' estimates of just what the state could accomplish. Promises such as that made by Lloyd George that he would build 'homes fit for heroes to live in', were to generate a revolution of rising expectations which demanded more thorough peacetime state intervention than anything yet attempted.

Arthur Marwick has identified the political pressures generated by total war as fourfold: first, total war tests political institutions and assumptions; second, it demands concessions to previously undervalued sections of the population in recognition of the importance of their contribution; third, it produces a dislocation and a disruption of peacetime patterns of social relationships which in turn opens up opportunities for major reconstruction; fourth, total war also has a psychological dimension – the reaction to the fact that so many were killed, for instance – that alters fundamentally, albeit unquantifiably (because psychological change is, by definition, so difficult to document) the balance in the social formation. Though Marwick's 'four-tier model' is by no means as helpful as it looks (it can be applied, after all, to any of the many pressures which produce social change in history, in peace as much as in war), and though it is by no means as predictive as the use of the sociological term 'model' would suggest, it does at least provide a useful analytical distinction for describing the manifold ways in which the pressures of twentieth-century wars have not simply accelerated but have also actually generated those pressures which produce social change.[1]

The most obvious political casualty of the test presented by the Great War was the Liberal party, though the Liberal decline was in fact already measurable before 1914 and was by no means completed by 1918. Important as the Great War undoubtedly was in altering the frame of reference of British politics, just as significant is the evidence of the remarkable resilience of traditional political loyalties. This was in turn a reflection of the quite extraordinary ability to adapt demonstrated during the war by the state institutions and indeed by the social fabric itself. It might have been expected that nothing was better calculated to destroy the careful synthesis between collectivism and individualism built by the New Liberals before 1914 than a mobilisation for total war. In fact, though the process undermined the Liberal party, the state machinery itself adapted remarkably rapidly to the extraordinary demand. At the same time, largely because the need for increased state intervention was seen to be out of the ordinary and merely short-term, the damage done to the liberal tradition of thought by the war was by no means fatal. The period 1918 to the mid-1920s was characterised, above all, by an attempt to return to normality – which meant, largely, an attempt to rebuild the landscape of pre-1914 values – as if the Great War had simply been a hiccup rather than a turning-point in the historical process. This produced the danger of serious conflict in the postwar period: not until the impact of the first ten years of the Great Depression had made themselves felt were there to be clear signs that political thought was adjusting to the fact that a permanent change had occurred in the direction of British history. The Great War further undermined classical liberal political values, but not even the superimposed effect of the depression was to kill them entirely.

The fact is that government adapted pragmatically to war demand, without ever conceding that the increases in state intervention were anything more than expedient and short term. Though, early in the war, Asquith's government failed to see the need for widespread controls, the Western Front proved to be a bottomless pit for resources. 'Business as usual' was the slogan of 1914, but by April 1916 the war was costing the nation £3.75 million every day. Already, £1222 million had been borrowed. The inevitable result was a major shift in the concept of national finances, with swingeing increases in both direct and indirect taxation. By 1918, 7.75 million people were paying income tax, six times as many as in 1914. This reflected the fact that individual incomes in most instances rose steeply during the war, of course, but it also signified a much wider and deeper intrusion of the state into the lives of ordinary people than anything that had hitherto been contemplated in other than socialist circles. Still, massive increases in taxation were not enough to offset the cost of the war. The National Debt had risen to £7000 million by 1918, a burden that was to prove almost unbearable as Britain moved from the war into the Great Depression.[2]

Control of industry was another inevitable consequence of wartime demand. The most remarkable example of many, perhaps, was the development of the Ministry of Munitions. Formed in May 1915 with David Lloyd George as its first, energetic Minister, Munitions expanded rapidly and enormously. By 1918, it had spent £2000 million in all and, at the end of the war, employed a staff of 65 000.[3] Yet the Ministry of Munitions was also the most obvious of the 'extraordinary' demands made by the war, a simply temporary phenomenon, the ideological significance of which was dismantled along with the rest of the state machinery as soon as the demand for weaponry had evaporated. Areas of the economy such as coal-mining, however, were to prove less adaptable to temporary demand. Virtually nationalised during the war, and heavily subsidised in order to maintain full production and minimal labour disruption, the mining firms had become by 1918 an omelette that proved virtually impossible to unscramble. The dismantling of the state control of the coal mines was to become the critical issue of the early 1920s, leading directly to the General Strike of 1926. Mining, however, was an exception to the general rule of ad hoc, piecemeal state intervention in industry during the war, in which the principle of temporary expediency was paramount, and the implication of an irreversible increase in state direction no more than minimal. Though a Ministry of Shipping was created in late 1916 in response to the toll in the Atlantic and the need to rationalise Britain's mercantile needs, it was not until late 1917 that the government was prepared to go so far as to introduce food rationing. For a country which relied so heavily on imports for simple survival, this was an extraordinary example of the tenacity of laissez-faire principles.

Modern techniques of mass communication were also used purposefully and on a large scale for the first time. A Department of Information was set up in 1917 and in 1918 a full Ministry was set up under Lord Beaverbrook. Full use was made of posters, films and the press to propagate the Germanophobe message.[4] The intention was to boost home-front morale at the fag end of a long war, particularly important once Labour had gone public on the demand for a negotiated peace. But the fact that a state-organised campaign could be left until so late in the war was once again a significant tribute to the longevity of traditional liberal, or at least libertarian ideas. Freedom of thought, after all, had always been the keystone in the structure of liberal thought. It was also, however, a tribute to the vigour of national patriotism that the need for such a Ministry was not apparent earlier in the war. The Imperialist urge of the late nineteenth century, the jingoism which had permeated the popular press and the music hall, had clearly been extremely effective in the psychological preparation of the population for war. The popular association of Germany with 'Prussianism' and authoritarianism, moreover, had created an atmosphere in which stories of German atrocities could become credible, and anti-war feeling marginalised. Alone among the great military powers in Europe in the nineteenth century, Britain had never conscripted, and could still afford to rely on a voluntary system to produce recruits until the great battles of the middle of the war. Nothing, perhaps, testifies more effectively to the stability of British society, and the strength of British political institutions, in 1914.

Early in 1916, however, it became inevitable that government would have to take the unenviable step of introducing compulsion. By December 1915, recruiting had shrunk to 55 000 a month (compared with 450 000 in September 1914). Not only did increased wages and job opportunities at home make enlistment less enticing, but the casualty lists hardly made good recruitment material. The problem, however, was not simply one of finding enough recruits but also of protecting vital war industries from losing valuable personnel to the Army; the voluntary system in the Great War pulled into the Army not simply the unemployed, as had traditionally been the case, but skilled craftsmen in essential trades. Ultimately, only conscription could produce the basis for the full manpower budget which was essential to keep the armed forces and war industries working most effectively in tandem.[5] Even conscription did not solve entirely the problem of producing adequate forecasts of the manpower budget, however; in 1918 men had to be pulled out of uniform for essential industrial work, just as major German offensives were threatening to tear holes in the British front line. Working its way through wholly uncharted territory, government was only slowly learning the rudiments of the concepts of state planning, an alien business which was undertaken only because it had to be. The experience of government in these fields was to be invaluable in framing the much more thorough and pervasive developments in state control in the Second World War, but were only undertaken in this period in a spirit of pure and short-term pragmatism. To this extent at least, the spirit of liberalism was merely submerged temporarily by the war, even if it seemed on the surface of things to endure massive dents.[6]

For the soldiers, whether volunteers or conscripts, there were to be few comforts in the war itself, and precious few in the immediate aftermath. Unlike the armies of Russia, Germany and France, on the other hand, there was to be little evidence in the British Army of major radicalisation by the war. There were problems of morale similar to those suffered by other armies, notably the mutiny at the Etaples base camp in September 1917, and the panicky premature surrender of some elements of the Fifth Army faced with the German spring offensive of 1918. Desertion ran at a rate of approximately 10 per cent annually. The ratio of military police to soldiers climbed steadily during the war, and courts-martial ran at 160 a day, compared with 10 a day in 1913. On the whole, however, it would appear that the 'culture of consolation' that had begun to characterise the late Victorian working class as a whole carried over into the wartime armies, a sardonic acceptance of the inevitable and a tendency to keep one's head down, both literally and metaphorically.[7] Two notable consequences of the soldiers' experience, however, were to play an important part in the shaping of postwar Britain. First, it is noticeable not just from the writings of the anti-war poets, but also from the diaries and letters of ordinary soldiers, that there developed a very distinct gap, a lack of comprehension between front line and home front. Soldiers on leave found it virtually impossible to discuss their experiences with family or friends, often finding themselves longing to return to the trenches, to leave behind the unreality of life on leave. Letters from home to soldiers do indeed often reveal a complete absence of understanding of conditions on the Western Front.[8] The effect of this rift may well have been to create a bond in the generation of young men that survived the trenches unlike anything that had happened before. The bond among the British survivors may not have been as dramatic as the commonly-used phrase 'the brotherhood of the damned' suggests. It certainly did not have such devastating consequences as it was to have in countries like Germany, where old comrades' associations and *freikorps* took the military spirit into the streets, playing an important role in the development of Nazism. On the other hand many rootless young men in Britain, trained only in the use of arms and grown used to violence, did drift into organisations like the 'Black and Tans', the Auxiliaries used with punishing consequences to restore order in Ireland after the war. In some of the expressions of labour and political protest in the postwar period, too, it is possible to discern elements of a restlessness with peacetime codes of conduct and politics. Certainly, the government did show signs of worry that the training of a whole generation in the use of arms could prove as devastating a political factor as it had become in Russia in 1917.

On the other hand, there was a second significant element in the soldiers' experience, and that was the reaction of many young officers to their first close cross-class experience. Undoubtedly, one of the many reasons why the British Army was able to tolerate the war for so long was the strength of its system of organisation, the group loyalty inspired by the regimental, company and, in particular, the platoon system. There is enough evidence to suggest that the interdependence generated by platoon loyalty provided in most cases a tight knit between men, NCOs and junior officers. For many, the trenches provided a revealing glimpse across the class divide for the first time, in a way that does not appear to have been nearly as true in the case of most other belligerent nations. The paternalist training of British officers combined with the traditions of duty and service imbued in the public schools, from which so many of the young officers came, to provide the basis of a generation of socially-conscious politicians who were to begin to break through into prominence in the 1930s. Harold Macmillan, Anthony Eden and Clement Attlee were among the most prominent. Though it was to become a cliché in the interwar years that the division which split Britain was not one between classes, but between those who had fought and those who had not fought in the Great War, it is fair to say that in some measure the class divide was indeed overlaid by the shared experience of combat. The major generators of the welfare state mentality were in fact to come from the younger commissioned survivors of the generation which fought the Great War.[9]

It would clearly be unwise to come to any simple conclusion on the effects of the test of the Great War on the millions of British men who fought it. Yet the physical evidence of the destruction of life and limb remained a constant scar on the collective conscious of the interwar generation. The three-quarters of a million British dead were to be mythologised as 'the lost generation'; they were to be iconised, too, in the building of war memorials in every city, town, and virtually every village throughout the country. The one and a half million wounded still walking the streets were everyday reminders, as were the widows and the young women who lived the rest of their lives as spinsters, of the deeper psychological trauma which did not end with the Armistice.

WOMEN AND THE WAR

As problematic as quantifying the long-term impact of the Great War on the system of government and on the men who joined the armed services is its effect on the role and self-perception of women in British society. The Great War is often portrayed as the period in which women moved into a new and more equal relationship with men. True, women did gain the parliamentary vote for the first time in 1918, and it is tempting to see a direct relationship between women's participation in the conflict and the winning of the franchise. But the vote awarded to women in 1918 was limited; not for another decade were women given the vote on the same basis as men. Though it may be fair to say that the war provided major new opportunities for women, it is too easy to forget, first, that women were already making large strides in terms of economic liberation before 1914 and, second, that many of the 'gains' made during the war proved to be for the duration only. Indeed, women in the Second World War and even into the 1970s were still fighting battles they had good reason to believe had been won many years earlier.

There are, of course, major theoretical difficulties in treating women separately in any discussion of the development of British politics and society. The implicit assumption in any such distinction must be that the rest, the majority, of the discussion will be about men. Unfortunately, it is an insurmountable historiographical problem that unless one treats women separately, they may not be treated at all. It is historically accurate to say that British politics, even after the enfranchisement of women, has been predominantly about, by and for, men. The first female cabinet member took office in 1924, but it was to be sixty years after enfranchisement before Britain had a female Prime Minister. Female cabinet ministers and even female members of parliament remained a tiny minority among the normal lobby-fodder of men.

What this limitation on the political liberation of women underlines quite clearly is the limited nature of the original suffrage campaign itself. Rooted as the central campaign was in the traditional liberal assumption that political freedom was itself the key to economic, social and cultural liberation, many of the early suffragists failed to measure the deep pathological roots of patriarchy. In fact, the repression of women rested on more than simply legal disabilities. Traditionally, the role of women in British industrial society rested on four functions; first, as producers of labour, they were responsible as wives for keeping the predominantly male workforce clothed, fed and ready for work; second, as reproducers of labour, they were responsible as mothers for producing, bringing up and socialising the next generation; third, as shoppers for the family, they played an important role in the developing consumer economy, and were targeted as such by the growing advertising industry in the late nineteenth century; fourth, in times of economic boom, national emergency or other labour shortage, they played the part of a reserve army of labour that could be called upon to fill the temporary gap in the manpower budget. The problem with women's experience of the Great War was that while their fourth function in this list, their role as a reserve army of labour, loomed very large, and while their role as consumers was temporarily backgrounded due to the heavy industrial demand generated by the war, their important economic and social roles as producers and reproducers of labour were in no way diminished. Since, too, the massive boom in women's employment opportunity was to be simply temporary, there was to be no clear evidence that the vote would amount to anything more than a cosmetic exercise – however well-intentioned the prime movers of the campaign for the vote may have been.

Even before 1914, after all, five million women were working, out of a total female population of some eighteen and a half million. The distribution of this largely working-class female workforce through the economy, however, demonstrates fairly conclusively that job opportunity before 1914 rested on more than simply economic factors. In mining areas, for instance, female work in the pits themselves had been banned during the nineteenth century and, although there were women employed on the surface in some areas, these 'pit-brow lasses' were considered socially disreputable.[10] With no other lighter work available in most of the mining areas, women were fairly tightly restrained to the home and the family; the powerful patriarchal system that resulted endowed the mother-image of women with full cultural weight, and it was this mother-image which so heavily underpinned the sense of community of the mining areas, a prime example of gender being overdetermined by class. In the textile-producing areas, however, where mechanisation had occured much earlier, a very different pattern of female employment was discernible. In Lancashire, for example, there was proportionately a much larger female workforce than in South Wales. It is also clear that the stable tradition of work led to a much fuller politicisation. On a purely organisational as much as on an ideological level, it is much easier to politicise people in stable work than in the home – this applies as much to unemployed men as to women – because it is in the workplace that the corporate sense of solidarity develops, and the power of labour is most obvious. The work of the Lancashire working-class suffragists before the Great War was notable for its insistence on seeing the female suffrage as only one element in a wider struggle for adult suffrage, and the general improvement of the lot of the working class. In fact, Lancashire feminism tended to be an element in working-class consciousness rather than a discrete feminist ideology as such.[11]

This socialist feminism stood in increasingly marked contrast to the development of the Pankhursts' Women's Social and Political Union (WSPU), in which the issue of gender, and above all votes for women, quickly overdetermined issues of class. The WSPU was largely though by no means wholly middle-class in its membership; its early links with, for example, the Lancashire working-class feminists soon faded in significance. Middle-class females in late Victorian Britain tended to be almost entirely housebound: middle-class male status depended on the household, and middle-class wives acted, in effect, as their husbands' social chief of staff. Marriage was the aim of all middle-class education, and incarceration in household duties the major prospect for the typical member of the 'silent sisterhood'. The prospect for unmarried women was, typically, to become the governess to someone else's children, or else to live in the virtual purdah of Victorian spinsterhood.[12] It was largely those who objected to this regime who became the backbone of the militant suffrage campaign of pre-1914. With the spread of family-planning among the middle class, to limit the size of families as the Great Price Fall ate into salaries and savings, and with the mechanisation of household duties, the educated middle-class woman had more time and thought to devote to political issues. For many, the furore over the Contagious Diseases Acts – which virtually legitimised prostitution, thus formalising the sexual exploitation of women and underpinning the Victorian moral double-standard – was the *entrée*.

The demand for votes for women was by no means new in pre-1914 Britain; it had featured as a plank in the Chartists' platform, and had enjoyed the life-long advocacy of John Stuart Mill. It was, however, the anger caused by the Contagious Diseases Acts which gave it a new vigour, and which led to suffragism becoming a mass movement. The militancy of the WSPU campaign in the decade before the Great War undoubtedly forced the issue into the forefront of national political interest, where it was continually stymied by the tactics of a dismissive Prime Minister, H.H. Asquith. Even the best supporters of female suffrage, however, were somewhat worried by the militancy, and by the social and political make-up of the WSPU. Though the Labour party as a whole backed the right of women to vote, they saw female emancipation as only an element in the campaign for adult suffrage; only Keir Hardie and George Lansbury appeared regularly on WSPU platforms. Some of the Labour worries appeared to be vindicated later; though the Pankhursts had long connections with the ILP, Sylvia Pankhurst was to move sharply to the left while Emmeline and Christabel were to move just as sharply to the right. Sylvia, indeed, played an active part in the foundation of the Communist Party, while Christabel was to stand as a Coalition candidate in 1918, and Emmeline as a Conservative in 1926.[13]

With the outbreak of war, the militant campaign ended, the leaders hoping to show that in the defeat of Germany, women were to be as important as men. With the rapid growth in the demand both for volunteers for the armed forces and recruits for industry, female work opportunities boomed. In industry, however, this involved the process of 'diluting' skilled trades, mechanising traditionally male-dominated crafts so that the jobs could be performed by unskilled or semi-skilled women.

Though the Trades Union Congress accepted this process as an inevitable consequence of massive demand, it was by no means wholly accepted on the shop-floor by men who saw their livelihoods threatened thereby. Many female workers were likely therefore to have found themselves targeted if they had stayed in these 'men's jobs' after the emergency was over. Much of this increased demand for female labour, moreover, came in industries specifically geared to war production, and the demand evaporated as soon as the war was over. In the munitions industries, for example, female employment grew from 212 000 in July 1914, to 819 000 in July 1917, and then to a peak of 947 000 in November 1918. Thereafter, naturally, it fell away sharply. Indeed, the comparison of the size of the total female workforce over the first thirty years of the twentieth century in Table 2.1 shows that the period 1911 to 1921 was actually a relatively poor decade in the overall trend towards greater female employment.

Table 2.1 *Total females employed 1901–31*[14]

1901	4 171 751
1911	4 830 734
1921	5 065 332
1931	5 606 043

Nevertheless, it would be wrong to minimise the impact of the war on female employment by reducing it to statistics. After the war, most young working-class females refused to go back to the drudgery of domestic service, a major area of female employment before 1914. Partly, no doubt, the erosion of middle-class living standards made it difficult for them to employ as many domestic servants anyway, but society magazines of the 1920s were full of letters and stories bewailing the difficulty of finding staff. New avenues for employment were opened up, some of which proved to be irreversible. In clerical work, for instance, the female typist was replacing the Dickensian male clerk on his high stool. In the professions, in particular, female doctors, dentists and veterinary surgeons moved from the realm of the notable to the unremarkable. This trend was backed by legislation, too; the Sexual Disqualifications (Removal) Act of 1919 made it illegal to refuse professional jobs or entry to the universities on grounds of gender. Though it may well be true that male-dominated appointment committees thereafter simply did not admit (or did not even realise) that gender bias continued to operate, this legislation was the first important recognition of the possible role of the state in countering irrational prejudice.

Nor must the psychological significance of even a short-term liberation in terms of job opportunity be overlooked. Though women in war work were consistently paid less than men for similar work, the independence granted by having a wage of one's own, and by learning some of the skills that had previously been part of the impenetrable male/work mystique, played their role in eroding traditional values. Family life was disrupted both by men being away from home, either working or fighting at the front, and by the fact that many younger females were living away from home and earning their own keep. In these situations, women were able to adopt a higher profile in both making and implementing family decisions and traditional patriarchal authority was undermined.[15] Changing moral attitudes also had their effect on women. The employment of women on such a large scale involved a much freer mixing of the sexes in the factories, breaking down many of the traditional cultural taboos. Though young women working away from home were carefully chaperoned in their hostels, casual relationships could develop at work where, traditionally, they could only develop after hours in the patriarchal cultural climate of the street and the home. The impact of the soldiers coming home on leave, moreover, did much to break down a massive ignorance about sex and about methods of contraception. Indeed, 'giving the boys on leave a good time' came almost to be considered a patriotic duty. It was notable that the 'war babies scandal', the large rise in the number of illegitimate children born in the war, was couched by the popular press in terms not of outrage at the decline of moral standards but of outrage that any blame should be attached to the mothers of brave soldiers' children. The issue of condoms to the troops, to help prevent the spread of venereal disease rather than to encourage sexual activity as such, did much to spread knowledge of means of birth control down into the working class. This in turn was to help to control one of the biggest causes of poverty in pre-1914 Britain, and one which particularly affected the health of working-class women, the problem of over-large families. The publication by Marie Stopes of *Married Love* in 1918, in spite of that publication's continued heavy emphasis on the traditional ideology of motherhood, was to give concrete form to the debates both on family planning and on female sexuality, issues that the moral climate of the Great War had done much to inform.[16] In the longer term, merely to introduce those questions may have been the single most important change that the Great War inaugurated for British women, because it was in the core of such debates that questions about the traditional gender balance in Britain could be most effectively raised.

Nevertheless, the loss of job opportunities at the end of the war was a sad blow to the cause of female liberation. Oral evidence seems to suggest that women themselves had only ever considered their wartime role to be temporary, that they had always believed that they were simply keeping the bench seats at the factories warm for the men, when they came home from the trenches.[17] For those who remained in permanent employment, there were still to be basic discrepancies in pay between men and women. The argument still held good that young women generally should only work to supplement the family income until they were married, and that married women similarly did not need a 'living wage'. Explicit in this pay discrepancy was still the assumption that there should be no need for women to work; the fact that they did work reflected on their fathers' or husbands' ability to provide. Marriage, whether in unskilled or in professional jobs, was still considered in many cases to be a bona fide reason for terminating employment. Official interwar unemployment figures, moreover, are probably wildly understated, simply because many women – not qualified for state unemployment insurance – did not bother to register. The history of interwar working-class women, yet to be fully written up, will almost certainly describe social conditions only marginally improved from the late Victorian and Edwardian period. What evidence has been collected suggests a story of women going short of food themselves in order to keep their men ready for work, should it appear, and of chronic neurological and gynaecological problems going untreated except by cheap, available aspirins.[18] It is clear that, whatever psychological difference the Great War may have made, measurable material advances for women rested on continued job opportunity. The political emancipation of 1918 and 1928 did not lead inexorably to social, economic and cultural emancipation, because the Great War had only produced the necessary precondition of large-scale employment for a short period. Only when the traditional functions of women within the British industrial economy had been effectively contested could the psychic balance of the genders be re-ordered.

With the gaining of the vote, however, the steam temporarily went out of the feminist movement, the leadership of which had campaigned largely on that single issue. In the 1918 general election, moreover, the female suffrage was still limited. While men won adult suffrage, only women over 30 who were householders, wives of householders, had a £5 property qualification or were graduates were allowed to vote. Effectively, this meant that most of the women who had helped to win the war, the young 'munionettes', remained disenfranchised until 1928. The limitations on the female franchise in 1918 make it difficult to resist the conclusion that the granting of the initial vote was the long-term result of the pressure applied by the predominantly middle-class feminist movement of pre-1914, rather than the direct contribution of women as a whole to the war effort. Nevertheless, full adult suffrage was soon to follow. Yet, even then, women still found themselves the victims of political, economic, social and cultural circumstances which the mere granting of the vote would not alleviate. Socialist feminists were to find themselves tied, in the interwar period, to the Labour party or the Communist party at a time when politics were dominated by the Conservatives. The economy, moreover, was dominated through the 1920s by a Depression which threw their menfolk out of work; through the 1930s by a recovery based on consumerism, which re-emphasised womens' role in the home – a new, increasingly affluent home with fewer children, it is true, but still home for all that.

ORGANISED LABOUR AND THE WAR

While women had to wait until 1928 to get the vote on the same basis as men, the extension of the franchise to cover virtually all adult males in 1918 produced a situation in which the working-class dominated the electorate for the first time. The electorate had in fact been tripled at a stroke. This domination by the working class did not lead to the kind of radicalisation of politics that many on the political right had feared. In fact, the attitudes and assumptions which dominated the pre-1914 working class were not substantially changed by the experience of the war. The issues on which a new class friction could be built were undoubtedly present, and broke out in many instances in intense labour disputes, and complaints about profiteering, about conscription and about food prices. On the other hand, the state proved adaptable in its response, and developed a closely-listening ear to working-class opinion on the home front. For it was not simply at the level of overall organisation of the war effort that the state intervened during the war; the introduction of rent controls, price controls, rationing, the large increase in the number of people paying direct taxes, the de-skilling of certain trades, the regulation of drinking hours and the introduction of firm rulings on the circumstances in which one could leave a job, brought the state into the details of daily life in wartime Britain in a wholly unprecedented fashion. All of these intrusions by the state were potentially explosive, and it says a great deal for the fundamental stability of the class system in Britain at this time that they were achieved relatively painlessly, and indeed were largely believed to be both necessary and benevolent. In the process, however, certain assumptions and expectations about the state were built into working-class consciousness, and the withdrawal of the state from so many areas of national life in the immediate post-war years was to spark off the most serious instances of class conflict in modern British history. Only when the state re-learned the need to adapt did the working class respond with its characteristic moderation.

The outbreak of the war found Labour in real disarray. In July 1914 the Parliamentary Labour party resolved that Britain should stay out of any European war, but the Trades

Union Congress was seized by the patriotic fervour of the time and forced a reversal of the PLP decision. Ramsay MacDonald resigned and the largely pacifist Independent Labour party – the leading thinkers and strategists of the Labour party until this time – were forced into a temporary isolation. The patriotism of the TUC brought its reward in terms of a close liaison with government on matters of industrial and labour regulation. The unions used their influence to make the first six months of the war a period of profound industrial peace. Many industrialists, however – particularly those faced with heavy war demand, such as in the engineering and shipbuilding industries – were pressing for the end of restrictive trade practices which, they argued, were hampering expansion of production. The voluntary acceptance by the union leaders of such a proposal was a key indicator of their patriotism, though it was severely to dent their credibility among many of their members.

In February and March 1915 the Treasury, unions and management successfully negotiated a deal for the engineering industry under the terms of which the 'dilution' of the workforce, the replacement of skilled workers by unskilled or semi-skilled workers, was permitted in return for a guarantee that trade practices would be restored at the end of the war. In the wake of this deal, the unions were soon being pressured to widen it to cover all industry. The reported shell shortage on the Western Front provided a particular sense of urgency; the result was the so-called 'Treasury Agreement'.[19] This voluntarism, however, did not last long. When Lloyd George moved from the Treasury to the Ministry of Munitions the Treasury Agreement was given the force of law and considerably extended. Under the terms of the Munitions of War Act, the suspension of trade practices was authorised in all war-related industry, and industrial disputes were subject to compulsory arbitration. Munitions workers were also forbidden to leave their jobs without the consent of their employer. In return, the guaranteed return to prewar trade practices after the war was extended to all affected industries, and an 80 per cent excess profits tax was introduced to prevent profiteering by industrialists in the national emergency.

But a willingness to co-operate at the national level was not always reciprocated at the local level. Only days after the legislation came into force, compulsory arbitration failed to stop a strike for increased wages in the South Wales coalfield, and the government was forced to back down, conceding most of the strikers' demands. Not altogether surprisingly, moreover, many engineers on the shop floor were not wholly enamoured of the national agreement on dilution. On Clydeside, notably, shop-stewards led a significant rebellion against the leaders of their union. In 1916 the government responded with the use of force, suppressing radical publications in Glasgow and arresting and imprisoning a number of unofficial strike leaders. The Clyde Workers Committee, however, survived to become the basis of a National Workers Committee Movement, the 'first shop-stewards movement'. In many ways, the shop-floor revolt in the engineering union may be seen as retrogressive, an element of the traditionally sectional and self-interested Labour Aristocracy radicalising only when its privileged position within the working class was jeopardised. Certainly, its motives were questioned by an intensely nationalistic popular press. Mass support was also jeopardised when their sectionalism was further exposed in May 1917, with a rash of widespread strikes in the engineering industry caused by the withdrawal of the 'trade card', which had formerly exempted engineers from conscription. Nevertheless, the miners and the engineers had demonstrated the power of labour in a period of high employment and in a national emergency, a power which could not be curtailed by simple recourse to the law but only by constant negotiation, concession and conciliation.[20] In effect, the miners and the engineers acted unwittingly as a mailed fist in the TUC's velvet glove.

The high level of employment and the concommitant rise in wages generated by the war maintained the rapid growth in union membership that had already been a notable factor before 1914. Union membership doubled between 1900 and 1914, and doubled again over the war and immediate post-war years, to reach 8 330 000 by 1921.[21] The TUC had become, *de facto*, a power in the land. The incipient industrial unrest of the war period – albeit without the support of the TUC – in fact strengthened the TUC's hand in its dealings with the state, and in imaging itself as a major institution which it would be foolhardy for any government to ignore. And although labour unrest may have been the exception rather than the rule in wartime Britain, it is also clear that even the majority of moderate-minded trade unionists frequently resented the inequities of the burdens of the war, reinforcing a 'them' and 'us' view of the social formation. There was still evidence, in other words, even among the moderates, of that same incipient class consciousness which typified the late Victorian and Edwardian working class.

Profiteering, for example, was a frequent cause of working-class grumbles, eliding with the demand of the Labour movement that there should be a conscription of wealth, as well as of 'life', a capital levy to offset the burden of wartime taxation on the less well-off. The Industrial Alliance Conference of June 1917 called for the conscription of wealth in order to ensure an equality of sacrifice between employer and employee in the national emergency. The demand for the conscription of riches in turn became a political call for the public ownership and direction in the national interest of all vital sectors of the economy. In such a way did the previously alien and esoteric concepts of socialism align themselves with the habits of everyday moderate thinking, with traditional understandings of 'fair play' and equal dealings between the classes. Yet the demand for a capital levy to pay for the war lost much of its appeal, as popular patriotism and its associated demand for equal sacrifice came to be replaced by popular demands for revenge at the end of the war, the feeling that it was the Germans who should pay for the conflict. Moreover, as wage rises began to outstrip inflation in late 1917 and 1918, many of the grumbles about profiteering faded. These sentiments had, however, earned the detailed attention of the Cabinet Labour Situation reports for long periods of the war.[22]

Another major grumble associated with profiteering concerned food prices, and the long queues for food which accompanied the development of the German offensive against British shipping. Strikes in protest against food prices and shortages occurred in many areas, the common demand being for a thorough and fair rationing system. Early rationing in fact was based on previous consumption, which manifestly benefited the better-off areas. Censors worried that the depiction of conditions at home in letters to soldiers at the front was becoming demoralising. The way in which complaints about food shortages and price rises were being articulated into wider industrial disputes was also to force the issue. The government's response to the problem in early 1918 was to stop the rise in food prices and to co-opt Labour representatives onto Food Control Committees. As Bernard Waites has convincingly argued, what happened in response to the everyday privations and the annoyingly visible inequities of the war was an enunciation of the principles of the 'moral economy' of the working class. This took the form of demands for 'fair play' and equal treatment, rather than revolutionary changes in the organisation of society, gripes which were listened to by government and adaptations made in the details of the system of administration.[23] In this way, many of the pressures which might have headed Britain along a more socially-damaging road were contained and neutralised. The corollary was, however, that when the state abandoned the policy of intervention it would also abandon its role as social referee. If this happened, then the alternative tactics of those advocating direct action, largely marginalised though they were in wartime conditions, might well appeal in the working-class attempt to maintain the threatened balance.

Labour was in fact as much worried by the threat implied by the shop-stewards' movement as was the government. Indeed, it was to be largely an antipathy to the perceived threat from the left which was to reunite the party in the second half of the war. Even though the ILP had been isolated from the right wing of the party by their pacificism since 1914, the rift had never looked entirely irreversible. Labour representatives in the cabinet were careful not to ally themselves too closely to the government as a whole, in terms either of military strategy or of the development of peace aims. They could thereby disguise the inherent split in the movement over the war, by claiming that their role in government was simply to protect labour interests. Arthur Henderson, as leader of the party, still faced an inherent difficulty, however, torn between the collective responsibility demanded by his government post and the need for Labour unity. He showed real political skill in 1916 in getting the party to accept conscription *de facto* if not *de jure*, but he got a very rough ride from the Labour party conference in 1917, just after the Defence of the Realm Act had been used to arrest Clydeside leaders. Ultimately, of course, Henderson could always rely on the patriotic Right in the party to swamp the anti-war minority, but to do so would be to sacrifice many important party strategists, as well as to make the party too narrowly industrial in its appeal.[24]

The turning-point in Henderson's attitude to the war came as a result of his government mission to Russia in 1917, shortly after the February revolution. He returned convinced that the Russian provisional government's determination to continue the war would lead directly to a Bolshevik takeover; beyond that possibility was the real prospect of the far left outrunning social democrats all over Europe. It was in fact the Bolshevik revolution in prospect which first prompted the Labour party to rally round the call for a negotiated peace. And it was the Bolshevik revolution in being which was to lead to the genesis of a new unifying constitution and programme in 1918, a restatement of clearly social democratic as opposed to revolutionary aims. Henderson resigned from the cabinet and dragged the right wing of the party into a commitment to a peace conference on negotiated terms. Once the Bolsheviks released the details of the secret treaties concluded between the Allies, the pressure from the Left and from the ILP to keep the campaign going was irreversible; now the Left could justifiably claim that it was indeed a capitalist war. For the first time in its history the Labour party emerged as the only clear opposition to the government, leaving Asquith's 'sober and responsible opposition' a poor third. Henderson was also left free to concentrate on organisational efforts to transform the Labour Party's electoral position from the narrow class basis the unions had provided into a national party, based on a constituency organisation like the other parliamentary parties. This was a bid for that radical middle-class support which might have gone traditionally to the Liberals, and which was essential if the Labour party was to avoid the tag of being the potential instigator of bloody class war.[25]

With the emergence of a consensus of Labour Party opinion on the question of peace, Ramsay MacDonald was given the opportunity to re-emerge in the leading ranks. Since Ramsay MacDonald was then once again to dominate the party through the crucial period of development into the 1930s, it is worth looking in some detail at the evolution of his ideas as a result of the war. Before 1914, MacDonald had been one of the foremost exponents of the ILP line that the pace of change must be regulated to suit the slowest, that to get TUC support it was worth toning down the socialist content of the ILP programme. He had also been prominent in the tactics of engineering the electoral pact with the Liberals which had given Labour its first parliamentary breakthrough in the 1906 election, though the close alliance with the Liberals was seen as something of a sell-out by the Left. As a pacifist, MacDonald had seen Britain's entry into the war, and Labour's support for the war effort, as a disaster which would set back the cause of democratic socialism for ten years. He had become particularly worried by the oligarchical tendencies, as he saw them, of the TUC within the Labour party. As a result, he had become concerned with the need for a reorganised party which would combine all radical forces under one banner, and which could look for financial as well as electoral support beyond the unions. 'Money did not make the party, and money will not keep it going', he said, referring to the power of the unions within the party: 'ideas made it and ideas are necessary to maintain it.' MacDonald, in short, projected a movement away from the early years of the party towards a national rather than simply an industrially-based party. This brought him close in sympathy, in effect, to Henderson's interest in organisational changes. The difference was, of course, that while Henderson was primarily concerned with the threat from the revolutionary Left, MacDonald was at this point rather more concerned with what he saw as the dictatorial Right in the party. This is not to say that MacDonald moved further to the left as a result of the impact of war, indeed far from it. He became seriously disenchanted with the whole concept of the extension of state power when he saw it applied by a populist like Lloyd George to a war which he could not support in principle. His worries about the over-powerful state, later reinforced by his worries about Stalinism, were coupled to his worries about the over-powerful unions. He became, as a result, suspicious about the whole notion of nationalisation. It would be true to say that the war moved MacDonald along more libertarian, non-socialist lines, though his pacifism aligned him with the ILP and gave him a spurious appeal to the Left.[26] This continued appeal to the Left contributed substantially to MacDonald's balance of emotional capital within the party, though he was to spend that capital heavily during the 1920s and, by 1931, it was to have run dry.

Arthur Henderson had worked hard to prevent the original split in the party over Britain's entry into the war becoming too open. Whatever the factions within the party on the question of support for the war itself, they had always been able to combine on the need to protect labour interests during the conflict. The War Emergency Workers National Committee had been set up by the party as a watchdog group for this very purpose, but it also had the function of keeping the wings of the party in constant communication. In particular, it allowed an important meeting of minds between intellectuals and trade union organisers, which did much to narrow the ideological gap between the factions. Sidney Webb, in particular, was to use the Committee to educate trade unionists in the possibility of a viable social transformation, which did much to produce broad agreement in shaping the 1918 programme. Jay Winter has dubbed Sidney Webb 'the Lenin of the social democrats'.[27] As a Fabian, Webb was irretrievably commited to gradualism but, in much the same way as Lenin did for revolutionary socialism, Webb also saw a role for a vanguard movement in social democratic politics. Implicitly at least, Webb's argument was that the building of a mass party was unnecessary as well as extraordinarily difficult, and that the role of the Labour party in parliament should be to create the 'social tissue', using nationalisation and taxation as the spearheads of change. In this way would be created a network of local and national political institutions ultimately managing public affairs, thus directing and fashioning from the top a peaceful social revolution. In arguing in this fashion, Webb was able to articulate the empirical evidence provided by the experience of state intervention during the war to the implicitly moderate aims of that 'moral economy' represented by most of the unions and their members.

Put simply, Henderson represented the right-wing worries about the extreme left; MacDonald represented some left-wing disenchantment with the implications of state control and the tyranny of the majority; and Webb represented the radical elitist views of those who wished to see a cross-class reorientation on the left of centre of British politics. From very different start-points, and with very different motives, these three men were able to combine in an effort to show that the Labour party could bring about the democratic state without violent upheaval or dictatorship. They saw the new constitution and programme they helped to shape in 1918 as a bulwark of the British parliamentary system, which they were all agreed was a supreme instrument, and one which they intended not to subvert but to take over. In practice, however, the TUC was to retain if not actually to increase its hold on the Labour party with the new constitution. The affiliated socialist societies such as the ILP lost their separate representation on the National Executive Committee, though there was increased representation for the constituency parties and, for the first time, separate representation for women. The trade unions, however, remained in an overwhelming position within the party, as indeed befited their role in financing the party and in providing membership. In the 1918 election, local constituencies nominated only 140 of the 361 candidates fielded by Labour; the miners alone nominated 51.[28] The socialist societies were given something in return in the adoption of Clause IV, though the actual interpretation of that famous compromise was to remain a most significant bone of contention between Left and Right for the next sixty years. The word 'socialist' was noticeably avoided, and Clause IV was ambiguous about the system of control of nationalisation: the clause reflected, in fact, a tradition of trade-union collectivism, of working-class notions of 'fair play', equity and pragmatism, just as much as it pointed the way towards workers' control.

The 1918 programme, 'Labour and the New Social Order', committed the Labour party to a Fabian-style evolutionary socialism, reflecting the expectations generated by the Great War, without committing the party either to specifics or to a timetable. It included reference to the establishment of a national minimum wage, the common ownership of industry, and the use of the taxation system to redistribute wealth. Nebulous though the aims may have been, however, and subject to different interpretations, the new constitution and the new programme reflected the fact that the party had been relaunched as what James Callaghan was later to call a 'broad church'. 'Labour and the New Social Order', moreover, did fill a global vacuum of social democratic programmes, undercut as evolutionary socialism had been by the success of the Bolshevik revolution. With this constitution and this programme, the Labour party hoped to be able to get to power before Bolshevism or, indeed, Fascism came to Britain.[29] In the short term, however, they were simply to be swamped by the sentiments of the 1918 election. They returned from the polls with a disappointing 61 seats though, perhaps just as significantly, they won second place over Asquith's Liberals in 79 other seats. Many of their leaders, including MacDonald, Henderson and Philip Snowden, lost their seats. Between 1918 and 1922, moreover, they were to find themselves under powerful attack from both left and right, seizing on the clear failure of the Labour party to break through after so much had been promised.

LIBERALS AND CONSERVATIVES AND THE WAR

The high politics of the war period gelled into a split between socialists and non-socialists, once the Labour party became committed to a negotiated peace. This magnified the increasing predilection of David Lloyd George for Conservative company, and was to leave the Liberal party painfully divided in the 1918 election and the immediate postwar period. Lloyd George had been one of the most conspicuous of the doves of July and August 1914 but, once the war had started, he argued that it had to be won as quickly and as economically as possible. Transferred to the Ministry of Munitions in 1915, he began pressing for a more forceful leadership than the lackadaisical Asquith was prepared to offer. With the formation of the first coalition, Lloyd George found allies among the Conservative members of the new cabinet. The Conservative leader, Andrew Bonar Law, was also arguing the need for more dynamism at the top, pressed as he was in his own party by the alternative claims to the Tory leadership of Carson and Walter Long.

The crisis of late 1916 was precipitated by Lloyd George's developing disloyalty to Asquith, in particular his association with the demand that the overall direction of the war should be put into the hands of a small War Committee, the membership of which would perhaps even exclude Asquith himself. Lloyd George resigned over Asquith's refusal to meet this demand, creating a crisis in which Asquith himself resigned, perhaps assuming that no one else would be able to form a government and that he would be recalled, this time without the need to find a place for Lloyd George. In fact, at a meeting at Buckingham Palace, Bonar Law declared himself ready to support a government led by Lloyd George. Without the parliamentary backing to form a government himself, Bonar Law undoubtedly appreciated the energy of Lloyd George, and saw in such a reconstituted coalition the chance to head off any continued challenge to his own party leadership. What happened, in December 1916, was quite literally a 'palace revolution', and it was by no means as clear at the time as it was to become that a new major problem had been initiated for the Liberals. Though the personal clash between Asquith and Lloyd George might have been clear, Asquith in fact continued to be leader of the Liberal party and pledged himself to a 'loyal and sober opposition'. Lloyd George, as yet, made no attempts to form a separate political backing. At this point it could still be assumed that, after the crisis was over, Lloyd George could simply be subsumed back into the Liberal fold.

The new Prime Minister, however, could be an extremely difficult person to live with, politically. Without doubt, David Lloyd George was the most spectacularly successful British politician of the century. It was his name which was associated most closely with the pioneering social reforms of the pre-war period. Then, as Minister of Munitions in 1915 and in 1916, he had engineered the development of the total war economy. His war leadership from 1916 to 1918 was to transform him into a major international figure, as well as a national hero. After the war, too, his direction of the Irish negotiations, though initially accompanied by massive blood-lettings, secured a sort of peace in that troubled island for nearly fifty years, something which had eluded even the great Gladstone. Each of these accomplishments would have been enough to secure him a formidable historical reputation; together, they make him virtually unimpeachable. On the other hand, there were clear disasters. His handling of the military leaders in the war was sometimes almost diabolical. It may or may not be true that Field Marshal Robertson, the Chief of the Imperial General Staff, and Field Marshal Haig, the commander in France, had serious shortcomings, but Lloyd George doubted his political strength to replace them. Instead, he relied on intrigue to undermine them and, on occasion, to deny them the resources they needed. Lloyd George's penchant for intrigue, indeed, may have created unnecessary problems for himself and soured relationships in British high politics for a generation. Very few trusted him, outside that close circle of confidantes with whom he surrounded himself. A populist rather than a democrat, he was at times closer to being a demagogue than a statesman: finally it was to be the mould of the British parliamentary system, which his premiership appeared to break in its presidential style, which was to bring him down in 1922, and to deny him any further office for the remaining 23 years of his life. In the process, the Liberal party was again to be torn asunder.[30]

It is difficult to gauge Lloyd George's direct and positive support in the House of Commons during the war. While Asquith remained leader of the Liberal party, and as long as Lloyd George refrained from starting a separate political organisation, his power rested on a supra-political base, the parliamentary equivalent of the Indian rope trick. In his continued appeal to the Liberals, he traded heavily on his radical past, the reputation which he had built up in the two decades before the Great War. In fact, though, it was not entirely clear that Lloyd George cultivated the support of either major party at this point. He ran the war largely through professional administrators or managers from industry rather than through career politicians. Men like Sir Alfred Mond and Sir Alexander Geddes ran their departments with no political ambitions, loyal only to Lloyd George as the man who had appointed them, and with every intention of returning to non-political life when the national crisis was over. Lloyd George expanded the orbit of the Cabinet Secretariat and ran the day-to-day business of wartime government indirectly through prominent members of the Secretariat, such as Thomas Jones and Sir Maurice Hankey. Behind the official realm of government, moreover, lay the Prime Minister's 'garden suburb', – so called because it had its offices in the grounds of 10 Downing Street – a private secretariat often used as supernumerary cabinet members on important governmental tasks. The private secretariat, however, was not a simple British equivalent of the professional White House staff in the American presidential system, for its members were often chosen for their extra-political links, particularly with newspapers. Through the close links he developed in the private secretariat with, for example, Lords Astor and Harmsworth, Lloyd George cultivated his populist support in the press.

Though Lloyd George's position appeared impregnable, this supra-parliamentary governmental system in fact left him politically vulnerable. Though Asquith was anxious not to oppose Lloyd George too obviously, for party political as well as patriotic reasons, increasingly he became the focus for growing discontent about Lloyd George's methods, the increase of state power and the presidential style of government which threatened the notion of parliamentary accountability. This was particularly clear in the Maurice debates, occasioned by the disciplining of General Maurice, who had leaked from the War Office the story that the Prime Minister had refused to release reserve troops to Haig at a moment of particular danger on the Western Front. The government chose to make the issue a matter of confidence, but a large number of Liberal MPs still voted, in effect, for Lloyd

George's resignation. It may have been at this moment that the Asquith–Lloyd George clash became a real matter of division within the party.[31]

The Conservatives, on the other hand, learned to live with Lloyd George, though they may never have trusted him. He appeared to them to offer, in his figurehead role, the only chance of national unity in prosecution of the war effort. Increasingly, moreover, the calls from the Left for a negotiated peace cemented the links between the Tories and the Prime Minister; and a united front against the peace campaigners turned increasingly into a united front against socialism. As revolution spread over Europe in the last months of the war, many Conservatives became convinced that the postwar world would be an alien one for traditional Toryism. Facing the prospect of an election on the basis of universal manhood suffrage, and with clear signs that the Labour party might be emerging from its prewar tutelage, a significant element within the Conservative hierarchy was not at all sure that their values could survive. 'Resist socialism or perish' declared Lord Birkenhead. Given the crisis of confidence in the Conservative party, there were solid grounds for maintaining and developing the links with the charismatic 'man who won the war', perhaps the only leader who offered the chance of heading off the Labour challenge. If Liberal votes could be tempted over to the coalition, and if the Asquithean element in the Liberal party could be crushed, an overwhelming combination of the Right and the centre in British politics could see off British socialism.

Lloyd George, too, was interested in such a prospect. Working with Conservatives in the wartime cabinets had dented his ingrained distaste towards his erstwhile political enemies.[32] His attempt to undercut Labour's appeal, notably his promise to build 'homes fit for heroes to live in' after the war, needed framing in a specifically anti-socialist context, something which the Conservatives could provide more effectively than the party to which he belonged but had no immediate prospect of leading. This notion of a Progressive Centre Alliance, electorally undefeatable, formed the basis for Lloyd George's 'coupon election' idea, which he then bounced on Bonar Law as the war in Europe came to an unexpectedly rapid conclusion. Lloyd George secured the coupon – a seal of approval both from the Prime Minister and from the Conservative leader – for 150 Liberals as his personal power base in the new parliament. Of these Coalition Liberals 134 were elected.

On the face of it, the concept of the Progressive Centre Alliance had been extremely successful. Coalition Liberals in 1918 proved to be especially strong in areas where Labour might have hoped to make real inroads – in the industrial areas of the North and North East – as well as winning over traditional Liberal strongholds in agricultural seats in Wales, Scotland and East Anglia. Lloyd George may have burned his political bridges – the Asquithean Liberals had been effectively smashed – but he also appeared to have redrawn the political map of Britain at a stroke, leaving himself in control. In fact, however, Lloyd George was unable to turn the alliance of convenience of 1918 into a reliable political base. It was, after all, an alliance of opposites, united only in the belief that it was necessary to keep Labour out. Lloyd George had hardly begun to think seriously about how to flesh out his proposals for social reform, so concerned had he been with the pressing military problems. Three Reconstruction Committees had laboured fairly fruitlessly and briefly during the war. Even the establishment of a Ministry of Reconstruction in 1917 may have been designed simply to move Christopher Addison sideways to allow Winston Churchill back into the cabinet at Munitions, probably the only ministry the dominant Tories would allow him. Nevertheless, Addison laboured hard at a scheme to create a Ministry of Health and to give substance to the Prime Minister's promise to provide homes fit for heroes to live in. But the war ended too quickly for the schemes to be given the time they needed to mature. Though Lloyd George began his campaign giving equal platform time to his twin planks of a just peace and social reconstruction at home, he reacted quickly to the electoral intelligence that the majority of voters wanted revenge for the war. By polling day, the Coalitionists were campaigning almost entirely on the need to 'squeeze Germany until the pips squeaked'. Electorally, this may have been successful, for it was an issue on which Labour could easily be made to look very vulnerable, given their

attitude towards the war as a whole. But it also meant that the
Conservatives could be allowed to dominate the new
parliament to an extent that threatened the whole idea of
the progressive centre alliance. In fact, the whole notion of
coalition served only to disguise, as it was to do again in 1931,
a conclusive Conservative victory.

The Coalition Liberals battled gamely for the Liberal idea
against the tide of opinion on the Conservative-dominated
government benches. As the postwar boom turned into
depression and the axe was turned on public spending,
however, their hopes for social reform were soon eroded. At
the same time, Liberal economic thinking was fundamentally
challenged by the tariff reformers among the Conservatives,
with Austen Chamberlain at the Treasury and Geddes at the
Board of Trade. Coalition Liberals and Conservatives alike
refused to consider the prospect of fusion into a new party.
Coalition Liberals began drifting back to the Asquithean whip
and the man who had won the war found himself increasingly
the prisoner of the Conservatives. Finally, too, even their
patience broke. With the Chanak Crisis bringing Britain to the
brink of war with Turkey, Tory backbenchers revolted. At the
Carlton Club meeting in 1922, Stanley Baldwin labelled Lloyd
George 'a dynamic force' who might end up destroying the
Conservatives just as he had seemingly destroyed the Liberals.
Though Conservative leaders were still convinced that the
Prime Minister was an important figurehead to lead the anti-
socialist crusade, the back-benchers were adamant. The
coalition collapsed, and Lloyd George found himself suddenly
in the wilderness.[33]

The parliamentary system had triumphed, and Lloyd
George discovered that a politician – no matter how massive
his personal reputation – is only as strong as the party to which
he belongs. In fact, subsequent elections were to prove that the
anti-socialist campaign was to succeed equally well without the
need for a Progressive Centre Alliance. It still did not need a
formal electoral alliance of Right and centre to keep the Left
out of power: Labour could still not force a clear electoral
passage around the corpse of the Liberal party. In the general
elections of 1910 the Liberals had still commanded more than
43 per cent of the total vote. The split in the party in 1918 left

the Asquith Liberals with just over 12 per cent of the vote, whereas the Coalition won 48 per cent. Thereafter, however, there were some signs of a Liberal revival. In 1922, the various Liberal groupings won over 29 per cent of the vote and 116 seats, maintaining this share in 1923. The election which followed the resignation of the first Labour government in 1924 saw the Liberals dip to below 18 per cent, but the old party's refusal to die created complicated cross-currents in the electoral politics of the 1920s. Labour, winning only 7 per cent in 1910, won over 22 per cent in 1918, but could only manage less than 1 per cent more than the combined Liberals in 1923. Not until the 1924 election could it clearly be seen that Labour had broken away from the Liberals. Even then, the complete collapse of the Labour vote in 1931 was to call into question whether Labour would ever mount a sustained challenge to the Conservative ascendancy. The Conservatives, on the other hand, could not afford complacency. Though they emerged triumphant in 1918, in 1922 they were to slump to below 40 per cent of the popular vote for the first time since 1886; rather less of a problem than that facing the Liberals but a significant psychological blow, nevertheless. They recovered in 1924 but dropped again to 38.2 per cent in 1929, a mere 1 per cent more than Labour. Though, with the benefit of hindsight, it is easy to see the Great War simply as the period in which the Liberals collapsed and Labour broke through, the pattern of the popular vote in the 1920s in fact reveals a rather more complicated picture of genuine three-party politics. The Conservatives as well as the Liberals had serious reasons for worry at Labour's growth – though certainly the Conservative decline was nowhere near as catastrophic as that of the Liberals – but at the same time Liberal survival meant that Labour could not make the decisive electoral breakthrough. Indeed, Labour would not do so until another equally traumatic war had wrought even larger changes in the national political consciousness. As a result the Conservatives were to dominate interwar politics, almost by default. By 1922, Lloyd George had effectively helped the Conservatives through a difficult period of loss of confidence and adjustment to new conditions. Thereafter, under the leadership of Stanley Baldwin, the Tories were actually to take over the mantle of the centre progressives, though Baldwin was to use rather less dramatic flourish in his approach.

The Liberal party had suffered what proved to be an irrecoverable electoral setback, though liberalism was by no means finished. With the final return of Lloyd George to the fold, the party began a frantic search for new ideas that would take them back into political centre-stage: it was to be among the Liberals that the transformative ideas of Keynes made their first impression, from which they spread out to dominate the centre stage of politics from the 1940s to the 1960s. Nevertheless, the Liberals' chance of power was to remain remote, though there were to be periodic hopes of a revival. It was by no means simply the dispute between Asquith and Lloyd George that had caused the Liberal demise. Since the onset of the Great Price Fall, the central political issue in Britain had been one of adjustment to the emergence of a quiet but clear class divide in the British social formation, overlaid and complicated by the intricacies of the Irish problem. Before 1914, it had been the Liberal party – under challenge from emergent Labour – that had carried most of the political consequences of these difficulties, and had been at the forefront of the dangerous process of adjustment. The test of the Great War added only a further challenge, to which the Liberal party again responded admirably on the whole. This time, however, the resultant split proved to be near-fatal, simply because Labour had finally reached the organisational stage at which it could effectively challenge a divided party for electoral second place. In the 1880s, the lack of an alternative organisation had allowed the Liberals the chance to regroup. This was not the case in 1918.

On another level, however, it is also clear that what the Liberals had suffered, in their struggle to adjust to twentieth-century conditions, was the loss of that ideological clarity which had given them such a distinctive political position in the years of Gladstone. In trying to adjust to maintain the cross-class appeal to the national family, over thirty years of trials and tribulations, the Liberals were destined to appear ambivalent, even opportunistic. The characteristically moderate class divide in Britain became the touchstone of politics when the Conservatives in the 1920s learned to show the

conciliatory face of the middle class, and when Labour
continued to show the conciliatory face of the working class,
leaving the Liberals with no clear political role. It was not so
much, then, that the Liberals ceased to be relevant, for the
adaptive spirit that had emerged before 1914 in New
Liberalism became the core ideology of both the other parties;
it was much more the case that the Liberals had simply lost
their political constituency to both Tories and Labour. The
Liberals' historic mission, to represent capital and labour as a
unity, had been a losing battle: the role that the Liberals had
played in the political education of both Conservatives and
Labour, on the other hand, had been a telling one, and as
former Liberals moved into the ranks of the other parties, they
took the spirit of conciliation and compromise with them. In
this sense, though the Liberal party may have ceased to have a
realistic chance of government, the legacy of nineteenth-
century liberalism continued to dominate concepts of the state
in Britain.

─────3─────
THE IMPACT OF THE DEPRESSION

THE ECONOMIC SETTING: THE GREAT DEPRESSION

The crisis of economic confidence which began in Britain with the Great Price Fall of the last quarter of the nineteenth century had, indirectly and in conjunction with the resulting social difficulties, set in train a process of events that shifted the terms of reference of politics by 1918. Important as economics became in politics, however, there had been no long-lived evidence of a changed perspective on the role of the state in the economy. The debate, rather, had been on the role of the state in offsetting the social consequences of the inexorable and natural laws of supply and demand. Economic policy was to dominate politics much more thoroughly after 1918, on the other hand, as the Great Depression ground into the social fabric year after year. The extension of the franchise in 1918 had brought the problems of poverty even more directly into the public arena than had been the case after 1867 and 1884. Moreover, abroad, communists and fascists were proposing radical solutions to economic problems which demanded in Britain a thorough appraisal of liberal methods, simply in order to defend liberal values. In recent years, the traditional image of the interwar years in Britain as a period of unrelieved economic depression and mass unemployment has undergone a substantial moderation. The revisionists have argued that the view of the interwar period as 'the locust years' needs to be set against the clear evidence of economic and social advancement that the period also provided. The 1930s, in particular, saw major developments in the consumer economy, as well as the lengthening of the dole queues and, even with never less than one million unemployed from 1919 to 1940, the average standard of living increased very significantly. This paradox, of some sectors in the economy developing while others stagnated, warrants some attention, for it was here that the shape of the changes wrought in British society and British politics in the interwar period were ultimately fixed.

The Great Price Fall had already shown the dangers of overcommitment in the British economy to the staple export industries. British industry suffered from a structural imbalance. Textiles, coal, heavy metal production and shipping had demonstrated their vulnerability to foreign competition before the Great War, though this had been temporarily offset by imperial expansion, by the rearmament boom and finally by the unprecedented demand of the Great War itself. Indeed, the temporary boom provided by the international conditions of the first eighteen years of the twentieth century had encouraged still greater commitment to the traditional giants in the industrial economy. The state had helped in this respect, desperate for all the coal and shipping, for instance, it had needed to fight the first total war. Between 1918 and 1921, moreover, the demand created by the re-entry into the peacetime economy, and the temporary incapacity of the German economy in defeat, continued to offset the consequences of the fact that British exports were finding it hard to compete in a free market. In the so-called 'return to normalcy', the government began to demolish the complicated structure of controls on prices, production and wages that had been necessary to maintain both production and industrial peace during the war. By 1921, however, the full blast of the international depression began to make itself felt. Already vulnerable to competition, the world slump in overall demand was likely to have particularly gruesome effects on Britain's export-led economy. While Britain's early start in the industrial revolution had certainly given her the lead in the world economy for most of the nineteenth century, it is also clear that this very success had bred a complacency, and a reliance on the concept of the free market economy, which provided no ready solution to the problems of the 1920s.[1]

The lack of competitiveness of Britain's export industries, coupled to the slump in world demand, was further complicated by government financial policy. Not only was an uncompetitive export economy chasing diminished world demand, it was being forced to do so under a deliberately depressive regime from the Treasury. Before 1914, the City of London had been the capital of the world money market, and had thereby been able to play an important function filling the inherent gap in the balance of payments through invisible exports in the forms of loans and insurance. During the war, however, the enforced sale of many of Britain's overseas assets, and the growth of the national debt, had forced the decision to go off the Gold Standard. Thereafter, the value of the pound had slowly floated down against the dollar. After 1918, government policy was aimed at restoring the former primacy of sterling and the City in order to win back the many beneficial spin-offs which went with that primacy. This took the form of following a depressive financial policy designed to force up the price of the pound to the point at which sterling could go back on to the Gold Standard at prewar parity with the dollar. By 1925, the Treasury believed, such parity had virtually been reached. In fact, Britain went back on to gold with the pound anywhere between two and a half and ten per cent overvalued. Britain's export difficulties were thus made even more acute, as British goods in effect rose substantially in price on the world market. A further complication was caused by the rapidly overheating world money market, with Europe financing her postwar debts with short-term loans on the New York market. This produced the giant speculation in US bonds and the Wall Street Crash of 1929. As New York began to call in its debts from Europe in the immediate wake of the crash, the European and then British crash followed inevitably in 1931.[2]

Faced with this matrix of problems, British economists and politicians held broadly to the belief that the only way to undercut these difficulties was to make industry competitive again by cutting the costs of production. If industry were faced with the full blast of competition it would be forced to rationalise, so that the recovery of world trade would find Britain leaner and more efficient, ready to repeat the rapid economic growth of the nineteenth century. The paying-off of the National Debt, meanwhile, would help to restore international confidence. The Labour party, for all its quasi-socialism, proved in fact to be almost purely Gladstonian in its economic philosophy. The Conservative party, on the other hand, did at least prove adaptive and pragmatic in its approach, though only within very limited parameters. It is perhaps not too surprising that governments seemed relatively powerless; they were, after all, living with a wholly new complex of circumstances – as well as inheriting institutionalised problems – and they were also the inheritors of an economic philosophy which seemed to have stood Britain well for over a century. The most thorough analysis of the cause of Britain's problems, and the most daring solution proposed, was that of John Maynard Keynes. Keynes's most famous suggestion amounted to a proposal for the complete reversal of the traditional means by which governments controlled the economy, an argument for counter-cyclical investment which would iron out the peaks and troughs of the trade cycle. Yet perhaps it would have been hoping for too much to have expected governments to accept Keynes either rapidly or wholeheartedly. There was, after all, no real 'Keynesian alternative' until relatively late in the depression: Keynes developed his ideas piecemeal through the interwar years, and only reached a fully-developed theoretical breakthrough with the publication of the *General Theory* in 1936. Keynesianism was a reaction to the depression, not a fully-blown alternative just waiting to be implemented. Even after 1936, it would have been extraordinary if such revolutionary and potentially anarchic ideas of economic management had been adopted quickly. As it was, it is remarkable that the first Keynesian budget in fact came only five years after the publication of the *General Theory*. But even if Keynesianism had been rapidly accepted, there is no evidence that it could have dealt with problems so large as those that Britain faced for most of the depression years. Keynesianism was designed only for fine-tuning of the economy, not for the massive reflation of a globally burst balloon.[3]

By far the most prominent of the contemporary alternative solutions offered was that of tariff reform. In fact, tariff reform was almost as hot a political potato as it had been in Joseph Chamberlain's day. Baldwin campaigned on a tariff reform platform in 1923. He lost the election, let in the first Labour government, and dropped the issue forthwith. In 1932, however, the Chancellor of the coalition National govern-

ment, Neville Chamberlain, finally introduced measures of
protection with an Imperial preference, thus bringing to a
conclusion the campaign his father had begun thirty years
previously. Though, by that stage in the depression, protection
was only the simplest of shelters from the international
blizzard, it certainly helped Britain edge her way through
some of the worst of the depression years. On the other hand,
protection had more dubious side-effects. It was during this
period that the United States, in order to circumvent
protection, began investing more directly in British industry,
with Ford putting money into Vauxhall, the opening up in
Britain of companies such as AEI, Hoover and Remington
Rand. The growing economic competition of the Americans,
which had been developing apace since the 1880s, was now to
be supplemented by what many were to see as an insidious
penetration of the British economy. Protection and Imperial
preference may also have had, indirectly, some deleterious
effects on international relations. Though Britain was hardly
the only villain in this piece, it may well be that it was the
threat of being forced out of potential Far Eastern markets
which reinforced the tendency of Japan to solve her economic
problems by military means.[4]

Protection, as a temporary expedient, may at least have
prevented things getting worse in the 1930s. Changes in
financial policy may have had slightly more positive results. In
1931, Britain went off the Gold Standard again in the wake of
the sterling crisis; this eased the six-year old problem of the
over-pricing of sterling. The National government maintained
low interest rates through the 1930s in order to make its
international debts cheaper to repay, with the added benefit
that it made investment cheaper and thus encouraged growth.[5]
Government was no longer content, however, with simply
managing the national finances. In the industrial rationalisation policies of the 1930s, the National Governments took the
state into significant new areas of economic management and
planning. The object of the rationalisation policy was to help
industry to help itself, by scrapping spare capacity.
Government backed the formation of the British Iron and
Steel Federation in a bid to make the industry more
economical and efficient. In 1936, the mine-owners success-

fully resisted the government in its attempt to enforce the amalgamation of smaller pits, but mining royalties were nationalised two years later and the money obtained thereby was used to help to overcome some of the industry's problems. A similar pattern in the textiles and agricultural industries showed government – in an ad hoc, piecemeal, perhaps faint-hearted but nevertheless significant way – preparing the ground for the much larger efforts in intervention that were to occur during and after the next war.[6] Rationalisation in the 1930s was significant for the way in which it amounted to a recognition that industrialists were not voluntarily going to work in the national interest by rationalising themselves out of existence, that government had a role to play in the shaping of the industrial structure, that government in fact should act not simply as referee in the economy but should campaign actively for the most effective deployment of the national resources. The experience of the Great War, in other words, could not simply be forgotten. In industrial terms, the attempted return to normality was ground down by the effect of the depression. In turn, the rationalisation policies of the 1930s, inadequate though they may have been to deal with the contemporary problems, were important experiments on which the nationalisation policies of post-1945 were to build.

It was ironic that the problems left in the aftermath of the Great War only found some temporary solution in the preparations for another. The rearmament boom of the 1930s had much the same effect on the economy as it had in the 1900s. Though the Treasury kept strict financial controls on rearmament in the 1930s, the demands of the international situation overcame the government's reluctance to spend, and particularly to spend on arms. The financing of rearmament through large government loans from 1936 on amounted to a notable U-turn in traditional budgetary policy. By 1937, in spite of the traditional view that the National Governments were parsimonious in their attitude towards arms, the state was actually spending a larger proportion of the national budget on arms than ever before in peacetime.[7] Ultimately, however, it was not government financial policy, nor rationalisation policy, nor the rearmament boom that brought about what recovery there was in the 1930s. Insofar as it came at all in the interwar years, recovery occurred in spite of, rather than because of, government policy. The general fall in prices through the 1920s was not matched by an equal fall in wages and salaries, with the result that those who remained in work were actually enjoying a substantial rise in real income, a rise which in some estimates amounted to something like 24 per cent over the interwar period as a whole. It was this rise in real income that began to feed a consumer boom in the 1930s, particularly in housing, but also in motor cars, electrical goods and other consumer durables.

Certainly, the only industries which showed any real rise in employment in the period were the consumer industries, the building and distributive trades and the service industries. Car production rose by 114 per cent between 1930 and 1937; one million new cars hit Britain's roads in the 1930s, creating for the first time what became known as the 'traffic problem'. Three million new houses were built in the 1930s, amounting to a 29 per cent increase in the total national housing stock. Of these houses 75 per cent were built for the private sector, and their appearance is often argued to have been the root of a new development block within the economy. Private houses bred the demand for consumer durables, and this development block in turn dragged the basic industries out of the depression in its demands for metal production and power.[8] On the other hand, though it is fair to say that the consumer economy was doing relatively well in the 1930s, and though it is fair to add too that the new suburban housing estate was as 'typical' an aspect of life in the 1930s as the depressed areas, it is still not entirely clear that this consumer boom was the basis for a new beginning in the British economy. The old industries continued to predominate in terms of the value of their net output and, in particular, the value of their exports. The development of the domestic consumer economy could not compensate for the continued relative decline in the export potential of the staple export industries, and Britain's share of the world market continued to fall through the 1930s. Indeed, not only did the consumer sector do even worse than the staple industries in terms of exports, they were also in fact extremely hungry on imports; Britain's share of world imports rose from 15.5 to 17.5 per cent over the 'recovery' period. Nor was there a great deal

of evidence that the consumer economy was any more efficient
than the older industries; in fact, many of the new industries
came relatively low in the table of increased productivity when
compared with the so-called declining industries. Finally, too,
it is not clear that the consumer boom really did help the ailing
industries to pull themselves out of the depression. Industries
like coal and steel were organised for and geared to a
previously massive world demand, and no home-grown
demand could soak up anything but a small percentage of
that capacity. The new industries, moreover, tended to rely on
new power sources and alternative materials as much as on
coal and steel. Indeed, it could almost be said that Britain was
developing a second, separate and discrete economy on the
ailing back of the old economy. It was, after all, the fall in basic
prices and the continuing depression in the basic industries
that made the consumer boom possible.

A growth rate of less than 2.5 per cent per annum through
the 1930s perhaps hardly merits the term 'recovery', though it
is true that Britain's economy was doing relatively better than
many of her competitors in this period, having done relatively
worse during the 1920s.[9] But it was unemployment, more than
any other factor, which remained the biggest negative among
Britain's economic performance indicators during the interwar
period. An average registered unemployment rate of one
million every year after 1921 – 10 per cent of the insured work
force – with a peak of three and a half million in the winter of
1932, is proof enough of the serious weakness in the interwar
economy. Even at the time of the dire national emergency in
the summer of 1940, there were still one million unemployed.
It was to take a full year after the declaration of war for the
impact of the depression on employment finally to be
eliminated. Recovery, where it did take place in the 1930s,
was both patchy and regionalised, centred on the South-East
of England and on some areas in the Midlands, and hardly
bore directly at all on the lives of those who lived in the
depressed areas of the traditional export industries in Wales,
the North of England and the Central Lowlands of Scotland. It
was this real and visible economic divide that gave
geographical point to the Disraelian notion that there were,
in fact, 'two nations'.

Though the relative prosperity of large areas of the electoral landscape may have done something to dampen the explosive potential of the impact of the depression, it was this divide that was also to create most of the tensions. It was in this context that government learned the need to intervene, too little and too late perhaps, but with important implications in terms of the notion of the role of the state. Not only could a bad economic performance lose a government elections, given the extension of the franchise, it could also, on the evidence of contemporary events in Europe, create the preconditions for social revolution. The question in economics by 1939 was no longer whether government should intervene but, rather, how far it should go down the road to state control of the economy. The attempt to make a bonfire of what had been assumed to be simply temporary wartime controls, and to return to pre-1914 normality, had to be abandoned under the sheer weight of the depression. In this largely pragmatic process, the notion had become established that the social democratic state had the duty to intervene to save the economy, which was itself nothing less than a fight to save liberal social democracy from the extremes of fascism and communism which had been the response of other countries.

'THE TWO NATIONS': STATE AND SOCIETY IN THE DEPRESSION

Benjamin Disraeli's novel *Sybil*, published in 1845, had the subtitle 'The Two Nations'. Disraeli pictured the two nations 'confronting each other for the most part with mutual disapproval and lack of understanding, and incapable of living together in terms of mutual trust'.[10] He meant, broadly, the rich and the poor, and in the process he defined the function of that tradition of Conservatism which has attempted to bring together the two nations, particularly as British society shaped into a classical class structure as it did in the late nineteenth century. Stanley Baldwin similarly saw his role during the depression as blurring the harsh edges of class conflict and, on the surface of things at least, he was remarkably successful. In America, Roosevelt brought his new broom to Washington, and began that large increase in the power of the presidency that was only to be challenged by Watergate. In France the Third Republic collapsed in factionalism. Spain descended into civil war and Germany into Nazism. Britain, on the other hand, came through the interwar crisis relatively unscathed from a political point of view. Apart from the General Strike, there was relatively little evidence of mass upheaval in Britain, in spite of the fact that the period has become a by-word for mass deprivation, mythologised in such phrases as 'the locust years' and 'the hungry thirties'.

Baldwinism – the spirit of compromise, conciliation and adaptation which characterised the Conservative party as it dominated interwar politics – may be part of the reason for this remarkable apparent quiescence, but it is also clear that the class divide in Britain was overlaid and disguised by a different sort of divide, a function of the depression itself. The working class was in fact divided by the regionalised impact of unemployment, which seriously affected the areas of the traditional export industries, but which had a relatively lighter effect on the the South-East and some areas in the Midlands – areas which, moreover, were to enjoy the relative prosperity provided by the consumer boom in the 1930s. Table 3.1 shows that the discrepancies were very marked.

Table 3.1 *Average unemployment, 1929 – 36*[11]

	%
London	8
South East	7.8
South West	11.1
Midlands	15.2
North East	22.7
North West	21.6
Scotland	21.8
Wales	30.1
Great Britain	16.9
South Britain	11.1
North Britain and Wales	22.8

A Ministry of Labour report in 1935 showed that although Northern England and South Wales contained less than 50 per cent of the insured population, these areas accounted for over 70 per cent of all unemployment. Broadly, this discrepancy in unemployment reinforced other traditional divisions within the working class, particularly the cultural division between north and south. Unemployment, indeed, has always proved to be a source of overall division and weakness in the British working class, much more than it has been a cause of militancy, largely because of the way it has tended to reinforce and widen these other divergences of culture, tradition and outlook. There is evidence from the 1930s to suggest that the powerful sense of community in areas of high unemployment, the long history of job insecurity, as well as the realisation that 'everyone was in the same boat' locally, tended to reinforce a fatalistic acceptance of circumstances, and provide solace in the traditional 'culture of consolation'. It may have been in areas of relatively low unemployment, particularly where evidence of the consumer boom was close at hand, that the deprivation of unemployment was felt most keenly, precisely because the unemployed were in a minority.[12] Unemployment, then, affected Britain differently from other Western nations, and this may well explain the rather more moderate political response. While in Germany and other countries which suffered mass unemployment, the proportion of unemployed may not have been that much larger in percentage terms, the effects were not nearly so regionalised: the impact was the same over the working class as a whole, and the political response in those countries may consequently have been that much more marked.

It is certainly clear that some sections of the working class in Britain enjoyed a relatively high standard of living, as the first effects of the development of the affluent society began to make themselves felt in the middle of depression. Even for the unemployed, the dole at least kept them out of the workhouse and in relatively better conditions than their parents had known. A slow redistribution of wealth was taking place as, from the 1920s on, the working class was getting more back in social benefits than it was contributing in taxation. The problem was one of relative rather than absolute deprivation.

But there was no point telling the unemployed that they were better off than their parents had been. One of the major causes of friction among the unemployed was undoubtedly the fact that they were, in national terms, a minority in danger of being politically marginalised by the employed majority. The prime purpose of events such as the Jarrow March to London was simply to force recognition of one nation upon the other. The large majority in Britain were only made dimly aware of the problems of the distressed areas by the mass media of the time. Though there certainly were radical attempts to prick the public conscience, in *Picture Post* for example, the large majority of publications that centred on the problems of interwar poverty were written by and for the liberal middle class, a continuation of the charitable Christian traditions of their parents' generation.

On the other hand, this period saw a growing intervention by the state, a rapid development in the principles of social policy, even more significant than the sea-changes taking place in economic policy. There were, moreover, some even more radical shifts in the direction of social policy proposed which, even though they were not accepted in this period, provided the blueprints for the larger framework of reconstruction of 1940 and beyond. The whole question of the depressed areas, for instance, was the subject of a continuous political debate. In areas with typically only one source of employment, the closing of the factory or the yard could have a devastating impact on the whole community. In Jarrow, where ship-building provided the only jobs, 75 per cent of the male workforce was unemployed in 1932. Similar or even larger percentages could be found in the mining villages of South Wales and other areas. Clearly, such areas could not 'seek their own salvation' as Walter Runciman is said to have advised Jarrow.[13] The initial governmental reponse was the Industrial Transference scheme, to siphon off the unemployed to areas of greater job opportunity. This scheme, however, only institutionalised the problems of the community left behind; not only did the project break up communities by taking young people away, it also meant that there would be no one to take the jobs on in the area if the depression ever lifted. Labour proved much less mobile than capital had proved to be; family ties and traditions meant that many were understandably resistant to the idea of transfer. From 1934, the emphasis shifted to attempts to revitalise the areas themselves, in the Special Areas Act of that year. Unpaid commissioners were put in to the areas to attempt to attract new industry. The funding of the scheme was a mere £2 million. Clearly, the Act was a mere sop to the critics of government inertia, hardly scraping the surface of the problem. The Special Areas Act was replaced in 1937 with the Special Areas Amendment Act, under the terms of which rate, rent and tax remissions were granted to industries moving into municipally-run industrial estates. On the whole, however, it was only light industry which was attracted by these concessions and, given the powerful macho culture of so many areas affected by heavy unemployment, they provided 'only women's work'. The net effect was probably to bring more women into the workforce rather than to provide employment for men, as was originally intended. Government training centres were also set up to retrain the redundant labour force for new jobs; men could be thrown off the dole for refusing to accept a training scheme, with the result that the scheme was dubbed 'slave labour' by Wal Hannington and the National Unemployed Workers Movement. Nevertheless, paltry and in many ways chillingly patronising though government measures to deal with the distressed areas seemed to later generations, they do at least indicate a shift of emphasis, an understanding that the state did have the right and the responsibility to intervene in the economic process for reasons of social engineering. Between 1937 and 1940 some rather more far-reaching ideas were suggested by the Barlow Commission on the Distribution of the Industrial Population, in particular the concepts of the redevelopment of congested areas and the dispersal of industry from the big conurbations. One of the results of the Barlow findings was to be the new towns policy of post-1945.[14]

The system of administering unemployment benefits proved to be the most contentious theme in social policy. There was to be at least one new parliamentary act dealing with unemployment benefit every year through the interwar period. The pre-1914 National Insurance Act was expanded in stages, with the result that virtually the whole male workforce was covered by 1939. Normally, however, the national insurance scheme only provided statutory benefit for six months, the scheme inheriting the pre-1914 assumption that it was designed only to deal with short-term unemployment. Undoubtedly, many unemployed did indeed find more work within six months, but the problem of the long-term unemployed was particularly real in the depressed areas. In July 1936, for example, the Ministry of Labour reported that no less than 24 per cent of those receiving benefit had been out of work for more than a year. The Transitional Benefit scheme had been introduced in 1921 to tide over the long-term unemployed. An important element in this scheme was the fact that it appeared to be a straight hand-out from the state, not an insurance as such (hence the term 'the dole'). In fact, the scheme was actually charged on the Unemployment Insurance account. It soon became clear that transitional benefit, originally conceived as simply a temporary measure pending the recovery of trade, was in fact going to become a permanent part of the unemployment benefit structure. As a result, the Unemployment Insurance account went seriously into the red and became a very serious problem in the financial crisis of 1931. Moreover, vestiges of an older attitude towards unemployment persisted, in spite of the significant extension of national insurance and the introduction of transitional benefit. Any gaps left by the statutory insurance scheme and by transitional benefit were still filled by the Poor Law, or Public Assistance as it became known after 1929.[15]

The major problem occurred with the administration of schemes of unemployment relief. Transitional benefits and public assistance were administered locally in the immediate postwar years. The result was that very big differences occurred in the rates being paid out, depending on the political complexion of the local Board of Guardians (Public Assistance Commission, or PAC, after 1929). In 1926, however, in response to what was known as Poplarism – the tendency, in some Labour-controlled areas, to pay out higher rates and on less stringent terms than the government deemed advisable – the Board of Guardians Default Act empowered government to replace local guardians. This was a thrust at the delicate balance between national and local responsibility for social administration and part of a developing pattern of conflict between central and local government, particularly in periods when Labour was doing relatively well at local level but relatively badly at national level. The crunch came in 1931 with the financial emergency and the public expenditure cuts which followed, especially the decision to make a 10 per cent cut in unemployment benefits and to impose generally the means test. A significant number of labour-controlled PACs refused to implement the means test, with the result that sometimes wildly different rates were being paid out in different parts of the country.

The Unemployment Act of 1934 in effect nationalised unemployment benefits. Unemployment Assistance Boards (UABs) were set up, controlling all three types of benefit and working to standardised national rates. There was an immediate outcry because these standardised rates were less than had been paid out before the new legislation came into force in some areas; the government was forced to relent and increase payments. The aim of the 1934 legislation was not progressive, in the sense that it was actually designed primarily to economise. The means test, too, institutionalised as it was by the new act, was to become the most hated symbol of the developing mythology of the interwar years, of a crass and uncaring governmental attitude.[16] But embedded in the 1934 Act was a major change in the principles of social administration in Britain. National responsibility for unemployment benefits was now fully accepted, a fundamental break from the Poor Law concept of unemployment as a problem of the locality. This fundamental breakthrough in turn made it easier to argue that, on a wider level, the problems of the distressed areas were problems of the nation as a whole, that unemployment itself was not simply a disaster for individual and community, but also a national responsibility.

For all the shortcomings and the petty, mean elements involved in the system after 1934, it remains true to say that the dole, the means test and the UABs between them allowed a rational, nationally-applicable, comprehensible, comprehensive and therefore ultimately fair system of distributing unemployment benefits. The means test undoubtedly caused great distress, especially where it impinged upon patriarchal culture by docking a father's dole because of the income of his wife or his children. The amounts paid out, however, were relatively higher than those in other countries, and generally given on less onerous terms.[17] Part of the reason why Britain remained relatively stable through these difficult years must be put down to this fact. Unemployment, especially long-term unemployment, still led to severe hardship, but not at least to starvation. Seebohm Rowntree calculated that a typical family of five on the dole in the mid-1930s only received two-thirds of what they required to maintain a fully healthy life, though it must also be remembered that Rowntree's definition of what constituted 'a fully healthy life' was a notable improvement on the subsistence level he had used as his bottom line in his 1899 survey;[18] this in itself is a measure of the revolution in rising expectations that had been generated by the pre-1914 legislation, and given added impetus by the experience of the Great War and the arrival of manhood suffrage. It would simply be anachronistic to apply the standards of the post-1945 welfare state to the years of the depression. Traditional notions of budgeting still applied, and all the major political parties were agreed in their perceptions of the depth of the crisis in national finances. The shortcomings of the interwar system of unemployment benefit are clear enough, but it can still be said that the depression in fact saw Britain stumbling somewhat blindly down progressive paths in the treatment of her unemployed.

There were to be fewer signs of progress, however, in the treatment of health. The effects on health of long-term unemployment were bound to be severe. In 1935, the War Office found that 60 per cent of would-be recruits fell below the required medical standard. This proportion fell to 30 per cent when conscription was introduced in 1939, an indication of the extent to which voluntary military recruitment had traditionally relied on the pressure of poverty. Dietary ignorance probably played its part, as much as low living standards, but in York in 1935 Rowntree found that the average child on the poverty line was three and one quarter inches shorter, and twelve and a quarter pounds lighter than the average child from further up the social spectrum.[19] Health care and national insurance were extended and broadened in stages during the interwar years, but the dependents of the insured, working-class wives in particular, still remained largely outside the state health care system. The 1926 Royal Commission on Health recommended extensions of the medical services whenever it was financially possible. A minority report, however, recommended complete nationalisation of the health service, a line to be taken up by the British Medical Association, and eventually to become the keystone of the Beveridge Report of 1942. For the time being, good health was to remain largely the prerogative of the better-off, the educated and the employed. For the still-silent sisterhood of working-class women, meanwhile, lives could still be led in the physical agony of untreated gynaecological and nervous complaints, as well as in the spiritual agony of unemployment and the means test.[20]

Housing was another major area in which little material progress was achieved. Lloyd George had promised 'homes fit for heroes to live in', and the 1919 Housing and Town Planning Act was designed to achieve that end, local authorities being required to make good their housing deficiencies with the help of funds provided by central government. Government funding fell victim to the axe on public spending in 1921, however, and there was to be no proper slum clearance programme until the Housing Act of 1930; even then, progress was dependent on financial circumstances. The giant boom in house-building that occurred in the 1930s was mostly private construction in the South-East; of the two and three quarter million houses built in Britain between 1930 and 1939, only 600 000 were built by local authorities. By and large, slum clearance was left for Hermann Goering and the Luftwaffe to do a quicker and more efficient job in 1940 and 1941.[21] The pressure of poverty in the depressed areas in particular led to chronic overcrowding in insanitary housing to reduce the cost of rent. The classic pattern of housing decay that Rowntree had found in York at the turn of the century – the vicious circle of impoverishment of an area – he found repeated in the 1930s, with 30 per cent of the working class living in unsatisfactory housing conditions.

In educational policy, the interwar period was typified by financial stringency. One of the few concrete results of the Lloyd George coalition's commitment to social reconstruction had been Fisher's Education Act of 1918. This had raised the school-leaving age to 14, allowing greater opportunities for working-class children to ascend the educational ladder through the scholarship scheme. But it has to be said that most of the improvements which occurred in British education between the wars occurred in spite of, rather than because of, government policy. The growth of the school population which resulted from the 1918 Act prompted many elementary schools to begin their own reorganisation to cater for older children who did not win places at grammar schools. This consisted of providing a separate secondary education for children over 11. The Hadow Commission of 1926 accepted and suggested acceleration of this system so that, by 1939, two-thirds of elementary school children over 11 were in fact in reorganised schools. This exercise in self-reform on the part of the schools was to be taken up and developed into a new philosophy of secondary education in the 1944 Education Act, an attempt to establish equal but different forms of secondary education to meet the needs of pupils with different capabilities.

While the state responded pragmatically to the immediate political dangers attendant on mass unemployment, the steps taken in health, housing and education were much less certain, involving far fewer irreversible commitments on the part of central goverment. In this sense, the claim made by some historians of British social policy that there existed a welfare state in embryo by 1939 is surely an overstatement of what happened in response to the depression. There was, in fact, a patchy and uneven development in social policy, in most areas involving only piecemeal additions to the minimal framework, the safety net, laid down by the pre-war Liberal governments. Only with the establishment of the principles of comprehensiveness and universality in social policy, an interlocking network of social services, can we talk of the Welfare State. This would require not simply the breadth of administrative vision of William Beveridge, but also a change in the perception of the function of national finances which the acceptance of Keynes finally allowed. Only then would the quantum leap into welfarism take place. In the meantime, however, below the surface of political events, a struggle was developing for control of the direction of the state, a struggle which would finally produce Keynes and Beveridge as a new compromise equilibrium between individualism and collectivism. The Barlow Commission and the Minority Report of the Royal Commission on Health were early signs of the blueprint for a New Jerusalem that was to emerge more definitely in the Second World War.

THE BRITISH CLASS STRUGGLE IN ACTION: THE GENERAL STRIKE

The General Strike of 1926 provides, in a close sequence of events, the clearest single example of the ideological tensions at work in British society and politics in the interwar period, and it is worth dwelling on at some length for that reason. The General Strike was the nearest Britain came to revolution since the 1830s, though it proved in the event to be nothing like a revolution. The Trades Union Congress was not prepared for a General Strike, had not realised the full political implications and proved scared of its possibly revolutionary effect. The concept of Direct Action, only vaguely formulated and half thought through, blew up in the face of the TUC in just nine days. In particular, there was no co-ordination between the industrial and political wings of the Labour movement. The Labour government of 1924 had in fact had access to the strike-breaking plans produced by the former Conservative administration, but had neither changed them nor told its industrial colleagues. This was symptomatic of a rift within the Labour movement that the General Strike did much to rectify. The result of the failure of the strike was to be a much closer fusion of the industrial and the parliamentary wings of the Labour movement, an unequivocal commitment this time to evolutionary and constitutional change, which marked the coming of age of the Labour movement.

Not that the General Strike was politically motivated as far as the TUC was concerned, but it did have enormous political implications and these were underlined by the government. As a result, the real issues which led to the strike became clouded; it became instead the constitutional issue of the TUC defying a legally-elected government. The real issue was that the government refused to intervene in the contemporary mining dispute, arguing that it was purely a matter for the miners and the mine-owners. The TUC, on the other hand, argued that the dispute was a government responsibility, because the situation had been created by the effects of governmental decontrol of the mines after the war and by the impact of government financial policy, particularly the return to the Gold Standard. Underpinning this union argument, however, lay the more basic assumption that it was the duty of government to protect the standard of living of all the electorate and to prevent mass unemployment; industrial disputes, it was implied, were matters of national importance, not simply narrow and localised conflicts between employers and employees in which the state could remain neutral. In short, the issue was that the TUC was arguing that government was abrogating its duty, whereas government argued that it had no such duty, and that any attempt by the TUC to force government to accept a responsibility it had no intention or mandate to take on had revolutionary constitutional implications. What was at stake, on the one hand, was the relationship of the state to the economy and, on the other hand, the power of organised labour to force the hand of government.

In one sense, the General Strike took place too late in the depression for it to be effective; unemployment and changes in the structure of the TUC had robbed the strike of the solidarity it needed to be successful. Membership of the TUC had stood at two and a quarter million at the turn of the century, but had shot up to eight and a half million by 1920 under the impact of the Great War. However, 1920 proved to be the peak of membership. As unemployment began to bite, membership was down to six million by 1922. The industrial warfare of 1920 to 1926 proved to be part of a typical pattern in British industrial relations; while union membership leaps in a boom, it falls as the economy takes a downturn, causing a backlash of industrial strife until this union counter-attack is snuffed out by the effects of unemployment and falling membership. In a boom, employers and governments may concede, whereas in a downturn they do not have to. The Great War had seen not only a large rise in union membership but also a wide-ranging structural change in unionisation. In 1914 the miners and textile workers between them accounted for 30 per cent of union members, but by 1926 they had shrunk to just 20 per cent of the membership. What was happening was the overtaking of the old Labour Aristocracy by newer, unskilled or semi-skilled unions such as the Transport and General Workers Union, formed in 1922, or the National Union of General and Municipal Workers, formed in 1924. Even some of the former Labour Aristocrat unions were being transformed into larger amalgamations of skilled and semi-skilled labour to cope with the changes that mechanisation brought to industry. The old engineers' union, for example, transformed into the Amalgamated Engineers Union in 1921. Though this structural change in unionisation did much to break down some of the old problems associated with status and hierarchy within the Labour movement, and to that extent produced more solidarity, it also tended to make concerted industrial action more difficult to organise. The leaders of the large new general unions tended to be more conservative in their attitude towards industrial action. Typically, they did not have the economic power of the skilled unions, and their strikes consequently had to be organised on a massive scale to have real impact. As unskilled workers they were also more open to blacklegging, particularly in periods of prolonged unemployment. They also needed the strong backing of other unions and co-ordination from the TUC. The power of direction of the TUC over its member unions, however, was very problematic. It was in an attempt to increase the central authority of the TUC that Ernest Bevin of the TGWU successfully argued for the replacement of the old Parliamentary Committee of the TUC with the General Council. Even then, it was by no means clear whether the General Council could supercede the authority of individual unions.[22]

Equally complicated was the theory of industrial action itself. It is easy to overstate the importance of syndicalist ideas in the TUC before the Great War and thereafter. The Triple Alliance of miners, railwaymen and transport workers of 1914, for example, was constructed to provide mutual support in the event of a strike by any one of the unions involved, an apparent manifestation of the syndicalist belief that major change can and should be accomplished by direct action and working-class solidarity, rather than through the ballot box. Yet there was no clear organisation to the Triple Alliance; it was in fact a bluff, designed for its assumed deterrent effect, which the member unions hoped would never be called by the employers. Nevertheless, there was clear evidence of unions flexing their political muscles for direct action immediately after the war. In May 1920, dock workers refused to load an ammunition boat headed for Poland during the Poles' war with the Bolsheviks. In July 1920 the TUC called a ballot on strike action in protest against government policy in Ireland, to the consternation of the Right in the Labour party.[23]

The problems of the coal industry provided a particularly telling test case for labour militancy. Padded from competition during the war, with prices and wages subsidised, the coal industry enjoyed a short boom even after the war when its German competition still lay in ruins. The miners' case for nationalisation of the mines lay as much in the demand for rationalisation as it did on purely socialist principles. The industry still consisted of nearly 1500 firms, some of them very small and at the very edge of financial viability once government subsidies ended. The tradition within the industry of settling wages by district rather than nationally had always been a major complaint of the miners, too, since profitability varied wildly from coalfield to coalfield, depending on the quality of the coal and on geological conditions. All these problems were simply pushed into the background during the period of government control of the mines. They clearly could not remain in the background if that control was to end. In 1919, the Sankey Commission recommended the nationalisation of the mines, but only on the casting vote of the chairman, and a government anxious to decontrol and hand back to private ownership used the split in the Commission to ignore its findings. The subsidy came to an end in March 1921 when decontrol went ahead. Up to this time, the effect of the subsidy was that the export price of coal had been three times that of domestic prices, and it was clear that grave readjustment would be necessary. The owners announced cuts in pay and refused a national wage settlement. The miners, for their part, conceded the reduction on wages but stuck fast on a national settlement, calling on the Triple Alliance for support.[24]

On 21 April 1921, 'Black Friday' as it became known, the Triple Alliance simply collapsed, underlining the inherent problems of mutual reinforcement in industrial disputes. The railwaymen and the transport workers withdrew their support for the miners because it appeared that the miners' leaders themselves were not entirely clear on what was negotiable and what was not. In the aftermath of 'Black Friday' the government was able to move swiftly to decontrol the rest of industry without fear of trade union reaction. But 'Black Friday' also put pressure on the TUC to make sure that such a surrender never happened again. Dissatisfaction with the economic performance of the first Labour government in 1924 also rejuvenated the idea that the unions would have to solve their problems on their own. The return to the Gold Standard in 1925 created further problems for the mining industry, the overpricing of sterling causing them to lose £1 million a month. The owners gave notice of a cut in wages and the miners appealed for support from the TUC, arguing that failure to support them would open the way to a general cut in wages, just as Black Friday had led to general decontrol. The miners, moreover, this time put their case and their negotiating position in the hands of the General Council, thus circumventing the problem that had broken up the organisation of the Triple Alliance in 1921. On 27 July, Baldwin's government refused a government subsidy to prevent wage cuts. Three days later the TUC issued notices for a general strike. Next day, 'Red Friday', the government caved in and provided a subsidy for nine months, also setting up the Samuel Commission, the fourth Royal Commission on the mines since the war.

It is clear that the cabinet was somewhat divided. Baldwin himself wanted to avoid a confrontation. William Joynson Hicks, Winston Churchill and Lord Birkenhead, on the other hand, were convinced that confrontation would have to come sooner or later. The only reason that they voted for the subsidy on 'Red Friday' was because they believed the government was not yet ready for the confrontation. Lord Salisbury was worried even about a temporary subsidy, arguing that it could be the thin edge of a socialist wedge which would eventually force the government into the position of controlling the economy. Joynson Hicks, in typically direct fashion, merged the class struggle with the constitutional issue by asking rhetorically : 'Is England to be governed by Parliament and by the cabinet or by a handful of trade union leaders?' As the cabinet agreed to the nine months' subsidy the Permanent Under Secretary at the Home Office, Sir John Anderson, began work on the preparation to keep essential services going in the event of a general strike. The private Organisation for the Maintenance of Supplies was given official blessing, and was to have ready some 100 000 volunteers by 1926.[25]

The government was preparing for confrontation in nine months' time, but the TUC did not even begin preparing for a general strike until January 1926. Pinning their hopes on the findings of the Samuel Commission, they assumed that the bluff of 'Red Friday' could be applied again. The Samuel Commission did indeed report almost wholly in favour of the miners. The owners' argument for lowering wages was accepted but so, too, was the miners' case for a national wage settlement. Above all, the Commission argued that the real need of the industry was a thorough reorganisation and rationalisation. The cabinet did not like the proposals, but said they were prepared to implement them if both miners and mineowners agreed. In fact, neither side accepted Samuel, though the TUC believed that the miners might be prepared to negotiate, using the Report as a basis. Once again, government had failed to act on the recommendations of a Royal Commission, the most august form of enquiry available in the British constitution. The physical weakness of the miners' case, moreover, lay in the fact that they had implicitly invested control of negotiations in the General Council, who continued to believe that Samuel's findings were still on the table. In fact, Baldwin did get the owners to accept a national wage settlement, but only on the condition that the miners accepted a 13 per cent pay cut. The cabinet had little sympathy with the owners; even Lord Birkenhead called them 'the stupidest men in England'. But government was not prepared to force the owners to see reason; it was, on the other hand, prepared to teach the unions a lesson. Negotiations were broken off by the government on the pretext that the printworkers' refusal to set an anti-union editorial in the *Daily Mail* was an infringement of the freedom of the press (in fact the note to the union negotiators calling off the talks was written before the *Daily Mail* incident was even known to the cabinet), and the General Council found that it had to put its money where its mouth was.[26]

The TUC had evolved no detailed plans for the strike. Ernest Bevin found himself building up an *ad hoc* organisation. Many union leaders undoubtedly did not relish the prospect of being forced to support what they considered to be the extremist tendencies of men like the miners' secretary, A.J. Cook. In spite of the poor organisation, however, and in spite of doubts in the General Council, the General Strike enjoyed very wide grass-roots support; it was not to be broken by lack of rank and file support, nor by the efforts of the volunteers, but by a crisis of confidence on the part of the Negotiating Committee of the General Council. The derailing of the 'Flying Scotsman', manned by volunteers, by strikers at Cramlington, the government's provocative use of troops to defend unthreatened food convoys in London, the Lord Chancellor's declaration that the strike was unconstitutional, all combined to convince the Negotiating Committee that they had unleashed a revolutionary juggernaut. As Patrick Renshaw has put it: 'The government was prepared to fight a revolution; the TUC hoped it would not have to lead one'.[27] The Negotiating Committee simply caved in after nine days, with no guarantees even that returning strikers would not be victimised by their employers. The miners fought on alone for another six months before being forced back to work, a most substantial defeat.

With the end of the miners' strike the miners ceased to be a problem for government for over forty years, until they re-emerged as the 'shock-troops of the labour movement' to bring about the collapse of the Heath government in 1974. There was to be no nationalisation of the mines until after the Second World War. In some sense, however, the General Strike was a success as much as it was a failure. Its object lessons became part and parcel of interwar ideology. After the General Strike, government and employers were reluctant to push down wages again, so that if the miners lost their own case, it may well be true that the furore that surrounded their struggle probably won it for others. More than that, the memory of what might have been during the strike galvanised both sides of industry into a new mood of conciliation and compromise, as the Mond–Turner talks on industrial relations proved in the late 1920s. A dangerous double-edged myth had been blown, about the revolutionary potential of British trade unionism and about the ability of the right wing simply to confront the labour movement and crush it. If the TUC had pushed the issue through to a successful conclusion, then at the very least the government would have fallen, but union leaders such as Walter Citrine, Ernest Bevin and James Thomas were simply not cast in the role of revolutionary leaders. On the other hand, if the TUC had gone on and ultimately lost its struggle, then a rampant right wing might have destroyed trade unionism for a generation, and the consequent development of British politics in the interwar period might have been framed in more extreme terms. As it was, a new truce had been concluded. The power of organised labour had been demonstrated, but also the limits to which it was prepared to go to achieve its aims; the constitutionalist and evolutionary tradition predominated over the innate instinct of any pressurised group to 'seize the time'.

THE LABOUR PARTY AND THE DEPRESSION

The apparent failure of the Labour party finally to break through electorally in the immediate postwar years, and the desultory performance of the first Labour government of 1924, had been among the factors that had prompted the TUC to take matters into its own hands in 1926. In fact, the Labour party was fighting an acute tactical battle in these years, in an attempt to win new electoral backing without losing its traditional support to alternative socialist strategies. Apart from the idea of a non-parliamentary road to workers' control through Direct Action, expressed by a few trade unionists, there was the appeal of the faster revolutionary road to socialism of revolutionary Marxism, with the example of Bolshevik Russia to hand. Equally worrying, in these immediate post-war years, was the outstanding success of the anti-socialist coalition that Lloyd George had forged in 1918. In its attempt to ward off Lloyd George's populist appeal, and to counter the taunt that Labour would plunge Britain into class war, Labour reacted swiftly and punishingly to the 'internal threat'. The formation of the Third (Communist) International in March 1919 had prodded a number of the socialist societies affiliated to the Labour party to form a Communist party in Britain; the Communist Unity Conference took place in July 1920.[28] Affiliation of the new party as a whole to the Labour party was refused and, in 1922, individual membership was refused to anyone belonging to another party. Throughout the interwar period, indeed, Labour was to show itself steadfastly anti-communist, and to be terrified at the prospect of infiltration into its own ranks and into the ranks of the TUC.

In effect, this vigorously anti-communist stance meant a refusal to work with groups like the Minority Movement and, later, the National Unemployed Workers Movement, to tackle some of the worst examples of deprivation caused by the depression. On the other hand, it was an impressive display of respectability and moderation, designed to strengthen Labour's appeal as the true heirs of nineteenth-century Liberalism as well as the prophets of socialism. The failure of the Third International to secure European revolution between 1919 and 1924 lessened whatever danger there had been that the Communists would effectively challenge Labour for direction of the British Left. At the same time, the threat from the populist Right faltered as the Lloyd George coalition began to crack up under the impact of the depression. But the end of the alliance between Lloyd George and the Conservatives spelled a new danger for Labour, that of a revitalised Liberal party. Though Lloyd George could not yet rejoin the Liberal fold, it was a wry fact that the election of December 1923, which was to bring the first Labour government to power, found Labour with less than one per cent more of the popular vote than the combined Liberal vote

(30.5 per cent as against 29.6 per cent). Baldwin's decision to go to the country on a tariff reform platform had rallied the supporters of free trade around the old party of Gladstone. The Conservatives in fact remained the largest party in the House of Commons in 1923. Asquith, however, could hardly agree to support Baldwin on tariff reform. He had little option but to agree to limited support for a minority Labour government. This was to prove to be another important tactical break for Labour.

The ensuing, brief Labour government may have dismayed its more optimistic supporters, but it did at least show that British streets would not run with blood with Labour in power. MacDonald's intention was not to lead the country immediately to the socialist millennium, but, rather, to use the opportunity of very temporary power to lay out his electoral stall in an attempt both to widen and to deepen Labour support, to put Labour's case not just for socialism in the longer term but as the only viable alternative to Conservatism in the short term. Indeed, only by earning respectability could the firm electoral base be established which would allow Labour the time in power to create the 'social tissue' to transform the state. Though Labour's minority position meant that they were unable, anyway, to achieve radical measures, this fact only served to strengthen MacDonald's predilection for the moderate alternative to Conservatism. MacDonald dropped the idea of a Capital Levy for reducing the National Debt, excluded left-wingers from the cabinet, offering posts instead to former Liberals such as Lords Thomson, Haldane, and Chelmsford, who also gave the party a presence in the House of Lords. The Chancellor, Philip Snowden, dropped the import duties which had been imposed by the Lloyd George and Baldwin governments, and abolished the corporation tax. Snowden's was a free-trade budget, virtually a Liberal budget, and therein lay its major significance. Labour had always been virtually indistinguish-able from the Liberals in terms of immediate policy. Before 1914 this had allowed Labour to sieze hold of the Lib-Labs; now the strategy was to attract the rest of the Liberals' traditional support. Temporary occupation of 10 Downing Street also allowed MacDonald to choose the time of the next election, and the issue on which it would be fought. The recognition of Soviet Russia, the *causes célèbres* of the Campbell case and the Zinoviev telegram, guaranteed that the election would be fought on the issue of a red scare, in which the Conservatives attempted to smear Labour as communist fellow-travellers and in which Labour could point to their clear anti-communist record. The Liberals were simply irrelevant. Though Labour lost seats, they increased their share of the popular vote, gaining over one million votes on 1923. The Liberals were almost annihilated in England, reduced to 40 seats and 17.6 per cent of the vote overall. MacDonald's limited objective had thus been achieved. Labour had governmental experience, and their right to be considered the principal opposition to the Conservatives was now unquestionable.[29]

It was a position that Labour consolidated during the rest of the 1920s. Their strategy on unemployment reflected their growing concern to move into the political centre, increasingly confident that the left wing in the party, though it might be angered by the direction the leadership was taking, in fact had nowhere else politically to go. Labour's policy was almost purely orthodox, concerned with the Sinking Fund to reduce the National Debt, arguing that the international credibility of sterling was crucial to Britain's recovery. Even before 1924, MacDonald had criticised the Conservative use of budget surpluses to accelerate housing construction on the grounds that the money should have gone to the Sinking Fund. After 1924, Labour's economic spokesman, Philip Snowden, constantly criticised Churchill as Chancellor for not making bigger cuts in public expenditure and for not making bigger contributions to the Sinking Fund. The result was, however, a deepening rift with the Left. Though it might be true that the Left had nowhere else to go, the deepening depression strengthened their hand in the attempt to wrest control of the party from MacDonald's consensual strategy.

The return of Labour to power in 1929, though again as a minority government reliant on Liberal support, found MacDonald unchanged in his attitude. Left-wingers were excluded even more firmly from the cabinet than in 1924, and Liberal support was cultivated by the offer of an investigation into the possibility of electoral reform. The frustrations of the left wing were intensified by the mutilation of the government's education, labour law and agricultural policies by the opposition and by the House of Lords. Even more distressing was the fact that unemployment, much of it inherited from the Conservative administration of 1924 to 1929, spiralled upwards in the first eighteen months of the new government. It was, of course, most unfortunate for the reputation of the second Labour government that it came to power at just the point when the depression was to hit its ultimate low. The Wall Street Crash of October 1929 soon sent reverberations through the European financial system. The rigidly orthodox economic and financial policies of MacDonald and Snowden, for all their apparent appeal to the middle ground of the political landscape, were extremely vulnerable to an increasingly vociferous left-wing attack. The first open revolt came from Sir Oswald Mosley, who proposed an alternative programme of direct state intervention in 1930, some of this programme more proto-Keynesian than it was socialist as such. Mosley demanded the expansion of home purchasing power to increase overall demand, the development of home agriculture to offload the import burden of foodstuffs, a liberal credit policy through public control of banking, nationalisation of industry under public control, the insulation of the economy through tariffs and the full development of the social services to offset the social consequences of the depression. Snowden rejected Mosley's suggestions outright, and Mosley in turn began that erratic movement out to the Right which was to lead to his isolation and finally his ostracism from the mainstream of British politics when he formed the British Union of Fascists.[30] In fact, though, much of what Mosley had argued for in his last months with Labour had been duplicated by the ILP in their programme 'Socialism Now'.

With the increase in the unemployment benefit, the Insurance Fund began to fall heavily into the red. The Treasury agreed to wipe out part of the debt, but believed that this was a further heavy burden on public expenditure at a time when gold was beginning to drain out of the Bank of England. The minority government was unable to resist opposition pressure to set up a commission of enquiry under

Judge Holman Gregory, to which the Treasury gave the damning evidence that the effect of large unemployment benefit pay-outs on British credit abroad was becoming critical. This led to opposition pressure for a full review of public expenditure, set up under Sir George May. On top of the increasing worries about what May would find, there was a further nervousness caused by the collapse of the Credit Anstaldt bank in Austria. Through June and July 1931 the Bank of England lost £22 million in gold. In July, the bank rate increased from 2.5 per cent to 4.5 per cent, and a £50 million credit was obtained from American and French banks. When the May Report appeared, forecasting a budgetary deficit of £120 million for 1932 and a deficit of £105 million on the Unemployment Insurance Fund, the run on gold turned into a rout; the Bank began losing gold at the rate of nearly £3 million a day. MacDonald saw Bank of England officials (the Chairman, Montague Norman, had collapsed and was incapacitated through the crisis) who told him that the Bank needed £80 million credit immediately, and that such a sum could not be obtained unless the government could restore international confidence. In effect, this meant accepting May's proposals for cuts in public expenditure, including £66 million from unemployment benefits.

Substantial cabinet agreement was reached for a package of cuts in public expenditure, but no agreement could be reached on cuts in benefit. The package was dismissed as inadequate by the Shadow Chancellor, Neville Chamberlain, which in effect meant that the government would be defeated if it tried to put its proposals to the House of Commons. The cabinet then agreed by a majority of 12–9 to further cuts, but the minority in the cabinet was too large to allow MacDonald a free hand. Arthur Henderson, leader of the cabinet minority, assumed that MacDonald would resign. The other parties, however, were reluctant to inherit what they saw as a Labour mess. The Conservatives also felt that a Labour presence in a reconstructed government would be essential to gain public acceptance for the proposed economies. The Liberals did not relish an election campaign and were therefore agreeable to a temporary coalition with MacDonald as Prime Minister, while Snowden could continue as Chancellor. It seems to have been the King who persuaded MacDonald that his presence was essential in the new cabinet. So, a 'temporary' coalition government was formed which, it was stressed, would not go to the polls as a unity but which was actually to fight two general elections and which was to last, in one form or another, for the next fourteen years.[31]

Two basic questions about MacDonald's motives and about the role of Labour in the political arena arise directly from this sequence of events; first, why did MacDonald accept the new commission in the first place; second, why did he stay on for another four years? In Labour demonology MacDonald has been castigated as vain, ambitious and with no real interest in the ultimate fortunes of the Labour party. This is simply silly. MacDonald had been the principal practical architect of the idea of the constitutional respectable alternative. He had given his whole career to that idea, and he had been remarkably successful. He believed that the Labour party was running away from a crisis which simply had to be faced if the party was ever to have credibility. If the Labour cabinet as a whole was not prepared to face up to the crisis then a Labour presence at least was essential; otherwise the traditional parties would take over like skilled craftsmen making good a botched-up job by a clumsy apprentice, and Labour would never get over the taunt that the party was 'unfit to govern'. It was an inevitable corollary of accepting the constitutional road to socialism that it also involved accepting the rules of international capitalism. The Left of the party were not only demanding more than MacDonald would, or indeed could offer, given the minority position of the government, it was in fact questioning the entire strategy that had dominated the Labour party since its birth and early development.[32]

Yet why did MacDonald agree to stay on and fight a general election as coalition Prime Minister? The answer really lies in the political straitjacket in which MacDonald was caught in the immediate circumstances that followed the collapse of the Labour government. Snowden presented his emergency budget of cuts in public expenditure and the credit of £80 million from the international banks was obtained. There were cuts in unemployment benefit, in the salaries of the civil service and the armed forces. On 15 September, however, there occurred the Invergordon Mutiny, a series of incidents involving naval ratings apparently refusing to sail because of the reductions in pay. The fact that the Royal Navy itself seemed on the point of breakdown caused another panic draining of the gold reserves. Within a week the government rushed through legislation taking Britain off the Gold Standard. It was yet another humiliation for the Labour party that the new National Government, less than a month after it had been formed to save the Gold Standard, simply did what the Labour cabinet had torn itself into pieces trying not to do. The immediate problem thereafter was to retain confidence in the period of transition from the Gold Standard to the floating pound. MacDonald and the Liberals concluded that the emergency was not at an end, though the Conservatives were adamant that an election was essential, with tariff reform on the menu as the only means by which Britain could survive the blizzard. Finally, the coalition parties agreed to go to the polls with separate manifestos and a covering note from MacDonald as Prime Minister, committing himself to no particular option but asking for a 'Doctor's mandate' to do whatever was necessary.

It was during the election of 1931 that the split between MacDonald and the Labour party became an open rift. Snowden shrilled invective against those who had 'run away' from the crisis and called Labour's manifesto 'Bolshevism run mad'. Labour, for its part, publicised accounts of the cabinet crisis which accused MacDonald and Snowden of treachery; both were to be expelled from the party. Though MacDonald still saw himself carrying the Labour flag in the cabinet, his political isolation was clear for all to see. Labour, meanwhile, had been reduced to 50 seats in the House of Commons, a defeat of such proportions that the rift that had occurred in the crisis and the subsequent election became impossible to patch over. The 'Great Betrayal' of 1931 was to become Labour's major contribution to the mythology of the 1930s, the moment at which, it is said, the future of the unemployed was handed on a plate to the Conservatives, along with the peace of Europe. Yet in practical terms it is difficult to see that there was a distinct alternative, within Labour's frame of reference at least, to MacDonald's course of action. It may certainly be true that the rigid orthodoxy of MacDonald's and Snowden's financial policy did not help the situation; it lacked imagination and flexibility. Yet most of the problems the cabinet faced in 1931 were not of their making. There were institutional difficulties in the British economy, the legacy of six years of an overpriced pound and the uncontrollable dynamic of international finance to weigh in the balance. Moreover, the alternative economic wisdom of the Left in the party had failed to make any decisive impact on the party as a whole, and if the Labour party itself could not agree on a socialist alternative, what chance was there that they could convince the electorate that one was needed? It was as the heirs of economic liberalism that the Labour party had developed to the point where it could form governments; the party, as ever, contained socialists but was not a socialist organisation as such.

The 1931 election forced Labour back into what had become its electoral citadels in the areas of heavy industry, the depressed areas of the North of England, South Wales and the Central Lowlands of Scotland. In these areas, their vote remained relatively solid or even increased. Indeed, the party still won a 30 per cent share of the popular vote in this electoral 'disaster'. But the political rationale of the concept of the respectable alternative was that Labour could not win general elections simply on this traditional base. What was required was to pick up seats in the South of England and in the Midlands, where the majority of the electorate was not unemployed, not badly housed, and not even fully aware of the problems that beset the depressed areas. With the distribution of the population the way it was in the interwar years, and with the distribution of parliamentary seats consequently favouring the relatively prosperous areas, there was simply no alternative way to reach parliamentary power. Given the electoral geography of the 'two nations', and given the commitment to the parliamentary road, MacDonald could realistically picture the options that faced the party as respectability and power, or radicalism and permanent opposition. The only alternative was to go back to theoretical basics, undo fifty years of work, and build from scratch a mass working-class party. It is in this sense that the Labour myth of the Great Betrayal is, basically, irrelevant. What is important about 1931 is not simply the crisis itself, but the context of Labour thinking in which it ocurred. Whether or not MacDonald plotted to rid himself of obnoxious Labour colleagues, and whether or not there was a 'bankers' ramp' intending to undermine British socialism, the fact remains that Labour had a socialist dream for the long term but no tactics for dealing with capitalist crisis in the short term.

MacDonald did not betray the Labour party, though the idea that he had done so enabled the party to blame its troubles on their former leader's personal failings, thus disguising the party's ineffective opposition through the rest of the 1930s. This displacement of blame also allowed Labour to retained its commanding position on the British Left, and thus retained mainstream British socialism within the constitutionalist mould; the party could claim that the disaster of 1931 was the result of personal treachery, rather than the result of fundamental theoretical flaws in Labour's position in the cirumstances of the depression.[33] Nevertheless, it was difficult to gloss over the fact that the party had suffered a severe setback. Only the coming of the Second World War, was to rescue the party from political marginalisation and present them with new opportunities for development.

'BALDWINISM': THE CONSERVATIVES AND THE DEPRESSION

The commanding position of the Conservatives in the politics of the interwar period depended, in part at least, on the fact that the Labour party remained unable finally to break the bedrock support for the Liberals. With the opposition divided, the Conservatives enjoyed a relatively easy electoral ride through the depression. With the developing consumer economy of important sections of the electoral landscape in the 1930s, too, they could rely on self-interest to work on the party's behalf. And with the further development of the lower-middle class (40 per cent of all families in Britain by the time of the 1931 census) the Conservatives had a source of virtually unquestioning support, probably even stronger than Labour's working-class base. Yet interwar Conservatism was by no means simply complacent in response to the problems of the depression. At the end of the Great War, many leaders of the Conservative party had not been at all sure that their traditional ideology could survive in a world of mass democracy such as the 1918 franchise seemed to present. Yet, just as the party had responded to the 1867 franchise, and picked up suburbia as its natural constituency through adopting a right-wing populism, so Baldwinism proved to be the pragmatic change of course that Conservatism would make to configure with the post-war world. Baldwinism represented that adaptation in ideology that taught the Conservatives that they could flourish in a mass democracy, without the need for the presidential and dynamic style of a Lloyd George, that by adopting a centrist approach the party could remain the 'natural party of government'.

Baldwin represented that stream of Tory thought which held that ultimately there were no hard and fast rules of political conduct; a political position or a theoretical assumption was only worth retaining as long as it proved its worth; theory, per se, counted for very little whereas practical politics, what R.A. Butler was later to call 'the art of the possible', counted for a great deal. Embedded in this essentially adaptive and pragmatic ideology of Conservatism was the assumption that it was rarely actually possible to solve anything in political life, though the provision of palliatives could offset the worst social and political consequences of the inevitable trials and tribulations that went with life in the advanced, industrial age. A policy of palliatives, within the limits of what was financially possible, could indeed transform capitalism by giving it a human face. Baldwin was the first British political leader to understand, in the age of mass communications which began with the age of mass democracy, the importance of political image. He understood that a political philosophy could be effectively popularised by giving that philosophy other, ostensibly non-political connotations in the popular imagination. Baldwin built for himself the image of the lover of the countryside, the tweedy squire figure that linked to a sentimental notion of the Old England of the agricultural economy. Only a week before becoming Prime Minister for the first time, Baldwin told the press that he saw his future in terms of a return to Astley, his country home, to 'read the books I want to read, to live a decent life and keep pigs'. With that image Baldwin sought to associate the Conservative party with the 'fundamental' British values of decency, honesty, conciliation and compromise. Baldwin had looked around in the House of Commons after 1918 and seemed to see, even on his own benches, 'hard-faced men who looked as though they had done well out of the war'. Baldwin's Toryism implicitly repudiated intellectual brilliance, which he associated with the trickery and immorality of the Lloyd George era in politics, in favour of duty and self-sacrifice. 'I never knew a good talker who was also a good worker', he said, 'nor a good worker who could talk.' It was his apparently transparent simplicity and honesty that made him the superlative politician of his time.[34]

The Tory party of the third quarter of the nineteenth century had been known as the 'stupid' party. The Liberal dilemma had brought a new wealth of intellectual talent into the party through the late nineteenth century and into the period of the Great War. Baldwin laboured hard to make the party 'stupid' again, but also decent. He also worked hard to rid the party of that patrician image with which it had become associated through figures like Lords Curzon and Birkenhead. There were definite efforts, too, to get on with the new men of the Left. Indeed, through his deliberate socialising with them in the lobbies and the bar of the House of Commons, it is probably true to say that the Clydeside MPs trusted Baldwin a great deal more than they did MacDonald. The party's conscious use of the mass media to construct the new image of Toryism was also, undoubtedly, a major element in its success. The press was dominated by the radical Tory press barons, Northcliffe, Rothermere and Beaverbrook, and Baldwin constantly found himself having to fight off the challenge they represented. On the new media, however, on radio and on cinema newsreel, he was a sensational performer. Baldwin could be said to have predated Roosevelt as the inventor of the homely fireside chat on radio. Throughout the interwar period, the British Broadcasting Corporation maintained a neutral stance on specific political issues. This was not always an easy position to maintain and the BBC's first Director General, Sir John Reith, had to fight hard for the Corporation's autonomy during crises such as that which surrounded the General Strike. To say that the BBC was neutral on particular issues, however, is not to deny that it was conservative with a small 'c'. In its news output as well as in its entertainment material, the BBC mixed populism with high cultural values, a mix which fitted particularly well with the spirit of Baldwinism.

On newsreel, the bluff country squire lauded the common sense of the British way, condemned the politics of division and the extremism of other countries, congratulating a weekly cinema audience of anything up to seventeen million on being British. Newsreel Toryism, in the Baldwin mode, was supra-political; it was the embodiment of traditional British values resident in Baldwin's own 'star quality'. Neville Chamberlain, Baldwin's successor as Tory leader, may have lacked the personal warmth that Baldwin seemed to exude on screen, but his newsreel performances were, if anything, even more cleverly contrived. Chamberlain's careful cultivation of the newsreel companies and their audience, in particular in his annual explanation of his budgets when Chancellor in the early 1930s, was to pay off at the high point of his career. The Munich settlement was the occasion of nothing short of adulation in the newsreels, Chamberlain being lauded as the politician who embodied the common sense of the man in the street: 'history will thank God, as we do know, that in our hour of need there was such a man – Neville Chamberlain'.[35]

In these ways, the Conservatives moved quickly to understand and to organise the new mass electorate. In just one newsreel appearance, the new leaders could reach an audience that Gladstone could not have reached in over a month of whistle-stop tours. By contrast, too, the Labour leaders never managed to use the media effectively before the Second World War. Though Ramsay MacDonald was no mean performer, it was only when he had the resources of the Conservative Central Office behind him, as Prime Minister of the National Government, that his full impact could be felt. This media-consciousness, though it was soon to become part of the everyday business of politics for all politicians, was at this time a revelation. Politics, it seemed to signify, no longer took place behind closed doors involving men in top hats and morning suits, with occasional circus-style elections for the masses. Baldwin, in spite of his own very establishment background, constructed and addressed an image of the common man in the age of mass democracy as decent and clean-living, neither unemployed nor syndicalist nor fascist but, typically, white-collar clerical with a wife and three children who lived in inner suburbia. Media-consciousness was in fact the central element in a sharply-focused attempt to capture the middle ground of politics, and thus minimise social divisions. Baldwin offered himself and his party's politics as the true British way to a quiet life and a warm heart, constantly juxtaposed in front of the public not only with the ineffectual neo-socialism of the Labour party, on the one hand, but also with the 'hard-faced men' on the other.

Baldwin's attempts to capture the middle ground of politics were, however, fraught with grave difficulties; in particular, the internal disputes of the Conservative party were difficult to patch over. His decision to go to the polls on a platform of tariff reform in 1923 he later described as a ploy to 'dish the goat', to offset the chance that Lloyd George might forestall him by adopting a similar platform to win back Tory hearts. Though the adoption of tariff reform led to electoral defeat, it did at least have the effect of rallying the Conservatives under Baldwin, and isolating Lloyd George even more thoroughly from his would-be supporters on the Right. Having thus brought back the former coalitionists to the Tory fold, perhaps somewhat grudgingly in the case of important figues such as Austen Chamberlain and Lord Birkenhead, Baldwin then immediately dropped tariff reform in order to make it easier for waverers such as Winston Churchill to rejoin the ranks. Baldwin may have disliked and distrusted him as a renegade, but Churchill did represent an important strain of the Tory tradition in the reorientation of politics that Baldwin was working to engineer. Churchill went to the Treasury in the mid-1920s as clear evidence of the party's new free trade intentions, bringing with him some of the populist ethos of his father as well as echoes of pre-war New Liberal progressivism. The placing of Neville Chamberlain at the Ministry of Health was an important balancing act, incorporating another Tory progressive tradition, that of Joseph Chamberlain's brand of community politics.

The 1920s saw an important and efficient development in that partnership between central and local government that had been such an significant element in the interface between electors and governors since the 1880s. Already in 1918 the creation of a Ministry of Health, merging the old Local Government Board with the National Health Insurance Commission and the Registrar's Office, had allowed local government to co-ordinate more effectively in national social policy. Chamberlain's Local Government Act of 1929 dealt with more of the problems which had accumulated as the scope of the responsibilities of local government had increased. The Act abolished the Board of Guardians, their powers being transferred to the Counties and the County Boroughs. Local government was also given increased powers in a number of areas which would allow authorities to spend to put the local unemployed back to work.

Yet, though the balance of the 1924–9 cabinet may have been important in widening the political appeal of Baldwin's Toryism, it in fact did nothing to make the government's policy internally coherent. Churchill's orthodoxy at the Treasury, the ruinous effects of the return to the Gold Standard in 1925, and his refusal to protect industry from the economic draught, were not entirely papered over by what Chamberlain was trying to do at Health. Churchill's almost contemporary decision to take some of the burden of rates off industry in effect undercut the ability of the Counties to make use of the powers given them by the 1929 Local Government Act. The Conservative administration of 1924 to 1929 was in fact peppered with examples of overall coherence in policy being sacrificed for the semblance of party unity, which allowed Conservatism to appear as all things to all men.[36] The Conservatives went into the 1929 election with one and a quarter million unemployed, and while they could still rely on the employed majority to give them a very good electoral showing, the rot was under way which would produce three million unemployed within two years, a major financial crisis and the very opportunity for social and political upset which Baldwinism was designed to avoid. As it was, the Conservatives were perhaps somewhat fortunate that it was Labour and not themselves who paid the price. With the return to government of the Conservatives in 1931, as the mainstay of the coalition formed in that year, Chamberlain's insistence on tariffs did at least make economic policy more coherent. Churchill's renewed disloyalty to the Conservatives, over the question of the movement of India towards independence, was to relieve Baldwin of the need to appease that wayward and increasingly isolated politician. The extent of the crisis also made it possible to ride roughshod over the free trade susceptibilities of Labour and Liberal members of the nominally cross-party coalition.

Baldwin had declared in 1924: 'There is one thing which I feel is worth giving one's life to, and that is the binding together of all classes of our people in an effort to make life in this country better in every sense of the word.' The economic policy of the Conservatives in the 1920s, however, put a great deal of the burden of achieving this aim onto public relations. The return to the Gold Standard, in particular, led directly to the General Strike, the clearest example of potential class conflict in the period. With the defeat of the General Strike, moreover, Baldwin was unable to resist backbench pressure for blatant class legislation. In 1925, Baldwin's intervention had been decisive in the defeat of a bill to curb the powers of trade unions; indeed, the phrase he used on that occasion – 'Give peace in our time, O Lord!' – was to become the catch phrase of Baldwinism. After the General Strike, however, the Trades Unions and Trades Disputes Act declared illegal any 'political strike', forbade unions for civil servants, made 'intimidatory' picketing an offence, and threatened Labour party funds by forcing unions to 'contract in' to the political levy. (Since 1913, unions had had to 'contract out' if they did not want to contribute to Labour party funds). These legislative powers were never invoked but while they remained on the statute book they created an atmosphere of friction and ill will, at odds not only with the ideals of Baldwinism but also with the will to moderation within both the TUC and the Labour party. One of the very first acts of the first majority Labour government in 1945 was to repeal this legislation, a highly symbolic rejection of what Baldwinism was by then deemed to have committed on the national psyche.

The signs of progressiveness in social policy, and also in economic policy in the 1930s, need in other words to be seen within the context of Baldwinism as a whole. The contribution of Baldwinism to the relaxation of social tensions amounted in effect to the pouring of ladles of soporific rhetoric over the evidence of class divisions. Labour could pick up massive majorities in South Wales or in County Durham but the party only got one seat whether their majority was 23 000 or merely 5. Fundamentally, the Conservatives controlled interwar politics because mass unemployment and real deprivation was always only a minority and a regionalised problem. Baldwinism blurred the harsh edges of the resultant divide, while doing nothing substantial to correct it.

On the other hand, the ideology of Baldwinism had substantial ramifications in terms of the development of concepts of running a country in economic decline. It was not simply that a personable, avuncular manner became an important prerequisite of any successful Prime Minister for the next forty years, it was also established in this period that consensus rather than conflict was essential to protect the social fabric in such circumstances. Social policy could be used to take the strain imposed by decay in the economic base, and the superstructure of political ideas must accommodate the fact that the state must be seen to be fair to all sections of the social formation. Baldwinism had thus rejuvenated centrist, pragmatic Toryism to complement the respectable alternative of the Labour movement in the battle for the centre ground.

THE APPROACH OF WAR

With Labour heavily punished by the 1931 debacle, the Conservatives were left in effective control of the 1930s. Snowden and some of the Liberal members of the coalition resigned over the Conservatives' insistence on tariffs in 1932, but MacDonald and the remaining Liberals within the coalition helped to maintain the necessary fiction of Baldwinism's claim to consensus. The National Governments did what they considered necessary, within the slowly widening confines of what they considered possible, to intervene and to rationalise. For the most part, however, their role seemed to be simply to sit out the depression and keep the social peace. Politically, they appeared to be in an unassailable position. Labour recovered to 150 seats in the 1935 general election but it is difficult to believe that, had there not been a war and had there been an election in 1940, Labour would have had a realistic chance of power. It is true that the accession of Neville Chamberlain to the leadership of the Conservatives threatened Conservative primacy in the medium term, because Chamberlain was not quite the master of consensus that Baldwin had been. Nevertheless, the break in Conservative hegemony was to come not in domestic affairs at all, but in the increasing vulnerability of the National Governments in their conduct of foreign affairs. In the political adjustments that occurred in reaction to appeasement, a new ideological avenue opened out which was to come to the foreground as the Tory consensus of the 1930s broke down as war loomed.

The next war was a much more frightening prospect in the 1930s than it had been before 1914. This was as true for mainstream right-wing opinion as it was for the Left, who were traditionally more prone to take an anti-war stance. The experience of the Great War had convinced most on the political Right in Britain that war was, politically and socially, simply too dangerous a prospect to contemplate. Not only had the conflict led to the toppling of the Old Order over most of Europe, but its economic legacy had produced chronic instability, a social friction sometimes held in check only by the flimsiest of social controls. Over wide areas of Europe, the resultant struggle between communism and fascism produced the danger that traditional politics would become simply irrelevant and the old elite rendered redundant. The prospect of renewed conflict was even more nightmarish for the British Right than the memory of the Great War. The advent of air war threatened, in its emphasis on targeting industrial centres and civilian morale, to bring about rapidly just that social and political breakdown that it had taken four years of trench warfare to produce in Russia and Germany. The airmen indeed claimed that social and economic breakdown was the main aim of air warfare, that the Great War had proved that a simple military victory was an impossibility in total war, and that only the destruction of the *materiel* and the morale of the enemy nation could produce victory next time round. To a generation of politicians who had witnessed the General Strike and the hunger marches, who had given their careers to offsetting the possible political and social implications of the depression, the claims of the airmen seemed all too credible. Significantly, it had been in the year of the General Strike that Baldwin had chosen to ask the House of Commons rhetorically, 'who does not know that if another great war comes, our civilisation will fall with as great a crash as that of Rome?' It is clear that the prospect of air warfare particularly deeply affected both Baldwin's and Chamberlain's attitudes towards foreign affairs: the point Chamberlain saved for last, the incontrovertible argument, in his justification of the Munich settlement to the Commons, was the prospect of 'people burrowing underground, trying the escape from poison gas, knowing that at any hour of the day or night death or mutilation was ready to come upon them'. In Hitler's Germany, moreover, the British government appeared to be facing a potential antagonist just about crazy enough to unleash the Apocalypse. On paper, at least, the Luftwaffe appeared a fearsome force, and in their *Luftpolitik*, the Nazis were determined to develop its full deterrent effect[37]

The air threat was complicated by other strategic factors, particularly the fact that Britain was unlikely simply to face Germany in a renewed conflict. The simultaneous emergence of threats in Japan and in Italy faced Britain with the prospect of a three-front war – against powerful opponents and on a truly global scale – for the first time in her history. Such a combination put the continued existence of the Empire and Commonwealth, as well as the home country, under the direst possible threat. The Chiefs of Staff in the 1930s consistently argued that Britain should not risk war until the number of potential enemies had been reduced. Though Britain might well be able to take on each of the threats separately, the combination of all three would prove the gravest possible risk, particularly at a time when it was by no means clear what sort of support would be forthcoming from the Americans or the Soviets. Chamberlain reasoned accurately that the Germans played the key role in the triple threat. If Germany could be appeased, then neither the Japanese nor the Italians would

dare to cut loose, but if Britain became involved in a war in
Europe, then the other two might well make the best of the
opportunities in the Mediterranean, in Africa and in the Far
East. It was on the basis of this reasoning that the appeasement
of Germany came to dominate British foreign policy to the
exclusion of other more traditional spheres of interest as the
1930s wore on.

For reasons concerned both with domestic and with
international politics, then, there appeared to the political
Right to be sound pragmatic justification for appeasement. A
renewal of the Anglo-German conflict could well spell disaster
for Britain; the war would hardly be worth winning, indeed
might be unwinnable. Appeasement also made economic sense.
The Depression had made the Treasury the single most
important ministry. The National Government had been
formed to save the economy, after all, and it was to that extent
inevitable that the traditional semi-autonomy of the Foreign
Office in framing international policy was whittled down. Not
only could Britain not afford armaments on the scale necessary
to fight a three-front war, but international friction itself was
deemed to be both cause and effect of the international
economic chaos. Germany, given the size of her population
and the potential strength of her industrial economy, must be
allowed to return to the community of nations, if European
economic difficulties were ever to be overcome. Britain could
not recover in isolation from Europe, and Europe could not
recover if Germany were kept permanently in chains by
international treaty.

Appeasement was not, then, simply an idiocy on the part of
the governments of the 1930s. Whatever moral qualms we may
feel about the policy with the benefit of hindsight, there were
solid political reasons why it should have come to dominate
foreign policy, and no clearly viable alternative appeared.[38]
Until the last eighteen months of the peace, Winston Churchill
appeared to be a political figure with no real future, and his
campaign against appeasement was shot through with
fallacies. As Churchill began his sustained attack on
appeasement policy and what he saw as the weakness of
British rearmament, the government could point out that, as
Chancellor in the 1920s, Churchill had not only understood

the need for a conciliatory policy towards Germany, but had in fact made the cuts in the defence forces which were currently making rearmament so difficult to achieve. As one leading military man at the time put it, armaments could not be built up merely by expressing the wish for them. It was not simply a case of making more money available, it was also a question of building up the infrastructure of the arms industry which had been allowed to atrophy since the end of the 'war to end wars'. In fact, more money was made available for armaments in the 1930s than ever before in peacetime in Britain. The problem was not financial but industrial, particularly that of gearing industry to arms production without interfering with the recovery of trade, the rock-solid bottom line of government policy since the 1931 Crash.

It was Hitler, however, who unwittingly contributed to the re-emergence of Churchill as a credible political figure, and began the process by which Baldwin's consensus was to be undermined. Churchill was, in fact, substantially wrong in his estimates both of German and of British military strength, particularly in the air. Hitler's air propaganda, however, maximising the fear of air attack and the belief that Germany had overwhelming strength available in the air, sowed seeds of doubt about the British government's figures which were subsequently difficult to weed out, simply because of the complications involved in compiling comparative figures of air strength. Churchill fed on the government's discomfiture and, given the popular fears of air attack, it was difficult for spokesmen simply to dismiss Churchill's alternative figures of German air strength without the government appearing complacent. Churchill's problem, however, was his isolation. Having changed parliamentary sides frequently in his political career, and having shown a lack of party discipline on a number of occasions, it is not perhaps surprising that few in the Conservative party trusted him. In Labour party circles, Churchill was the villain of Tonypandy, of the General Strike, and the racist of the debates on Indian independence. Had it not been for the growing disenchantment with appeasement, it is reasonable to conclude that the ageing Churchill would never again have achieved public office.[39] As it was, the alternative strategic wisdom that began to group around Churchill was bizarre in its diffusion.

Churchill rarely made determined efforts to gather support in his own party. His Tory supporters tended to be those other resentful misfits on the Right who had little chance of advancement in Baldwin's or Chamberlain's party. They were very rarely prepared to go to the extent of actually voting against the government, in spite of the fact that the government's majority was virtually unassailable; neither, indeed, was Churchill himself very often to walk into the opposition lobby when it came to a division. Nevertheless, the fact that they were at least prepared to speak out allowed them to forge a tenuous bond across the political spectrum with the Left. Labour's international policy in the 1930s veered alarmingly from pacifism to militant anti-fascism. The inconsistencies are in fact explained by the changing make-up of the parliamentary Labour Party as it began its recovery from the 1931 disaster. Many of the big names on the Right and in the centre of the party had lost their seats in 1931, with the result that the leadership fell to the pacifist George Lansbury. It was only after the election of 1935 that men such as Hugh Dalton reappeared in the House, and only with the onset of the Abyssinian crisis that Labour found it possible unequivocally to support the concept of collective security. Even then, Labour could make no impact on the huge government majority. They had nothing in common, either, with the small right-wing opposition except antipathy to appeasement; they even disagreed about alternative foreign policies. The astonishing spectacle of the communist Willy Gallagher agreeing fervently with Winston Churchill in the Munich debate remained, as yet, only a straw in the wind, a pointer to the still unlikely combination of Left and Right against the centre.

More significant, perhaps, were the signs of possible co-operation between the right of the Labour party and the younger left of the Conservatives, soon to emerge as the Tory Reform group, who could agree not only on matters of foreign policy, but also on a broader range of issues in social and economic policy, and the need to extend and to modify substantially the consensual policies of the National Governments. Coalition after 1931, though it isolated the Left, did produce a number of opportunities for cross-party contacts which may have gone some way to fray the edges of political conflict in the centre. Harold Nicolson even converted to the new coalitionist Labour grouping from the Right, though it must be said that his action was more startling than typical. On the other hand, younger Tories like Harold Macmillan frequently and publicly rubbed shoulders with members of other political parties in groups like Political and Economic Planning, and contributed to the coalitionist National Labour *Newsletter*. In the Next Five Years group, scientists and other intellectuals combined with politicians from both Right and Left backgrounds to proselytise the mixed economy and the use of a steeply graduated taxation system to ease the problems of poorer sections of society. But it was above all, perhaps, the threat of the next war which produced the strongest currents towards agreement. The League of Nations Union, hopelessly idealistic though its aims may have been with the benefit of hindsight, did at least allow an apparently dyed-in-the-wool Tory like Lord Cecil to appreciate the collectivist arguments of some of his left-wing fellow members. In the notion of the Popular Front, moreover, came the strongest evidence of the nascent development of a new political centre, prepared to sacrifice specific party loyalties and traditions for the sake of defending democracy as a whole against fascism. Thus, although coalition between Churchill and Labour still appeared highly unlikely in the 1930s, even with their growing agreement over issues of foreign affairs, there were signs of developing links at the edges of the political parties which might give such a coalition real ideological weight, should a great enough crisis ever appear. Such a crisis was indeed to occur in 1940.[40]

Finally, Neville Chamberlain was to sacrifice his political reputation to the consensus which he had helped to found, and which had helped to bring the British establishment relatively unscathed through the Great Depression. Appeasement was to convince all sections of political opinion that there simply was no other way. Even George Lansbury, convinced pacifist though he was, admitted on the day that war was declared that the public accepted that there was no alternative.

Chamberlain appeased until he could appease no more and mentioned publicly, as war was declared, that all he had fought for in his political life was crashing in ruins about him. When Hitler invaded Poland in September 1939, and as Chamberlain still delayed issuing an ultimatum to Germany, the right-winger Leo Amery shouted across the House to Arthur Greenwood, as he rose to reply for the Labour party: 'speak for England, Arthur!' It was an invitation that many on the Left found acutely embarassing but one which, having accepted, they were to find immensely beneficial.

Though Chamberlain's government was to continue into the summer of 1940, it had been fatally undermined by the failures of its foreign policy. Winston Churchill, as leader of the coalition that replaced it, was to prove either unwilling or unable to provide the kind of initiative in domestic affairs that had characterised Baldwin and Chamberlain. As a result, there was to appear a vaccuum in Conservative political philosophy, and an opportunity for Labour to engineer a rapid shift to the Left, replacing the interwar consensus. It was an opportunity Labour could not realistically have expected to have placed before them, given their electoral form between the wars, but it was to be an opportunity firmly seized as the party entered the most decisive and confident phase in its history. In response to the new Labour initiative, the younger Tories who had rubbed shoulders with the Labour Right in the 1930s were to move the Conservatives to the left to complete the new consensual alignment of the 1940s and beyond.

THE IMPACT OF THE SECOND WORLD WAR

THE PEOPLE'S WAR

The impact of the Second World War on Britain is still clouded with some of the most powerful mythology in modern history. Phrases such as 'the Dunkirk spirit', 'backs to the wall' and 'the finest hour' have a profoundly iconographic quality which has survived more than forty years of mobilisation at every level from academic history to television drama. The war became more than just another series of events to be lived through: it became an historical ideal, against which to measure the values both of the period that had gone before and the period that has elapsed since. What is deemed to have happened in the war, and in 1940 in particular, has become central to the concept of British national identity, a belief that there exists a national family with a shared memory, a collective consciousness which cuts across class, gender and regional divides. The year 1940 has become a constant point of reference for what Britain could achieve, and of appeals for further effort, for further sacrifice, for further heroics to recapture that sublime 'finest hour'.

Yet, looked at it in closer detail, the mythology of the impact of the war on Britain is not actually as clear-cut as it might at first seem. It has, in fact, been used for entirely different purposes. For the political Right in Britain, the Second World War was fundamentally important for the moral stance Britain is believed to have adopted in international affairs. Britain stood up to the dictators alone, when others failed, thus providing the opportunity for the world to be kept safe for democracy. This particular view of the war was to be mobilised to underpin British attitudes (with varying degrees of success) towards the Soviet Union in the Cold War, towards Colonel Nasser in the Suez Crisis of 1956, and towards the Argentinian military junta during the Falklands War. It has even at times been used to decry the internal 'dictatorial' enemy in the shape of 'over-powerful' trades unions. For the Left, on the other hand, the war was more important as a rejection of all that the interwar years are deemed to have stood for, not simply fascism in international affairs but also the dole queues and means tests at home, created by a regime of hard-hearted conservatism which itself bordered on neo-fascism. In this view, the Second World War was a 'People's War', a fight for a new brand of social democracy, for a New Jerusalem. For the New Left, on the other hand, these were ideals which were never fulfilled because of the failings of the leadership of the mainstream Left in Britain. The New Left was to blame the Labour Party for not being prepared to seize the revolutionary moment in 1945. It remains the case of the mainstream Left, however, that the New Jerusalem was indeed built by the Labour governments of 1945 to 1951, in the shape of the Welfare State and in the nationalisation of the 'commanding heights' of British industry, and was to survive until the ravages of the New Right of the 1970s and 1980s destroyed the fruits of that victory. The postwar consensus was founded on the national unity supposed to have been engendered by the experience of the Second World War. On the other hand, with the benefit of hindsight, it is now possible to see that that consensus was founded on a compromise between very different political positions and was eventually to founder when that compromise was no longer tenable. The New Left and the New Right have their roots in a rejection of that compromise and in conflicting interpretations of the circumstances which gave it birth.

The interpretation of the Second World War, and 1940 in particular, as a new beginning, a new opportunity, whether in the right or the left analysis of the form which that new beginning and new opportunity actually took, is clearly founded in turn on a rejection of the consensus of the interwar years. This rejection can be dated quite precisely to the wartime years. The coalition that came to power in May 1940 was composed of groups which had nothing in common except their antipathy to appeasement and their determination to fight the war through to a succesful conclusion. It was of supreme importance, in the circumstances of 1940, that a scapegoat be provided for the perilous position to which Britain was reduced by the military debacle in France. It was no basis for national revival to admit what was probably the case, that Britain's international bluff had been called in the 1930s. On the contrary, it had to be argued that Britain had been brought so low not through basic weaknesses in the economy but through the personal incapacity, not to say cowardice, of the nation's leaders in the preceding years. *Guilty Men*, written by three journalists in 1940, was set on the beaches of Dunkirk and traced back the history of that disaster to the appeasers of the 1930s, ending by demanding the dismissal of those 'guilty men' who still held high positions in the country.[1]

Guilty Men in fact marked only the beginning of a sustained campaign against the men of the 1930s, not just for their foreign policy but for their domestic policy as well. And in the development of this campaign, mainstream conservatism temporarily lost the initiative to the Left. In fact the political Right in Britain gave ground readily, apparently convinced that concessions would have to be made to secure national morale for the efforts that would have to be made if the war were to be won. Much of this campaign against 'the locust years' was actually state-inspired. The Ministry of Information, in particular, was convinced that if home morale was to be strengthened sufficiently to withstand the expected onslaught from the air, then some new commitment must be made; peace aims must supplement war aims. Much of the worry that the Ministry of Information felt in the early stages of the war was no doubt fuelled, in turn, by the reports of their Home Intelligence team and of the Mass Observation organisation. What both sets of social surveys seemed to indicate was a gap between leaders and led, with potentially dangerous consequences if the bombing war ever started. Early propaganda campaigns, for instance, were deemed disasters by the survey teams, for the explicit distinction they seemed to draw between 'you' and 'us'. The poster that read 'Your Courage, Your Determination, Your Cheerfulness, Will Bring Us Victory' was perhaps the most obvious gaffe in this area made by MoI in the early days. The campaigns against fifth columinists and 'careless talk' were similarly thought to have failed because of their patronising attitude and the insulting assumption that every man in the street was a potential traitor. Even the intelligence survey teams themselves came in for some stick, the press dubbing them in Duff Cooper's days at MoI as 'Cooper's snoopers'.[2]

Determined to avoid the stigma of being seen as the catspaw of authoritarianism in Britain, the MoI developed a liberal attitude in censorship (as far as the defence ministries would allow, at least), and actively encouraged what can only be described as a swing to the Left in their own output. Their films are a case in point. Early in the war, the MoI's film division was run by Sir Joseph Ball, previously head of film in the Conservative Research Department. In 1940, however, the documentary film-makers of the 1930s were brought into a reconstructed films division, and immediately began producing propaganda shorts with a wholly different social ethos. There were to be no more middle-class heroes and working-class spies and, most noticeable of all, there was to be a new imaging of the 1930s as the 'locust years' and of the war as an opportunity for a new commitment to social advancement. There had, of course, been many such 'alternative' views of the 1930s produced in that decade, by the documentary film-makers among others, but the difference was that whereas in the 1930s these views had been effectively marginalised by the mass media, they were now going out as government information. As such, the many thousands of films, newsreels and millions of pamphlets put out by MoI may have contributed to a revolution of rising expectations in the country.[3]

It was not only official publicity material which constructed this view of the war as a rejection of everything the 1930s stood for; similar views were to be found in the mass media generally, particularly in the quality press and on radio. *The Times*, a notable supporter of Chamberlain in the 1930s, was forthright in drawing the implications of the Blitz for social policy. As early as October 1940, the *Times* leader commented:

> The reconstruction of England will reshape many ways of life and will attack poverty and slumdom, ignorance and ill-health, the insecurities of employment, the closed door of opportunity. Indeed a solid, stable and not slow social

reconstruction, and some considerable industrial reconstruction, will be the task of reformers after the war – nothing less than a replanning of the national life.[4]

Early in the war, too, the BBC moved away decisively from the staid presentation and programming of the Reith era of broadcasting, adopting a new populism which was as apparent in its coverage of current affairs as in light entertainment. The inclusion of J.B. Priestley in a peak-listening spot for his *Postscript* series in 1940 not only allowed regional accents onto radio for the first time, but also allowed the opportunity for the expression of a somewhat anodyne quasi-socialism. Priestley argued the need to make the war

> a colossal battle, not only against something but also for something positive and good. If all this, together with certain obvious elements of social justice and decency seems to you Socialism . . . then you are at liberty to call me a Socialist . . . but there's a danger that as this high mood passes, apathy will return, and selfishness and stupidity.[5]

How much such views were genuine reflections of a popular move to the Left as the war began, or how much they simply demonstrated the ability of British institutions ideologically to reform to offset expected new demands, is difficult to say. But George Orwell was clearly right in his remark that the left-wing intelligentsia of the 1930s had been sucked into the machinery of the state, moving from the periphery of public affairs which they had occupied in the 1930s to the centre of the massive wartime exercise in public relations.[6] It is also clear that they took their political opinions with them. Arguably, this had the effect of changing public attitudes towards the state, as these views filtered through the mass media over nearly six years of war. It would be wrong, however, to describe the development of the idea of the 'People's War' simply as an invention of the mass media, for it is clear that mass involvement, civilian as well as military, played a critical role in determining new avenues along which politics would develop in the war years themselves and for twenty years thereafter.

On a practical level the war years, and particularly 1940, demanded major new involvements by the state which, because of their cumulative effect and because they were in force for so long, were very difficult simply to dismantle as they had been after the *ad hoc* and piecemeal interventions of the Great War. The Blitz, for example, faced government with a whole range of relatively small and detailed problems of administration and rationalisation, which together amounted to a substantial redefinition of the role of the state in social policy. In the 1930s, government had planned for air war on the assumption that there would be massive fatal casualties, and that the major role of the state would be one of controlling incipient riot. Air raid precautions had been largely confined to sensible but rather inadequate measures such as the provision of personal shelters for erection in the garden (not very useful if one had no garden), or the provision of gas masks and stirrup pumps to deal with gas and incendiary attack. The government would not provide the necessary capital for Local Authorities to build mass shelters, arguing that a concentration of people in such shelters was likely to lead to greater casualties. Neither was government in the 1930s prepared to deal with the possible problems of post-raid welfare, arguing that this would largely be the responsibility of the Local Authorities.[7] The Local Authorities, understandably, had been angered by this planning assumption, the boroughs surrounding the Port of London, for example, arguing that the Port would be a certain target because of its national importance and that protection of the Port and the population which kept it going should therefore be a national responsibility. The onset of the Blitz was to prove decisively that the tradition of distinguishing between local and national responsibility in social provision, a tradition inherited from the 1834 Poor Law, was simply inadequate as well as inappropriate when dealing with a wartime emergency of this magnitude. Government had no option but to learn that the relationship between local and central government had to be recast. The burden of war preparation had to be borne nationally rather than locally, even if this involved superseding the local authorities to some extent in supervising the establishment of a fair and safe measure of civil defence. In turn, central government was to find itself superseding local government in a wide range of activities as the effect of the war underlined the importance of national planning.

In fact, the actual administrative problems caused by the Blitz were very different from those which had been expected. Fatal casualties were never to approach pre-war estimates. There was never to be any real evidence that German bombing could produce more than a passive and fatalistic numbness on the part of the victim communities, certainly nothing approaching the mass breakdown of morale that had been predicted. The pre-war air theorists had underestimated the stability of urban society, that network of inter-reinforcing social sinews that made a community out of family, work and leisure ties. The biggest threat to morale proved to be not the bombers themselves but the indirect effect of goverernment's lack of preparation for post-raid welfare. The typical victim of the Blitz was not a shop steward preaching class war, but a middle-aged man who had lost his house, his glasses, his false teeth, his ration book and his bicycle; he was hardly a threat to national security but, rather, the object of the most intense sympathy. Yet the scale of the homelessness, and the scale of the other relatively minor problems with which the local social services and voluntary services had to deal, was overwhelming. Nor was it acceptable that local communities should have to bear the whole burden of distress: civilians were being bombed because they were British, not because they were Londoners or Liverpudlians. Government neither wished, in the circumstances, nor indeed had the choice to do anything else but step in and allow local authorities virtually whatever capital and resources they required to set their communities back to work. In so doing, government set important precedents which were difficult to ignore in the future. The aftermath of the Blitz, moreover, provided both the need and the opportunity for substantial replanning and rebuilding of large urban areas in Britain. The members of the Barlow Commission on the Industrial Population, who reported in 1940 in favour of large-scale redistribution of Britain's congested and decayed urban areas, could not have expected their conclusions to get such an easy ride when they had begun work in the 1930s. An ideal social plan had been promoted to the level of immediate necessity by the impact of war.

In other areas, too, the Blitz was to have long-lasting consequences. The government, expecting large numbers of psychiatric as well as physical casualties as a result of bombing, had organised the Emergency Hospital Service out of the chaotic system of hospital administration in pre-war Britain. The Service involved the infusion of public money to provide extra beds and staff in the expected target areas, often providing a vital lifeline for understaffed and underfunded charity and voluntary hospitals. It became clear that this particular reorganisation was not one that could easily be dismantled once the emergency was over. As early as 1941, on largely practical grounds rather than in anticipation of wider reforms in the health-care system, it was agreed that the Emergency Hospital Service should be made permanent in a National Hospital Service. This development in turn made it that much easier to consider the possibility of a full rationalisation of health care in Britain in a National Health Service.[8]

It was, however, where the practical concerns of dealing with a wholly unprecedented form of warfare coincided with deep emotional issues that the dynamics of the 'People's War' assumed most importance. Air warfare, in targeting the workforce as well as the war economy, was warfare aimed against the whole of British society. Indeed, civilian casualties in Britain outweighed uniformed casualties through 1940 and most of 1941. MoI was worried that, if bombing concentrated on the East End or on the depressed areas, the resultant class tensions might be unbearable. Home Intelligence indeed reported growing class tensions in the first few weeks of the Blitz. But the Luftwaffe was unable to concentrate its warload geographically. The indiscriminate bombing of the whole of London, including the West End and even Buckingham Palace, produced instead a common distress that stretched across class divides. There were isolated instances of incipient class aggression, such as the occupation of the bomb shelter in the Savoy. On the whole, however, the reaction to bombing seems to have reinforced the sense of regional and national rather than class identity. East Enders, once they had become accustomed to the changed routines of living through the Blitz, developed a pride that they were at the forefront of the Battle of London. Similarly the Blitz in the provinces encouraged an advanced form of municipal identity. In Coventry and Southampton, Plymouth, Portsmouth and other regional cities, there were undoubtedly problems, breakdowns in local organisation, but the sinews of community revealed by such breakdowns served to underpin a renewed civic pride in the fact that 'they could take it'.[9]

Rarely did breakdowns in local organisation last more than a few days, and production was usually back at pre-bombing levels after two weeks, even after the heaviest raids. People 'trekked' miles into the surrounding countryside to get a good night's sleep while the raids were on, but trekked back again next morning to be at work. This may not have been simply out of a sense of national responsibility; the work ethic had been so heavily reinforced by the experience of unemployment in the previous twenty years that to miss work was seen as the least acceptable way out of difficulties. The Federation of British Industry found that the longest periods taken off work after a raid were rarely more than two or three days, and then only if the workers concerned had lost their homes. This in itself is quite extraordinary evidence of the strength of that urban industrial culture which had survived the Depression and which again proved so resilient when it was threatened root and branch by strategic bombing. Workers themselves organised roof-top surveillance in factories when raids were imminent, leaving it to the last moment to evacuate the buildings so that the loss of production should be minimal.[10]

War against civilians, moreover, threatened the funda-mental building block of society, the family. Not just male industrial workers but mothers and children were in the firing line for the first time. Nothing, perhaps, was more likely to conjure up the the primeval instincts of group survival, or to allay differences and frictions between the social classes. Evacuation had been designed by government to deal with what had been expected to be a panic rush to get out of the cities before the raids began. As originally conceived, evacuation was virtually an exercise in social control. The pre-war scheme was designed to ensure that those who had to remain behind did indeed remain and to police the removal from the cities of those elements who were not needed, and whose assumed nervousness might be a threat to morale. The emphasis of the scheme was on evacuation rather than on reception, and very little had been done in advance to ensure that appropriate billeting arrangements would be made at the other end. In fact, there was to be no wide-spread rush to evacuate at all, and many of those who did evacuate right at the beginning of the war soon returned, many of them just in time for the Blitz. There were many social and cultural mismatches between evacuees and receiving families, and no doubt much misery for many children away from home for the first time. On the other hand, the mismanagement of the scheme should not really be all that surprising; nothing like it had ever been attempted by government before. It amounted in practice to a massive exercise in social engineering with many unforeseen consequences. A significant proportion of the 1940s generation of urban school-children grew up with horizons not entirely limited to inner-city deprivation; Liverpool children experienced life in the countryside of North Wales, for example, while London children were schooled in the entirely different cultural environment of Oxford. Surveys of the social and educational needs of evacuated children played a major part in forming the basis of a new deal for young people in British society, which was formulated in the ensuing years.[11]

Above all, the 'two Englands' of the depression years met face to face for the first time in evacuation. The effects may not always have been benevolent. Many families in the reception areas no doubt had their prejudices about the urban working class confirmed by what they saw as rowdy and ungracious evacuees, and in turn many working-class families may have been astonished by the relatively comfortable lifestyles that they often encountered. On the whole, however, the effect of evacuation may well have helped to break down many divisive regional differences, by shaping a new understanding of the way in which other families in other economic, social and cultural circumstances lived their lives. Above all, attention was to be focused on the crucial significance of young people in social policy; as the next generation, threatened directly by the bombers, their future was nothing less than the future of society itself, and in guaranteeing their well-being and development the state should assume the role of parent in the national family.

The culture shock that Britain experienced during the Second World War was not confined to the fact that civilians were in the firing line for the first time. The refugees from Europe who came to fight on in Britain after their own countries had been defeated and occupied brought with them not only the harrowing experiences of just what it was like to live under Nazi rule, but also a sense of a common supra-national struggle. By the middle of the war, Czechoslovakia was no longer, as Chamberlain had put it at the time of Munich, 'a faraway country of which we know nothing'; neither was France nor Poland, as the shoulder flashes of Free Czechs, French and Poles became relatively familiar sights in pubs, shops, railway and bus stations. The arrival of the Americans, too, in the vast numbers necessary to develop the Anglo-American air offensive, and then in the build-up for D-Day, brought to Britain the vision of an alternative way of life, an affluence, a relative classlessness, a freshness and an openness in expression that had only been a fantasy image on cinema screens in the 1930s.[12] More worrying for the Right in Britain, perhaps, was the developing hero worship of the Soviet Union for its apparent ability to take on the Nazis succesfully. Soviet resilience raised doubts about the supposed inefficiency of the Soviet system and called into question whether Communism really was as evil as Churchill and others would have had the country believe.

Perhaps the biggest radicalisation that was to take place, however, was among the armed forces. Many of those conscripted in the early part of the war had lived their adolescence in the last years of the Depression; for many, the call-up had been their first job and 1945 was to be their first chance to vote. The new forms of warfare no longer demanded the conscripts to be simple cannon-fodder; gun-layers, tank crews and pilots were the lifeblood of the newly-mechanised armed forces, demanding skills and training unprecedented in the history of warfare. To be conscripted in 1939, and to live to see VE Day, was to undergo a quiet but major social and cultural transformation, to acquire a set of expectations very different from those with which the conscripts had gone into the war. The stance of the average serviceman might be summed up in the question shouted to the Minister of Labour by one soldier as the troops embarked for the D-Day invasion: 'what do we do when we've done this job for you, Ernie? Go back on the dole?' It has even been argued that conscription in the Second World War involved a species of socialist indoctrination. The Army Bureau of Current Affairs was said to be a hotbed of radicalism, through which tendentious views of recent history, of the Beveridge Report, of the nature of the Soviet system, were disseminated to the young audiences. Whether this is true or not, it must be said that the experience of war between 1939 and 1945 offered wider social and political perspectives than had been offered, say, in the Great War. Not only were conscripts more highly trained but the war was fought not just in France and Flanders, where trenches had probably looked much the same wherever a soldier was, but on a truly global scale. Aircrews were being trained in Rhodesia and in Canada. Soldiers were fighting in North Africa and the Far East, returning at the end of the war to find a home front which had suffered in many ways as badly as they themselves had done, again unlike the Great War.[13]

Servicewomen, in particular, seem to have gone through a particularly telling transformation. Whereas most young women working in the factories on the home front seem to have been very willing to give up those jobs at the end of the war and look for a domestic life, the responsibilities and the opportunities offered to servicewomen in wartime made for a more restless and demanding view of the postwar world. As radar-operators, barrage-ballon crews and as drivers, they enjoyed not only that independence that had characterised women's experience of the Great War but also the sense of a more direct involvement in the war, as an intrinsic and vital element in the defence of the nation. This is not to say that women's involvement in the Great War had been mere tokenism, nor that the Second World War proved to be any more devastating a blow to patriarchy in Britain.[14]

All of these factors may go some way towards explaining why it was, as Mass Observation discovered in 1943, that the majority of people in Britain felt that they were fighting a war different in quality from those which had gone before, a radical struggle, the outcome of which would change fundamentally the domestic as well as the international order. Certainly, it was to be in the constituencies most directly affected by the war that the largest swings to Labour were to take place in 1945. Against a national swing to Labour of 13 per cent since 1935, for instance, the five Medway constituencies (known as 'Bomb Alley' in 1940) were to swing 25 per cent to Labour. The service vote seems to have gone overwhelmingly to the Left. Labour was to profit in 1945 from the fact that the experience of the Second World War laid bare many of the injustices and inequities that had characterised British society in the interwar years, but which had been disguised both by the narcotic effects of Baldwin's consensus, and by the fact that the effects of the Depression had been so localised. The idea of the Second World War as a new beginning for Britain involved a quite explicit rejection of the consensus of the 1930s as inadequate, unfair and inefficient.

This understanding was a result of the experience of living, working and fighting through the war in Britain, and was confirmed by official government projections to both the home and fighting fronts of what the war was really all about. This is not to say, however, that the Second World War involved a wholly irremediable shift in public opinion towards the Left. Labour's great majority in 1945 was followed by a welter of major reforms, but that majority was reduced substantially by 1950 and lost by a whisker in 1951. From the 1950s to the mid-1970s, moreover, the electorate seems to have been relatively content with the new moderate consensus established by the right wing of the Labour party and the left wing of the Conservative party. Clearly, any radical and progressive notions which may have been thrown up from the grass roots during the 'People's War' were relatively easily contained and neutralised by a reorganisation and reorientation of traditional political forces. Evolution, rather than revolution, remained the pattern, even though the pace of evolution may have accelerated rapidly to cope with the demands generated by the second total war in Britain's recent history.[15]

LABOUR AND THE STATE

There can be no doubting that the Labour party was lucky in 1940. On the evidence of its electoral showing in 1931 and in 1935, there was very little reason to expect that it might attain sufficient parliamentary seats to have a hope of power if there had been an election in 1939 or 1940, as the peacetime law demanded. In May 1940, however, a revolt in the Conservative ranks put Labour in the position of power brokers. Though Chamberlain still had an easily workable majority after the debates on the chaotic Norway campaign, it was clear that there would have to be some substantial recasting of the government to obtain cross-party support in the developing national crisis. The Labour party refused to serve under Chamberlain, and it was this that brought about his resignation and replacement by Churchill. Labour was lucky again in that Churchill was magnanimous to Labour in the formation of the new coalition, though it is more likely that the new Prime Minister did not fully realise the political implications of what he was doing. Labour's control of the Ministry of Labour and National Service, and the Home Office and Ministry of Home Security, left the party virtually in control of the home front while Churchill involved himself almost wholly with the military and diplomatic side of the war. It is probably true to say that, as a result, Ernest Bevin and Herbert Morrison impinged more directly on the lives of British people in the Second World War than Churchill himself. Churchill was the war leader, an almost supra-political figure, remote though magnificent, whereas Bevin and Morrison were part of the everyday pattern of getting on with the war and organising for victory. In a very real way, it is possible to argue that the 1945 election result was not so much a rejection of Churchill as a resounding vote of confidence in the politicians who had dominated the home front for the last five years.

Labour was in fact given an enormous responsibility in the Churchill coalition, as well as a chance to hold power for longer than ever before. The experience gained, and the credibility the Labour leaders established with the electorate, were no doubt of immense importance in creating a situation in which just under 48 per cent of electors would vote for them in 1945. Perhaps the most important of the figureheads established for Labour in this period was that of Ernest Bevin. Bevin was significant not only as a massive and instantly recognisable political personality but also for what he represented in the Labour movement, and especially for what he projected as Labour values to those outside the party. A severe anti-communist but a dedicated trade unionist, he was the archetypal right-wing working-class democratic socialist. He was the Winston Churchill of the working class. The fact that Bevin was able to work so well with Churchill – in spite of their diametrically different backgrounds, and in spite of their having crossed swords sharply on so many political issues in the past – is testimony not just to the political unity engendered in the short term by the national emergency, but also to the longer-term spirit of reconciliation and compromise which still underlay the British political system. The problems that Bevin faced in organising industrial labour were immense, and the potential power put in his hands in the war years to overcome those problems was virtually totalitarian. Only a trade unionist of Bevin's standing could have got away with it. Bevin never forgot that he was a cabinet minister, but neither did he forget that he was a trade unionist.

As a trade unionist, Bevin was determined that organised labour should benefit from the war, but as a minister he was equally determined that labour should earn those benefits by a display of discipline, patriotism and sheer hard work. Bevin's constantly reiterated thesis was that the war against fascism provided the opportunity for labour to show not only its muscle but also its sense of responsibility, so that it could be truly said at the end of the war that it had been won by the British working class.[16] The basis of Bevin's war mobilisation system was the Essential Work Order scheme, which allowed a full planning of the manpower budget, in particular a distribution of labour between the armed services and essential industries. If a factory was named a Protected Establishment under the Essential Work Order scheme, its labour force was virtually exempt from conscription. An almost military regime applied to conditions of employment: no worker could either resign or be dismissed without the approval of the local National Service Office and the Joint Consultative Committee of unionists and employers. As Chairman of the Production Executive, too, Bevin ensured that no public contract would be scheduled without satisfactory terms and conditions for workers, including a guaranteed weekly wage. Nevertheless, the necessary dilution of some skilled trades created just the problems with the unions that it had created in the Great War. Bevin set up consultative bodies at all levels of the process of administration but in the last resort had to rely on appeals to patriotism, and finally the letter of the law, to get his way. Bevin also won control of the administration of the Factories Acts, and of medical services in the factories, and established the principle that labour health and welfare were in themselves essential prerequisites of productivity and efficiency. Indeed, the state-run Ordnance factories were to become pioneers in progressive labour welfare schemes as well as in wage structuring, their use of bonuses and incentives teaching management in the private sector a good deal about labour relations.[17]

Unemployment still stood at one million at the time of Dunkirk, so long did it take to soak up the slack in the economy after the Depression. Thereafter, it decreased rapidly as a result of labour demand, but this in turn created a possible inflationary problem. The Ministry of Labour was determined not to interfere with labour power on the question of free collective bargaining. Indeed minimum wages were an essential part of the war production system, and wages boards were set up to regulate both wages and conditions of work in areas of industry where trades unions had been traditionally weak. These were to become an integral part of British industrial relations with the Wages Councils Act of 1945, covering some four and a half million workers in the retail trades and in agriculture. Bevin believed that to interfere with free collective bargaining in the case of the established unions would be to undercut the spirit of conciliation and the consultative network on which the Ministry of Labour ultimately depended. Compulsory arbitration could be resorted to where necessary but the control of inflation should be left to the moderating influence of union leaders, and to government action to control prices and to extend rationing.

Wartime inflation, after all, was a result not only of increased wages but of inevitable shortages in goods. Bevin could point out to the labour critics of the Essential Work Order scheme that capital was also being mobilised for total war in the Excess Profits Tax, which taxed the extra profit made in wartime at 100 per cent. If government had wanted to press ahead with wages control, however, Bevin would have pressed for large-scale nationalisation of British industry as a *quid pro quo*.[18]

The issue of nationalisation as a solution to the vexed problems of mobilisation was never far below the surface in wartime; it was the ultimate deterrent aimed at recalcitrant employers. Stafford Cripps nationalised the aircraft firm, Shorts, for continued managerial inefficiency and Bevin was pressured to take similar measures with other firms, and indeed with whole sections of industry such as mining. The Ministry of Labour faced particularly acute problems with the mining industry. Here the history of appalling industrial relations did not work in Bevin's favour, since he was seen by many in the miners' union to be one of the villains of the General Strike. The importance of coal in war was clear, and the unions argued that only nationalisation could surmount the involved problems of an aged workforce, low productivity and rock-bottom morale in the industry. Given the history of mining, however, nationalisation would have created immense political as well as administrative difficulties in wartime. The miners felt that Bevin had been overborne when the setting up of a Ministry of Fuel and Mines in effect requisitioned rather than nationalised the industry. In fact, Bevin sensed accurately that the requisitioning of mining meant that eventual nationalisation was inevitable, and saw little point in deliberate provocation of conservative interests on such a delicate issue[19]. Herbert Morrison was also keen to defuse the issue of nationalisation, potentially ruinous as it was to the coalition, seeing in the wartime practical experiments with rationalisation a plan for future implementation by Labour. The priorities, he felt, should lie in public control of industry rather than public ownership as such, enough to ensure that the economy was run for the benefit of society as a whole. Such rethinking of the fundamentals of socialism may not have endeared either Morrison or Bevin to the Left but they worked efficiently, and they did not create political problems, both of which were important factors in wartime. More importantly, statements like these did much to help Labour into the solid centre ground of politics which the Conservatives had occupied for so long. Morrison could even find himself supported by younger Tories who saw in his ideas a development of some of those notions that had emerged on the left of the Conservative party over the past ten years, in Political and Economic Planning, in the Next Five Years Group, and in Harold Macmillan's 'middle way'.[20]

Industrial labour undoubtedly earned a great deal from the war. Wage rises easily outstripped rises in the cost of living and trade unionism appeared to have been made safe by statute in areas where it had been struggling for decades. The most important gain, however, was in a commitment made by the wartime coalition to ensure full employment after the war: without this, all the other gains made might simply have withered away as they did after the Great War. Labour's introduction to the ideas of John Maynard Keynes was to prove of immense importance in the development of main-stream left-wing thought, providing the missing link in the theory of evolutionary socialism: in tandem with William Beveridge, Keynes seemed to provide the mechanical explanation of how the state could engineer the development of a socialist society without, in the process, creating massive dislocation and class friction. Keynes and Beveridge indeed seemed to offer the ultimate dream of the respectable alternative, the possibility of revolution by consensus. Judicious use of the public budget could iron out the peaks and troughs of the trade cycle, and the tax system could be used gradually to iron out the inequities of income. Public control of the mainstays of industry would ensure overall state direction of the economy in the name of the people and, with the wholesale development of the social services, would amount in effect to the structure of the 'social tissue' through which, the Fabians had always argued, the state could engineer and organise a peaceful revolution from the top.

It seems highly unlikely that Keynes could have gained the widespread acceptance that he did begin to enjoy in the 1940s without the impact of the war. The Left had been highly suspicious in the 1930s about his attempts to save capitalism by reforming it, and his ideas on counter-cyclical investment were heretical to a centre still wedded to classical liberal economic theory. Bevin, during the war, remained unconvinced about Keynes' ingenious plan to prevent inflation by siphoning off excess spending power into involuntary saving. Keynes had argued that swingeing increases in taxation would undercut incentives, while increased governmental wage controls would be anti-libertarian and difficult to enforce. Involuntary saving would not only close the gap between purchasing power and the goods available for purchase in wartime, but could also be repaid after the war in what would amount to a counter-cyclical investment to offset the expected depression.[21] Though the postwar credit idea was only to play a small role in wartime policy, the Treasury did move early on to accept Keynes's views on the possibility of using the budget to plan more effectively for dealing with inflation. The 1941 budget is often called the first Keynesian budget, founded as it was on a survey of expected national income and expenditure over the next twelve months, and a definition of the probable 'inflation gap'. Once it had been tried, and found to be relatively successful, there was no reason why the wider implications of Keynes's *General Theory* should not be applied.

The White Paper on Employment Policy of May 1944, quite explicitly committed government to making full employment a central political task. In fact, the White Paper did not give a *carte blanche* for unlimited use of the budget to achieve this end, and the commitment to full employment was hedged around with cautionary points about the need for efficiency and better productivity to improve exports in the postwar economy. Nevertheless, it was made quite clear that the 'social capital' invested in the industrial infrastructure was to be considered as important as the profit motive *per se*, and that 'where a large industrial population is involved the Government are not prepared either to compel its transfer to another area or to leave it to prolonged unemployment and demoralisation'.[22] Effectively, the experience of the 1930s was now branded as wholly unacceptable. The vilification of the 'guilty men', the myth of the 'People's War', and the practical implications of the increased power of labour in wartime had together conspired to produce a new commitment on the part of the state, in which central government could no longer claim simply to be an impartial referee in the workings of the economy.

BEVERIDGE AND THE SOCIAL SERVICES

It was, in fact, the TUC which was the main instigator behind what emerged as the Beveridge Report in 1942. A union deputation had asked the Ministry of Health in February 1941 to look into the deficiencies of existing health insurance. Clearly, health insurance could not be looked at in isolation but only in relation to the social services as a whole: the Minister of Reconstruction, Arthur Greenwood, therefore appointed a committee of civil servants under Beveridge's chairmanship to consider the problems. There is some suggestion that the committee was only set up in the first place to get Beveridge out of the politicians' hair, since his busy-bodying had annoyed Bevin among others. Although it was a high-powered committee, there were no politicians sitting on it, and no minister was to sign the Report. Indeed, ministers became so worried by what they heard of the political implications of the committee's work that they changed the status of the civil servants sitting on the committee from full members to advisers. This meant, as Greenwood wrote pointedly to Beveridge, that 'the Report, when made, will be your own report'.[23] It seems fairly clear that, although the committee was given the widest possible frame of reference, it went a great deal further than it was originally expected to go.

No one had more experience of the social services in Britain than Sir William Beveridge. He had experience of charitable social work, had held senior civil service posts before and during the Great War, and had been Director of the London School of Economics between the wars. Angus Calder has described him as 'the outstanding combination of public servant and social scientist'.[24] Certainly, the Report that he produced in December 1942 was worthy of a committee of civil servants. In over three hundred densely-printed pages it argued the case for a rationalisation of the social services which would, if nothing else, lead to greater administrative efficiency. The bureaucratic interests of the committee were evident enough in one of its principal recommendations, namely that a Ministry of Social Security should be set up to handle all the social services under one roof. Similarly, the idea that everyone should pay one flat-rate contribution, to cover all the areas of benefit, was an administrative simplification of the chaotic maze of contributions to different schemes that had been the legacy of the piecemeal extensions of the social services until this time.

Yet the Beveridge Report amounted to much more than simply a rationalisation of what already existed. What was different about the Report was its emphasis on the twin principles of comprehensiveness and universality. It was comprehensive in the sense that it recommended an intermeshing and extension of existing social service schemes, to ensure that virtually every mishap that could happen would be covered by the simple weekly contribution. It was universal in that it applied to everyone, irrespective of need. It would, in fact, provide a national minimum below which no one in foreseeable circumstances would be allowed to fall, 'from cradle to grave'. In these senses, the recommendations of the Report could be said to be qualitatively different from what had gone before. The rag-bag of *ad hoc* schemes developed to cover what could be isolated as 'blameless' causes of poverty, aimed at and partly paid for by the vulnerable groups themselves, was to be replaced by the concept of a Welfare State in which, in effect, everyone was to be equally financially responsible for everyone else's misfortune. Certainly, the richer sections of society could buy themselves extra and better provision through private insurance, though it was assumed that, for the large majority, the new national minimum would make redundant most of the voluntary contribution schemes. The national minimum in no way implied a national maximum, nor was it originally conceived that the rich should pay more to offset the cost of the services to the lower-paid sections. These were the flies in the ointment of equity as far as the Left was concerned, though Beveridge's notions were to secure a very positive response from the centre.[25]

The contributory principle, then, continued to dominate the social services, a sort of involuntary self-help ethic remaining as important in Beveridge as it had in the pre-1914 schemes of the New Liberals. The leadership of the Labour party, moreover, now accepted this contributory idea, where before 1914 they had urged that the social services should be wholly paid for from taxation. Nevertheless, the cost to the state of the new schemes would be very heavy, in comparison with the prewar social serices budget, and it was this that made the right of the Conservative party carp. The scheme might be acceptable in principle, they argued, but the question was whether postwar Britain would be able to generate the wealth to pay for it. The cost did not stop at Beveridge's specific proposals, either, for Beveridge suggested that improvements were necessary in other areas of social planning and provision, to ensure that his scheme would work most effectively. Family allowances must be given for all children, to offset the cost of bringing up larger families. Even more significantly, a National Health Service should be established, not only for obvious beneficial social reasons, but also to lessen the burden of claims on the social service budget for sickness payments. The state should also take the burden of planning to avoid unemployment; indeed, Beveridge reckoned that his scheme could not cope with unemployment of more than a few per cent. Beveridge added his own weight to the demands of labour and the suggestions of Keynes with his *Full Employment in a Free Society*, which he saw as a most important appendix and caveat to his earlier Report. Beveridge was prepared to go even further beyond the strict purview of social security, suggesting that improvements were also necessary in environmental policy and in education for, as he put it in that millenarian rhetoric with which the Report was sometimes enlivened:

A revolutionary moment in the world's history is a time for revolutions, not for patching .... Social security fully developed may provide security: it is an attack upon Want. But Want is only one of five giants on the road to reconstruction and in some ways the easiest to attack. The others are Disease, Ignorance, Squalor and Idleness.[26]

Beveridge's choice of words in such passages provides a clue to the significance of his Report, for this was the last huzzah of nineteeth-century Liberal Radicalism as much as it was the clarion call of a People's War. In an unguarded and over-exuberant moment, Beveridge claimed in an interview with a journalist that the Report would take Britain 'half-way to Moscow'; it was much more accurate to describe it, as Beveridge did in the Report itself, as the culmination of a 'British revolution' which had begun in the late nineteenth century. It was in this spirit, as well as in the contemporary popular radical feeling about the issues involved in the war, that Beveridge appealed to a new consensus emerging between the Right of the Labour party and the Left of the Conservatives. A rejection of the 1930s, after all, did not have to involve a rejection of the whole of British history: Labour was as interested in projecting the twentieth century as the period of the steady, progressive tramp of the working class as the Conservatives were interested in projecting it as the steady evolution of an integrated national family. Both political groupings could accept the Beveridge Report as the next big step forward.

The cabinet, however, was non-committal. Though Labour pressed for early implentation, Churchill and Kingsley Wood were not convinced. The Prime Minister no doubt remembered the fate of Lloyd George, who had promised so much to the home front in the Great War but had failed to produce in the peace. He prevaricated on the grounds that a wartime coalition could not bind the hands of a future government and also, no doubt, because he thought there were more important things to occupy cabinet time at such a crucial point in the war. Kingsley Wood was more concerned with the financial implications of the Report, arguing that Britain would have to wait until after the war to see whether she could afford the schemes or not. In the event, the cabinet agreed to accept most of the Report, but only 'in principle'. In the House of Commons, however, the government faced the biggest backbench revolt of the war in the debate on the Report. Almost the entire Parliamentary Labour Party outside the cabinet voted against the government, and a number of Conservatives were only prevented from doing so by a speech

from Herbert Morrison explaining the government's reluctance to accept speedy implementation. Within a few months,
these Conservatives were to form the Tory Reform Committee,
which by the end of the year could regularly count on up to
fifty MPs. It was at this point, in fact, that the famed
Conservative discipline began to go awry. By the end of 1943,
the Tory Right was countering the influence of the Tory
Reformers in the Progress Trust. With Churchill refusing to
lead one way or the other on domestic issues, the Conservatives
were drifting without a rudder to defeat in the next general
election.

In spite of Churchill's reluctance, much of substance in the
Beveridge Report had in fact been implemented by the time
the war was over. A Ministry of Social Security had been
established, and family allowances were being paid. The White
Paper on Employment, carefully phrased as it was to avoid the
implication that the budget would be used in any sense
'irresponsibly', had generated wide consent in the House of
Commons. Tory Reformers, moreover, had attempted to take
big strides to keep up with the pace Labour was setting in
laying out the political agenda for the next ten years. Henry
Willink at the Ministry of Health produced a White Paper on a
National Health Service which set out the broad lines on which
Aneurin Bevan was to develop legislation immediately after
the war, though the White Paper left opaque large areas of
substantial detail which almost threatened the concept.
R.A. Butler at the Board of Education moved through his
Education Act in 1944, a piece of legislation which bore all the
hallmarks of Tory Reform. Its rhetorical emphasis was on
building on the past as much as looking to the future. In detail,
however, the Act appeared to mark a significant shift away
from previous education policy, creating a clear division in
secondary education between grammar, technical and secondary modern. In theory, these areas of secondary education
were to be co-equal in status; in practice, however, as so often
with Tory Reform, the results were to look remarkably like the
old system. The grammar schools were to retain their clout and
threaten the development, which Butler originally seems to
have intended, of the comprehensive system. There was no
move to curb the public schools. It was an effective piece of

pre-emption on Butler's part, for Labour in power was not to alter the details of the Act.[27]

The Beveridge Report had been remarkably happy in its timing. Arriving as it did between news of the victories at El Alamein and at Stalingrad, it took its place as blueprint for the postwar world at just the point in time when people could look up and see light at the end of the long tunnel. The war was going to be won, though not yet, and the Beveridge Report encapsulated many of the hopes that this war would actually be worth winning. It was not a radical document but the circumstances in which it appeared made it look like one. At last, the vaguely-formulated aspirations associated with the rejection of the 1930s and the 'guilty men', and with the related mythology of 1940, could take on concrete form. In the political debate surrounding the Report, moreover, electors could spot the ghosts of the 1930s still alive and kicking in the Conservative party. They could also see, in the massive administrative competence of a Bevin or a Morrison as it affected their everyday lives, that a social conscience was not necessarily incompatible with governmental efficiency. 'Socialism' had become practical politics for the first time in Britain.

CHURCHILL'S WAR

Even at this distance in time, Churchill is almost too massive a political personality to confront directly. He has become the embodiment of a discourse on former British greatness against which, implicitly and often explicitly, the political Right and even the Left measure the decline of Britain and the capacity of British politicians who succeeded him. He embodies ideals of leadership, of national unity, and he embodies, in particular, assumptions about the role that Britain should still be playing in international affairs. Churchill is a potent political idea in the here and now, even if that idea is merely a caricature of the original. If Labour's capture of the direction of home front politics was to be the decisive factor in the shaping of the relationship between politics, society and the state over the next twenty years, it is equally true to say that Churchill's role in international affairs simultaneously moulded attitudes towards the outside world in Britain which were to co-exist rather unhappily with the consensus in domestic affairs. Overcommitment in defence, for example, was one major result of Churchill's legacy, and on a number of occasions this threatened to break up the consensus that had been established during the years of the home front. It is for this reason that Churchill's rearguard action for Imperial values in the war deserves separate treatment, for the rallying point it was to provide for an alternative view of 1940 and its implications for the future of the British national family. Churchill lies at the core of the right-wing interpretation of the significance of the Second World War, the development of which was finally to undermine the postwar consensus.

During the last twenty years of Churchill's life, virtually every word he uttered publicly took on almost biblical status. The core of his reputation rests on three tenets. First, he unequivocally opposed appeasement in the 1930s, and was wrongly ignored by short-sighted politicians who were bent, or so it is believed, on selling Europe to the fascists. This distanced him not only from the governing principles of Conservatism in the 1930s but also from some of the Tory Reformers who were tarred with the appeasement brush from their association with Foreign Office policy before the war. Second, with the failure of appeasement and the outbreak of war, Churchill was called upon to pick up the pieces. In 1940, the legend says, Churchill took Britain by the scruff of the neck so that she could take on the Axis single-handed until the Soviets and the Americans were forced into the war. Third, in the last stages of the war, with the defeat of the Axis assured, Churchill began to concentrate on the possible threat to world stability posed by the increasing power of the Soviet Union. Churchill was by now living testimony of the dangers of appeasement and his argument that Stalin must not be appeased as Hitler had been could not simply be ignored. Thus, over the course of fifteen years, the man who had seen himself as one crying in the wilderness in the 1930s was transformed into the guru of cold warriors throughout the Western world, lionised wherever he went not only as a prophet of international affairs but also as the epitome of all good British values.

Questions, however, have to be raised about this enormously successful self-projection. Why, for example, did success come to Churchill so late in life? When he became Prime Minister he was already 64. He had been a MP for forty years, during which time he had earned as much antipathy as any contemporary politician. And why, in spite of the popularity that he achieved in the 1940s, did he still manage to lose the general election of 1945 by a landslide? The electorate returned to 10 Downing Street Clement Attlee, a man as quiet as Churchill was exuberant, a virtual unknown who was once described by Churchill as 'a modest little man with much to be modest about'. Churchill, in fact, had two quite separate reputations, and the image of him that dominated his later years has to be contrasted with the reputation he had in the 1930s, that of an unreliable, erratic, disruptive and disloyal politician, out of touch with the electorate and with an enormously inflated estimate of his own ability. These two reputations to some extent overlapped during the 1940s, and to get a measured view of Churchill's role both on the home front and internationally in the war years, we have to bear both reputations in mind.

In Churchill's case, as in that of Lloyd George, the major lesson is that a politician is only as strong as the party to which that politician belongs.[28] In opposition to his party, Churchill was frustrated and helpless. In control of his party, on the other hand, he failed to provide leadership on the issues which really mattered. In the 1930s, Churchill was mistrusted by the Conservatives as a man who had deserted the party when it was in serious trouble in 1904. Many were suspicious that he had helped Lloyd George stab Asquith in the back in 1916, and had then deserted Lloyd George to come back to to the Tory fold when it became clear that Lloyd George was finished. His right-wing campaign against the Conservative leadership in the early 1930s, on the question of the future of India, looked like a mismanaged attempt at a coup. He had also deeply offended many coloured politicians in the Empire by his racist remarks about Gandhi. For the Labour opposition, his stance on India simply confirmed the reactionary position he seemed to hold on virtually every issue; his mythical role in Tonypandy and in the General

Strike continued to rankle. There is no reason to believe that Churchill had any future in politics after 1931, had it not been for what became the single, all-important issue of appeasement. But the fact that so few supported his stand over appeasement is not altogether surprising, given his record.

Nevertheless, with the onset of war, it was clear that Churchill had to have a seat in the cabinet. Not only was he virtually the only Conservative who had not, at some time or other, said nice things about Adolf Hitler but his experience of the defence forces was almost unparalleled. Not only had he served in the Army, he had held all three defence posts in government, indeed all the most important cabinet posts except the Foreign Office and the Premiership itself. The failure of the Norway campaign sealed Chamberlain's fate, but Churchill was still not the obvious choice to succeed. Chamberlain himself seems to have assumed that Lord Halifax would take over, but Halifax ruled himself out on the grounds that his peerage would not give him the necessary close links with the political parties in the House of Commons. The Labour party was prepared to accept Churchill and temporarily to forget the past, given the extent of the national emergency. Yet the men who would have to work closest with him in Whitehall did not relish the prospect. John Colville, later to become a close aide of Churchill's, later recalled that 'in May 1940, the mere thought of Churchill as Prime Minister sent a cold chill down the spines of the staff at 10 Downing Street'.[29] The fear was not so much that Churchill would make heads roll, but that he would make mistakes.

Yet there can be no doubting the massive importance of the symbolic role that Churchill immediately took up in the circumstances of the summer of 1940. The role of Prime Minister at such a time was one to which Churchill could commit himself totally, because it was the only role in which he could be successful: all his energy, at other times applied irresponsibly and sometimes destructively, could be brought into play. A national hero when he had escaped from the Boers forty years previously, misunderstood and distrusted ever since, he had finally been summoned to the Palace to 'save England'. His weaknesses were suddenly strengths and, above all, he could make the struggle transcendent. President Roosevelt, listening to the 'we'll fight them on the beaches' speech on radio across the Atlantic, exclaimed: 'It's extraordinary. It's like the whole of English history coming to life to the sound of trumpets.' In 1940, Churchill provided one of the two foci for unifying opinion in Britain after the divisive experience of the depression, the other being the idea of the People's War. Churchill's focus, importantly, was markedly different from the other. At the nadir of British fortunes, he promised an eventual victory made even more spectacular for the fact that the country had sunk so low before the tide turned. In objective terms, though, the early war years simply could not be Britain's 'finest hours'. In fact, from the moment General Guderian began pushing through the Ardennes forest to the moment General Perceval surrendered at Singapore, Britain suffered the most crushing series of defeats in modern international history. In the long term, too, these defeats proved to be irremediable, even though Britain was on the side of the victors in 1945.

Churchill provided a comforting and pain-killing narcotic during the worst years of the war, provided one rationale for going on but, in the long term, he fostered dangerous illusions about Britain's real place in the world. Such super-confidence, both in himself and in Britain, did not make him easy to work with as Prime Minister. Nearly every minister, civil servant or military man caught the sharp edge of his tongue at some time or another for not performing superhuman tasks at the drop of a hat. He could be deeply offensive, accusing those who came to him pointing out the practical difficulties of his latest idea, of being cowards and defeatists. Many of his schemes, however, were indeed hare-brained. Roosevelt once said, 'Winston has a hundred ideas a day: one of them is brilliant.' Churchill's almost demonic urge to win the war, at all costs and as quickly and as totally as possible, led him into some very questionable strategic decisions. Determined to strike at Germany wherever it was possible, he tended to favour strategies which offered attack in the short term, even if his advisers and allies felt that these would delay longer-term but more decisive strategies. His backing of Air Chief Marshal Sir Arthur Harris and the strategic air offensive, for example, directed air resources away from army support and away from the Battle of the Atlantic, to the consternation of the Admirals who had to wait until 1943 to get the long-range air support essential to win that critical battle.

Equally contentious was Churchill's determination on the Greek venture in 1941, which turned out disastrously in itself and so weakened the British forces in North Africa that Rommel nearly overran Egypt. Indeed, the whole of Britain's Mediterannean strategy was questionable. The escalating British commitment in that theatre began simply because it was the only area left for the Army to fight in, once France had fallen. But Chuchill also had visions of attacking the 'soft underbelly' of Europe and was to become almost obsessed with the significance of the North African campaign, perhaps to the detriment of preparations in the Far East, which allowed the Japanese to advance as far as the Indian frontier almost unhindered. The Mediterranean strategy was also to place a great strain on Anglo-American relations. All credit should go to Churchill for building up the so-called 'special relationship' in the first place, for that relationship really was the invention of Churchill and Roosevelt in wartime, overlaying the deep mutual suspicions that had characterised Anglo-American relations in the interwar years. On the other hand, Churchill constantly pushed the Mediterranean strategy on the unwilling Americans.

The reasons for Churchill's reluctance to give up on the Mediterranean strategy are fairly clear. First, the Mediterranean was bringing success, of which there had been precious little since the beginning of the war. The Allies were at least moving forward in the Mediterranean, if in the wrong direction. Second, and equally important for Churchill, the Mediterranean was a British-dominated campaign, and D-Day would not be. The massive preparations and logistics required for the Normandy landings were to take the direction of the Atlantic alliance entirely out of British control, and thereby place the future of liberated Europe firmly in American hands. Third, and this was a rationale for the Italian campaign that began to appear in the latter stages of the war, an Allied breakthrough in Italy might possibly get the British into Eastern Europe before the Red Army arrived.[30]

The D-Day strategy, on the other hand, had the inevitable corollary that the Soviets' advance into Eastern Europe would be considerably eased thereby. This was something that began to worry Churchill deeply as he began to picture a postwar Europe effectively divided between Soviet and American influence with Britain frozen out.

Churchill's attitude towards the Soviets changed considerably during the course of the war. Temperamentally and politically, he was averse to everything Russia stood for. In the 1930s he had found it difficult to argue, as the British Left had argued, for an alliance with the Soviets against Germany. In 1940, at the time of the Soviet invasion of Finland, he had described Communism as 'a doctrine that rots the soul.' In 1941, however, as the Germans invaded the Soviet Union, he issued an immediate declaration of support for the Russians, commenting privately that 'if Hitler invaded Hell, I'd be prepared to make a favourable reference to the Devil himself in the House of Commons.' Churchill never lost his distrust of Soviet intentions; he merely put it on a back burner while Hitler posed the greater problem.

Churchill, in effect, had lost control of the international situation by the time of the Yalta Conference. D-Day, in the long term, gave Western Europe to the Americans, if they wanted it, just as surely as the Battle of Kursk had given Eastern Europe to the Soviets, who assuredly did want it. It was inevitable that Britain would be squeezed out once it became clear that the war would be decided by the vast attritional potential of the United States and the Soviet Union. Stalin summed up the situation pithily when he remarked that 'in the defeat of Germany, Britain provided time, America provided money, and Russia provided blood'. By 1944 and 1945, the time that Britain had provided in 1940 was no longer a sufficient guarantee of a dominating voice in international affairs. What was surprising, though, was that Churchill managed to maintain a British initiative for as long as he did, through the Mediterranean strategy. Seen within Churchill's frame of reference, he had ultimately failed to maintain the world system that gave Britain control, but it was perhaps simply a fantasy to assume that that was even possible in the circumstances of the second total war of the century.

In his concentration on the military and strategic side of the war, moreover, he had also failed to maintain on the home front the domination of traditional values that he sought. Refusing to give a lead to the Conservatives on domestic matters, he proved to be no more of a party man as leader than he had been in the past. The Conservatives could not survive simply on the charismatic qualities of Churchill himself. The Conservative election manifesto in 1945, with the typically archaic title 'Mr Churchill's Declaration of Policy to the Electors', concentrated as much on issues of international politics as on domestic affairs. Though it committed the Conservatives almost to the same measures of social reform that Labour promised, it managed to sound unconvincing when contrasted with the carefully set out programme outlined in detail in Labour's 'Let Us Face the Future'. Churchill, once again, had his finger on his own pulse and assumed it was that of the people.

It is not unusual that old men get out of touch. Churchill lived for only a few years short of an entire century, and was naturally likely to be more out of touch than most. For someone of his particular generation and background, born into the English aristocracy at the time of British pre-eminence, the progress of the twentieth century was a particularly disturbing experience. The effect of international economic competition before 1914, the social and psychological impact of the Great War, the impact of the Great Depression – these events had effectively torn the heart out of the ideology that had dominated in Churchill's youth. Though the economic structure which underpinned the system of political power in Britain may have changed very little, the type of politician which manned that political system had changed considerably, adapting the system to the changing needs of the twentieth century. Reformism had subtly, almost undetectably, changed the angle of vision of politics from imperialism to welfarism. All this had happened in Churchill's lifetime, and it would be unreasonable to expect any man to make the adaptation that it took virtually three generations of politicians in their prime to accomplish. Churchill, indeed, had played his own part in this adaptation, in close harmony with Lloyd George in the Liberal government of 1908 to 1914. It was with much greater reluctance, however, that he actually oversaw the overture of the final stages of reformism as Prime Minister in the Second World War.

In Churchill's last years, when he suffered badly and almost permanently from deep depression, his daughter asked him why he should be so depressed when he had achieved so much. He replied that he had *done* a great deal, but *achieved* nothing. Churchill was indeed a failure, but only within his own impossible frame of reference. The spirit of national unity which had seemingly focused on his leadership led not, as he had supposed, to a British Empire lasting a thousand years but to the Welfare State and the retreat from Empire. Reformism rather than reaction was to capitalise on the spirit of 1940 over the next twenty years. In international affairs, far from maintaining British power, Churchill had actually overseen its collapse. Churchill had provided the most significant catchphrases of the 1940s, 'the finest hour' and 'the iron curtain', but the implications of these phrases were to be very different from what he had foreseen. The crowning irony is that Churchill's greatest political antagonist, Neville Chamberlain, had foreseen almost exactly what would happen if Britain became involved again in a major war, and it had been to maintain the cracking edifice of the prestige of traditional British values that Chamberlain did what he did in the 1930s. Churchill saw none of this as inevitable. He thought he would change the course of history, but he ended up simply being its agent.

Churchillian rhetoric, however, and the mystique which surrounded the man who had not only foreseen the Nazi threat but had also beaten Hitler, left an unfortunate legacy which amounted to a denial of the facts which had undermined Britain's international position. The attempt to maintain great power status after the war, moreover, was linked implicitly to an attack on welfarism. For the war had created two antipathetic self-images for Britain, involving two very different definitions of freedom. Labour's war had been a struggle for freedom through collectivism, whereas Churchill's war had been a war for freedom fought by rugged individualism against state tyranny. While the first of these definitions of freedom was to dominate the first twenty years of

British politics after the war, the latter was never far below the surface. As collectivism began to falter in the 1960s and the 1970s, however, the pugnacious, populist, patriotic indivi-dualism of Churchillism began to re-assert itself.

---5---
THE POSTWAR CONSENSUS AND ITS DEMISE

THE LABOUR LANDSLIDE

Labour's victory at the polls in 1945 seemed to signal a major change in British politics. A government that was both radical in intentions and experienced in administration looked set to alter the face of the nation. Labour had never even had a majority government before, let alone such a list of clearly competent ministers or such a manifesto full of viable schemes for major change. Churchill and Conservatism seemed to have been decisively rejected and with them, it appeared, not only the values that had dominated the interwar years but also a much longer tradition, the high-minded patriotism and rugged individualism of Churchillian rhetoric. It looked as though the electorate had voted for a new angle of vision, a decisive switch from Imperialism to Welfarism which would make the 1945 general election result the fulcrum of twentieth-century British history. In fact, the electoral system had once again warped the results somewhat. Large as Labour's victory was in terms of parliamentary seats, the Conservatives still captured nearly 40 per cent of the votes and Labour still won less than the magical 50 per cent. It was the distribution of the vote that won Labour their 148-seat overall majority. In the Home Counties, the South-East, the West Midlands, and even in the shires, Labour were winning seats they had never won before. Unfortunately for them, they were never to win many of them again. Clearly, the radicalism of the 'People's War' was a short-lived affair for those suburbanites who lent Labour a classless image for a few short years after the war.

Some in the Labour party could claim that the cross-class nature of Labour support in 1945 meant that the party could now truly call itself 'national'. In a sense, the victory could almost be taken as retrospective justification of Ramsay MacDonald's policy of establishing Labour as a 'respectable alternative', for it seemed to suggest that the nation was ready for revolution by consensus. It also seemed likely that this revolution would prove irreversible for, even though Labour was out of power within six years, the defeat of 1945 energised the Conservative party to accept in broad outline much of what had been done since the war. Through the 1950s and into the 1960s the alarms and excursions on such issues as the Suez crisis could not disguise the fundamental agreement of the two major parties on the broad issues of economic and social policy, the depth of the consensual commitment to welfarism and to full employment. It was for this reason that many in the Labour ranks claimed that the work of the immediate postwar governments had completed Labour's historic role, had ushered in a bloodless revolution, even if it was the Conservatives rather than Labour who were to enjoy the fruits of that revolution.[1] Yet, within twenty years, the postwar consensus was showing distinct signs of fraying at the edges, and by the late 1970s appeared to be in ruins. The Keynes–Beveridge axis established in the war years and after 1945 proved to be only another of the compromise equilibria which the British political establishment engineered to deal with the problems of relative economic decline. In particular, the economy after 1945 simply would not grow at the rate that was needed to maintain that revolution in rising expectations generated by electoral promises of an ever-more prosperous Britain.

Yet the euphoria of Labour in 1945 was understandable enough. There had been two previous 'khaki elections' in the twentieth century, in 1900 and in 1918, and the Conservatives had swamped the opposition in both. The effective discrediting of the Tory 'Guilty Men' of the 1930s in the war years, however, together with the demonstrable success of the notion of state intervention in mobilising Britain for the Second World War, had left traditional Conservativism looking extremely vulnerable. There may well have been a feeling among many sections of the electorate, moreover, now that the myth of the interwar 'locust' had been given full credibility by wartime propaganda, that the Second World War should not be followed by an even worse return to normality than that which had occurred after the Great War. Labour felt competent and confident enough to approach the task of putting through the huge reform programme which it had promised the electorate. Over the next six years it was to introduce a massive programme of reform which was to complete the evolutionary process begun by the Liberals before the Great War. So institutionalised was the role of the state to become, indeed, that it proved extremely difficult to reverse, even by so committed a set of politicians as the Thatcherites after 1979.

RE-ENTERING THE PEACETIME ECONOMY

The scale of the reform programme which Labour legislated after the war is all the more remarkable for the series of economic difficulties the government faced. First, there was the effect of the cost of the war. By 1945, Britain had external liabilities of some £13 000 million. Foreign assets worth £1 billion had been sold, with the result that income from foreign investment, traditionally such an important way of filling the balance of payments gap, fell from £175 million in 1938 to £73 million in 1946. The balance of payments problem was made worse by the fact that the price of imports had quadrupled during the war and the terms of trade were to worsen for Britain during the Korean war. It was calculated that, to fill the gap, Britain would need to raise her 1939 level of exports by 75 per cent. This would have been a nigh-impossible job in ordinary circumstances, but with the large majority of British industry geared to war demand, it required a truly prodigious reorientation. In 1945, 87 per cent of the employed population was directly engaged on war work, either in or out of uniform.[2] The new cabinet, not prepared to re-create the labour chaos that had followed the Great War, was clear that rapid demobilisation was not a satisfactory way out of the problem.

Britain's balance of payments problem was not helped, either, by the continuing commitment to expenditure on defence. The commitment to the army of occupation in Germany led on to longer-term commitments in Europe, notably in NATO. With the reaction to the failures of the 'Guilty Men' of the 1930s, most Labour politicians were as sure as the Conservatives that Stalin must not be appeased as Hitler had been. By the end of the Labour administration in 1951, defence was taking up 14.5 per cent of the public budget. This was to mean not only pressure on spending on the social services, with some malevolent effects on Labour unity, but also that a large proportion of the engineering and other industries remained geared to defence rather than export demands. In turn, indirectly at least, it may also have meant an increased financial reliance on the United States of America, to go with the united front in foreign policy.

In fact, British debts to the USA had begun mounting rapidly as soon as war had been declared. The Treasury had compelled the surrender of British investments in the US, and sold them to service this debt. By 1941, this source of income had dried up; it was only at this point that the US had adopted the Lend-Lease scheme. As many on the Right as well as on the Left pointed out, American wartime 'generosity' had only begun to operate when Britain had run out of money; that was the cost of holding the line alone for democracy. The extent of Britain's financial reliance on the US during the war can be judged by the fact that Lend-Lease from 1941 to 1945 amounted to some $26 billion, the equivalent of almost sixteen years of prewar imports from the States. At the end of the war, moreover, America abruptly cancelled Lend-Lease, with the result that Britain had no option but to negotiate an orthodox loan with the Americans. The British had no bargaining power in the ensuing negotiations, except that they had been close allies of the Americans, a fact which seems to have cut little ice in Washington. The conditions applied to the loan, though perhaps justifiable in normal circumstances, were particularly harsh when one considers the parlous state to which Britain had been reduced by fighting a war she could not afford to fight.[3]

The most onerous condition was the American demand that the Sterling Area should be abandoned. The Sterling Area had effectively begun in 1930 to protect British finance in the crisis which followed the Wall Street Crash. Continued during the war, a period of drastic over-spending, it was seen by the

Americans as a restrictive practice which could only be justified in wartime. By the time Britain restored convertibility in 1947, most of the $4 billion loan had in fact already been spent. The cost of the occupation of Germany, the deteriorating return from diminished foreign investments, the unhelpful terms of trade (particularly with America) and the difficulties of restoring Britain's exports together created a run on the pound as soon as convertibility came into force: sterling in fact began selling at the rate of $150 million a week and convertibility had to be suspended after just one month. It was a crushing demonstration of the relative economic status of Great Britain and the US in the postwar world. It was also a cruel and rather unfair blow to the prestige of the Labour government, which believed that it had lived down the legacy of 1931 and the taunt that, when it came to economic and financial affairs, it was 'unfit to govern'.

Both Labour and Conservative backbenchers had been worried by the domination of Britain's future by America that seemed implicit in the terms of the 1945 loan. In the House of Commons 72 Conservatives and 23 Labour MPs had voted against it, even though Churchill had pointed out that 'a vote against the loan is a weak yielding to the emotions which the long-term interests of state require should be strictly restrained'. *The Economist* no doubt voiced the bitterness of many, irrespective of their political opinions, when it judged that 'our present needs are the direct consequences of the fact that we fought earliest, that we fought longest and that we fought hardest. In moral terms we are creditors; and for that we shall have to pay $140 millions a year for the rest of the century. It may be unavoidable; but it is not right'.[4]

After the convertibility crisis, the Left of the Labour party secured the appointment of a Minister of Economic Affairs. The hope was that a minister freed from Treasury worries about short-term difficulties would be able to put up long-term plans for British self-sufficiency. The post went to Stafford Cripps, darling of the Left in the 1930s, but the divided responsibility between the Treasury and the Ministry of Economic Affairs (MEA) proved no more satisfactory in the late 1940s than when it was tried again by Labour in the 1960s. With Hugh Dalton's resignation, Cripps was to combine the Treasury with the MEA, and short-term difficulties continued to dominate. Cripps was nobody's fool, but it was difficult to avoid the logic of the economic situation. Determined to make Britain self-sufficient as soon as possible, he began an austerity programme, demanding cuts in public expenditure and wage restraints. In fact, wages were to rise more slowly than prices till 1950 and the TUC co-operated with the government for two years before it rejected restraint. The trade deficit with America had risen to over £600 million, however, and in spite of the help provided by Marshall Aid and the improvements that austerity brought to the trade figures, when the American recession hit Britain in 1949, it was clear that devaluation of the pound was essential. Cripps delayed too long and then devalued too dramatically, by over 30 per cent. One Tory backbencher accused Cripps of reducing sterling to the 'currency of a banana republic'. Similar jibes were to be thrown at successive governments by both sides of the House, as the development of the balance of payments problem slowly but surely began to undermine the new consensus in the years that followed.

It is important to remember, then, that an atmosphere of financial and economic crisis was the ever-present backdrop to Labour's reform programme. Indeed, the crisis was itself part of the very rationale of that reform programme, and it shaped it and limited it in important ways. Fears of an international or at least a national recession, similar to that which had occurred after 1918, were not unjustifiable after 1945. The priorities in domestic policy were, therefore, the provision of palliatives to protect the vulnerable before that recession made itself felt. The immediate alarms created by economic circumstances, in other words, were to confirm that pragmatic tradition in mainstream Labour thinking which complained to the Left that there was neither the time nor the need for ideological purity. Social democratic philosophy, moreover, relied on economic growth to allow a gradual and frictionless redistribution of national income, but throughout this period economic growth seemed to be in jeopardy. It was during this period that the 'national cake' analogy first began to impinge on popular politics: Cripps explained that 'there is only a certain sized cake, and if a lot of people want a larger slice, they can only get it by taking from others'. While the cake continues to grow, redistribution can take place with relatively little friction; everybody gets a larger slice, so the better-off sections of society will not care that their extra crumbs are relatively fewer than those received by the previously worse-off. If the cake stops growing, or if it gets smaller, then either redistribution or a failure to redistribute is likely to cause friction. Thus did promises of progress towards social equity and calls on the nation to work harder elide in the political culture of postwar Britain. Economic growth became synonomous with, and the *sine qua non* of the future of social democracy.

NATIONALISATION

Nationalisation was perhaps the most important of the strategies Labour developed to attempt to offset the dreaded post-war recession and to generate that growth which would allow a relatively frictionless redistribution of the national income. Nationalisation really never had more than these limited aims in mainstream Labour thinking: as it was developed in the postwar period, it really amounted to evidence of Labour's commitment to Keynes rather than to socialism. Government control of the 'commanding heights of industry' would provide the filler cap in the economy through which public investment could be poured counter-cyclically in the event of depression, or siphoned off if the economy was in danger of inflating. In the process, of course, it would also act as at least a sop to the Left, by guaranteeing that society as a whole would benefit from any profit that there was still to be made out of God-given assets such as coal or steel, or those manmade national assets which were part of the infrastructure of the economy as a whole, such as transport or power.

In many ways nationalisation, as it was pursued by the postwar Labour governments, would have been the ideal solution to the problems of the interwar years. Many were to criticise Labour, indeed, for looking back to the interwar years rather than developing progressive policies for the future. Many of the industries chosen had been laid waste by the interwar depression, and had been so reorganised during wartime that they were virtually impossible to return to private ownership anyway. There was virtually no opposition from the Conservatives to the nationalisation of coal. Interwar Tory governments had had quite enough of both the coal-owners and the miners. The industry was barely viable financially and had been so reliant on government control and rationalisation in wartime that it was difficult to think up a credible alternative to nationalisation.[5] The transport industry, railways in particular, suffered similar problems to coal but, again like coal, could not be allowed simply to decay, because of the colossal effect its demise would have on the rest of industry. Nationalisation of the Bank of England made little difference in practice, since the Bank could hardly dictate financial policy to the government, but it was an important gesture for a party still suspicious that it might have been the victim of a 'bankers' ramp' back in 1931. In the case of the steel industry, however, the government found itself with a real fight on its hands. The steel industry was still profitable, marginally at least, and the Right of the party argued that nationalisation was not therefore necessary. The debate within the party and the delays in the legislation imposed by the House of Lords gave the steel owners and the Conservatives time to mobilise, particularly since the government already seemed to be on the run after the convertibility and devaluation crises. The steel owners were effectively to refuse to co-operate with the British Iron and Steel Federation after nationalisation, until the industry was denationalised by the returning Tories.

In no sense did nationalisation threaten private enterprise, then. In fact it was its best guarantor, for it is difficult to underestimate the impact on the economy as a whole if either the coal or transport industries had collapsed. The mixed economy was projected, in fact, as an historic and pragmatic compromise between socialism and capitalism which would produce a structure which was both efficient and humane. The management structure of the nationalised industries pointed to the fact that no really radical motives were involved in Labour's policy of public ownership. They were to be run as state businesses, along the lines Herbert Morrison outlined in his concept of state corporations, and workers' control simply did not figure as a principle. Since 1926 and the defeat of the always small syndicalist element in the Labour movement, no one had effectively worked out how the concept of workers' control should be applied to Britain. There was, therefore, little organised opposition to Morrison's ideas.[6] Unions and consumers were to be given only indirect consultative powers within the new management structures. Many were the miners who went back to work the day after nationalisation, only to find the 'same bloody gaffer' sitting in the office.

The result of the limited motives involved in public ownership and the limited changes to the system of management was to saddle the principle of nationalisation with an unenviable reputation, that of huge, grey-faced, monolithic institutions which devoured public money, and which provided an ever-more decrepit service. However, if the expected depression had in fact materialised, then post-1945 nationalisation might have made the reputation of the British socialist tradition inviolable. The publicly-owned industries would have been the channels through which public money could have been channelled in the Keynesian formula, and the multiplier effect might well have worked to iron out at least some of the effects of the depression. But the depression did not materialise for thirty years. Instead, Britain was faced with the rather different problem of inflation. The nationalised industries were to be used in effect to deflate without producing unemployment. Money was provided for jobs but not nearly enough for capital investment. The result was that nationalisation as a concept was to be burdened with the image of shabby old railway stations, labour inefficiency, and the retention of old-fashioned and commercially unprofitable fuel sources. Public corporations were asked simultaneously to break even financially and also to provide a public service: these demands were incompatible. The Beeching cuts in the railway network, and the slower, sadder cutbacks in British steel and coal production (steel was to be renationalised by Labour in 1965), were virtually unavoidable consequences of the weaknesses of forethought in the post-1945 legislation.

By the time that future Labour governments were prepared to take commercially viable sectors of the economy into public ownership, such as British oil assets in the North Sea, the political damage had been done. Nationalisation was something you did to industries that were dying, in order to save jobs. Public ownership was what happened, a joke of the 1960s had it, when you took a firm like Marks and Spencers and made it as efficient as the Co-op. It had been 'proved', ironically by the results of the work of the Labour government backed by the biggest majority the party had ever had, that 'socialism did not work'. The privatisation of so many public companies in the 1980s was to look like the auction of the contents of some great old house, the value of which the eccentric and now-defunct family had never really understood and which they had left covered in cobwebs in the attic. The 1940s debate over whether or not Labour should nationalise steel epitomised the problem of British parliamentary socialism. The heirs of Ramsay MacDonald and the 'respectable alternative' in office in the late 1940s argued, as MacDonald had done implicitly, that the role of an avowedly socialist parliamentary party was to protect the working class from the vagaries of capitalism as best it could. This inevitably involved compromise, because there was little point in putting through parliament a series of truly radical measures which would simply be overturned by the opposition when they returned to power. If revolution was to come through parliamentary democracy, to avoid the potential bloodbath of class war, then it could only come through consensus. Socialism in the 1940s, as much as in the 1890s, had to be regulated to suit the pace of the slowest. But the problem still remained what it always had been, that socialism involved at some point a radical break, an ideological leap into a system of values quite different from those which the Labour party had adapted from liberalism. It was this conundrum that Aneurin Bevan was to address centrally in his ministerial career in the 1940s and in what he came to represent after his resignation. The concept of the National Health Service, which Bevan piloted through public and professional opinion and parliament, was not only the lynch-pin of the legislation of the postwar Labour governments but also the major test site of the strategy and the tactics of parliamentary socialism as a whole.

ANEURIN BEVAN, HEALTH, HOUSING AND DEFENCE

The National Health Service was to become, in many ways, the equivalent of the regimental colours of the Labour party, the jealously-guarded symbol of the one certain and ineradicable achievement of parliamentary socialism, namely the right of every citizen to the best health that the combination of science and humanity could provide. The NHS has also become indelibly associated with the most famous exponent of the possibility of socialism through democracy in Britain, Aneurin Bevan. Yet even the NHS had its limitations in conception. Some historians have seen Bevan's work as Minister of Health simply as a completion of the work already begun in the wartime coalition by the Tory Reformer Henry Willink, after Beveridge. Certainly, the main lines of development of the Service, its organisational structure and the methods of finance, had been set out in the White Paper of 1944. Bevan's biographer, Michael Foot, sees the principle of universality enshrined in the preamble to the National Health Act as a transformation of the wartime preparations, making socialist what had previously been welfarist,[7] but in fact the principle of universality had been basic to Beveridge's assumptions, and was not anyway specifically socialist.

In fact, to get his Bill through, Bevan did indeed have to deal with many very important points of organisation and detail which had not been sorted out in wartime. In so doing, he had to make large concessions on significant points of principle to secure the co-operation of the doctors. The consultants, for example, demanded the retention of the private medicine system within the hospital service, the so-called pay-bed scheme. He had to concede to the British Medical Association, too, that there were would be no full-time salaried service for general practitioners, which the BMA believed would reduce GPs to mere civil servants: instead, there was to be a basic salary, topped up by a capitation fee for each of the patients on a GP's list. Even then the BMA was not entirely convinced, in spite of the fact that much of the impetus for a national health service had actually come from them in the first place. At this point, Bevan simply stuck to his guns, refusing to make further concessions and, in the event, 90 per cent of GPs enrolled within two months of the beginning of the new service.

Almost immediately, however, Bevan's department was faced with cutbacks. The devaluation crisis and Cripps' austerity programme led not only to the introduction of prescription charges, but also to £35 million being cut from the housing subsidy. This cut was a serious blow. By 1945, there were 700 000 fewer homes than in 1939 and the massive postwar rise in the marriage and birth rate created a large new demand. Bevan's Housing Acts, the New Towns Act and the Town and Country Planning Act opened the way for a Local Authority building boom. By 1948, almost 300 000 homes were being built a year, though many of these were prefabricated, temporary homes to deal with the short-term demand. Many of these 'prefabs' were in fact still in occupation in the late 1960s, in spite of the much-lauded home-building programme that Harold Macmillan launched for the Conservatives in the 1950s. Bevan fought hard in cabinet against the proposed cuts, and at least managed to stave off their introduction date. An open break with the Chancellor of the Exchequer, Stafford Cripps, was only just avoided before the 1950 general election.[8]

The crunch came, however, when Cripps was succeeded as Chancellor by Hugh Gaitskell. Gaitskell insisted that the financial changes be introduced immediately and Bevan was moved sideways to the Ministry of Labour to avoid a direct confrontation. Further than this, however, the Americans were expecting a three-year £6 billion defence programme from Britain. Such an expenditure could only lead to further cuts in the social services. Gaitskell threatened to resign if a large new defence programme was not accepted and demanded that another £23 million must be chopped from the cost of the NHS to help to pay for it. At this point, Bevan had had enough. He resigned from the cabinet, along with the President of the Board of Trade, Harold Wilson, and John Freeman, a most damaging blow to Labour's chances of re-election in the 1951 poll.

Bevan's resignation speech in the House of Commons demonstrates all the frustrations that face the parliamentary socialist. Of Gaitskell's budget, he said: 'it was a remarkable budget. It united the City, satisfied the Opposition and disunited the Labour Party. All this because we have allowed ourselves to be dragged behind the wheels of American diplomacy.' Prescription charges he characterised as the thin edge of the wedge which would legitimise further reductions in health spending. 'There is only one hope for mankind', he concluded, 'and that is democratic socialism. There is only one party in Great Britain which can do it, and that is the Labour Party. But I ask them carefully to consider how they are polluting the stream.' Above all, Labour must make sure that 'we are not going to allow ourselves to be diverted from our path by the exigencies of the immediate situation'.[9] Bevan was what might be called a 'ratchet socialist'; Labour could only hope to achieve socialism by the evolutionary method of winning a whole series of little victories; but each of those victories, once won, must not be conceded, must become instead part of the strength of the ratchet, applying an ever more vice-like grip to capitalism. For Bevan the introduction of prescription charges – though in itself only a small reverse, and the cost may not have been very great for patients – was a matter of bad tactics, as well as an abrogation of principle. It introduced a crack in the edifice which could be used to undermine the whole structure. It conceded that the evolution of socialism through democracy was reversible.

The whole problem revolved around the importance that should be placed on what Bevan called 'the exigencies of the immediate situation'. The current economic situation, and the demands of the international context, as Gaitskell and the right of the party saw them, demanded that compromises would have to be made. The direct linkage that Bevan's resignation had made between threats to the future of the newly-formed social services on the one hand, and defence policy and Britain's Atlantic alliance on the other, ensured that his resignation would lead to a savage fight over the whole range of Labour policies. Hidden away in Labour's rising defence estimates in the late 1940s had been the cost of producing Britain's A-bomb, kept secret both from Parliament and from the cabinet. When it appeared, the A-bomb was to deepen the fratricidal struggle developing between the Bevanites and the

Gaitskellites, which was to help to deny Labour office for the next thirteen years. Harold Wilson, having resigned with Bevan but thereafter distancing himself from the hard left, managed to appeal to both right and left of the party to reunite them after Gaitskell's death. But the respite proved only temporary as, once again in the 1960s and 1970s, the Labour party appeared to be blown off course by 'the exigencies of the immediate situation'. Even at the moment of its greatest triumph, then, the Labour movement was still divided on the basic issues of parliamentary socialism.

THE TRIUMPH OF TORY REFORM

Labour lost the 1951 election by the narrowest of margins. The party actually polled two million more votes and won a larger percentage share of the popular vote than they had in the 1945 landslide. Labour also did considerably better than they had in the 1950 election, when the government had been returned with an overall majority of five. The Conservatives and their allies, polling 200 000 votes less than Labour, had an overall majority of 21 seats in 1951 (to which should be added the 19 National Liberal seats). The reason for Labour's defeat was that the party had failed to consolidate the gains of 1945 in the South, in East Anglia and the shires. Once again, as in the 1930s, Labour began to pile up massive majorities in wholly safe seats, while the Conservative vote was distributed more thinly but more economically over the country as a whole, but particularly in the suburbs where so many seats lay. In 1955, the Conservatives came within a whisker of 50 per cent of the popular vote, but Labour was less than a million votes behind (out of a total vote of not much less than 27 million). The Conservatives held their share of the vote in 1959 while Labour, though losing a few percentage points to another in the series of Liberal revivals, still won nearly 44 per cent of the vote. It must be said, then, that though Labour lost three consecutive general elections in the 1950s, it was the distribution rather than the total size of the vote which gave the Conservatives their comfortable majorities. In spite of the much-publicised rows within the Labour party, there was no sign as yet that Labour support was actually on the wane. But, in an electoral system in which a near miss is as good as a mile, Labour might as well have been in the voting wilderness of the 1930s. By the time the party came back to power in 1964, only Harold Wilson had any ministerial experience.

The Conservatives moved rapidly to the political centre after their humiliating defeat in 1945 and capitalised on the consensus on welfarism. Though Churchill still proved unable to give a decisive lead in domestic affairs, the Tory Reform Group had seized on the opportunity the late 1940s provided to convince the party that they had little alternative but to accept much of what Labour was doing in economic and social affairs. The appointment of R. A. Butler to the Treasury and Macmillan to Housing was evidence enough that the Tory Right considered itself beaten. The Conservative economic policy, however, showed little understanding of the subtleties that Keynesianism actually implied. The new government was immediately helped by the dramatic improvement in the terms of trade, which allowed the balance of payments deficit to be wiped out by 1953. Butler was thus permitted to put forward a series of expansionist budgets which developed a mini-boom. Soon after the 1955 election, however, it was clear that the economy was over-heating and the brakes were applied. This pattern of 'stop-go' budgeting was to be one of the hallmarks of the thirteen years of Conservative rule. The brakes continued to be applied through 1956 as the Suez crisis led to a run on the pound. Britain was forced to go to the International Monetary Fund for a loan for the first time – a salutary lesson, though it was soon forgotten. Through 1957 and early 1958 the reign of the monetarist Peter Thorneycroft at the Treasury led to continued deflation. Macmillan stepped in and sacked Thorneycroft in January 1958, however, fed up with the restrictions on growth, and on populist Toryism, that monetarism had imposed. New expansionist budgets were to produce another boom in time for the 1959 election. Then, with the election successfully out of the way, the new Chancellor was also sacked by Macmillan for trying to deflate again. By 1961, the deficit on the balance of payments had produced another inevitable run on the pound.[10]

At this point, the whole economic policy of the government (if something so brazenly electioneering can be called 'policy') began to unravel and threaten dire social consequences. A new big loan was negotiated with the IMF but it was clear that the government could not simply continue with stop-go. Selwyn Lloyd decided to take on what he considered to be the basic problem, namely low productivity and wage-pushed inflation. What this meant, in effect, was resisting wage rises from public sector employees, the only ones over which government had any direct control. A National Economic and Development Council was set up in an attempt to secure voluntary wage restraint from the TUC, and a National Incomes Commission. The TUC could not be drawn, however, and private sector wages continued to rise while Selwyn Lloyd continued to deflate. Macmillan, not known for his loyalty to his colleagues, decided to revive the flagging popularity of his government with a 'night of the long knives', sacking Selwyn Lloyd along with one third of his cabinet. The new Chancellor, Reginald Maudling, prepared to take Britain through the inflationary sound-barrier by engineering the biggest boom yet. By 1964, as a result, Britain's balance of payments deficit stood at something like £800 millions.[11]

Nevertheless, the artificial booms did their political job, allowing the Conservatives to remove many of the controls inherited from the era of Crippsian austerity. And the denationalisation of steel and road haulage gave Conservative propagandists the chance to claim that they were involved in a policy of freeing the nation from the legacy of socialism. In fact, in the broad thrust of economic and social policy, there was not that much which divided Conservatives from Labour. The detailed differences, however, were important and were to have significant repercussions. The Conservatives' budgetary policy was often simply irresponsible, where Labour's had been mostly over-careful. Most important of all was the difference in housing policy. The Conservatives were determined to top Bevan's record in housing construction: the target of 300 000 houses a year seems to have been decided upon for no other reason than that it was more than Labour had built. Macmillan, moreover, intended to give much more emphasis to the private sector than Bevan had done, providing massive increases in the availability of mortgages to enable people to buy their own homes. Using the planning framework of the Town and Country Planning Acts and the New Towns Act which he inherited from Labour, Macmillan played the major role in transforming Britain into a property-owning demo-cracy, constructing in the process a populist basis for a progressive Conservatism. The traditional predilection of the lower-middle class for the Conservative party was thus further reinforced, but the Tories also began to make significant appeals to the better-off working class, for whom full employment and rapidly-rising standards of living began to bring home ownership within relatively easy reach for the first time. Looked at as a whole, it would be fair to say that the Conservatives maintained the structure of the Welfare State that they had inherited from Labour and that they maintained the commitment to economic growth, though largely through the use of sometimes irresponsible budgetary techniques. In the process, they had 'conservatised' welfarism. While Labour could claim that welfarism has brought more social equity, Harold Macmillan could subtly change the emphasis by declaring: 'you've never had it so good'.

Harold Macmillan, the dominant politician of the 1950s, managed to combine a flamboyant Edwardianism with a clear commitment to social progress. The Disraeli of his age, he performed an important bridging strategy for Conservatism, proving ambiguous enough to appeal both to traditional Conservative voters as well as to those younger electors who had reached maturity at the end of the depression and during the war. Macmillan combined for Conservatism an instinctive patriotism with an instinctive rejection of the 'guilty men' and 'the locust years'. Yet the Conservatives, on the whole, merely enjoyed the fruits of what had already been achieved: they did little to expand the Welfare State. No new hospitals were built, and the slowness in building new schools undercut the fine hopes enshrined in the 1944 Education Act. Employment within the expanded social services also lagged continually behind needs, so that nurses, teachers and social workers found themselves overworked and undervalued. The public services that had been built up in austerity in the 1940s were backgrounded by the new consumerism, setting the stage for the developing struggles of the 1960s. These battle lines, though only imperfectly drawn as yet, were made clearer by the necessities imposed by Britain's changing position in the world.

BRITAIN AND THE WORLD IN THE 1950S

The important nuances which separated Labour from Conservative in domestic affairs were mirrored in international policy. Again, though, the differences between the parties tended to be matters of detail rather than of overall policy, over Suez most obviously. Suez was, in fact, the exception which proved the general rule of bipartisanship, for it was Conservative worries which were to force Eden's resignation rather than pressures from the Opposition. On the other hand, though Gaitskell could not guarantee the undivided support of the Labour Party for nuclear weaponry, Gaitskell himself was determined to 'fight, fight and fight again' to save the party from what he saw as the insanity of unilateralism. Ernest Bevin's tenure of the Foreign Office found him as convinced a cold warrior as Churchill. Both parties also shared a suspicion of American motives and feared for British independence in the Atlantic alliance, but both were equally convinced that the relationship with the US was special and unbreakable. In the period in which Britain was famously described as a nation which 'had lost an Empire and not yet found a role', the party of Keir Hardie and Ramsay MacDonald found adaptation almost as difficult as the party of Disraeli and Churchill. Both became almost equally obsessed with the question of Britain's world status. Labour's grant of independence to India and Pakistan and the bonfire of Imperial commitments in Africa which followed took away Britain's material right to be called a great power, but the assumption that she still had a major, independent role to play in the world took a great deal longer to die. In the event, economic pressure was to prove as important in this process as any moral reassessment by either of the major parties. In turn, the cost of maintaining great power status was to have important repercussions at home.

Churchill's status as supreme statesman of the West seemed to confirm the right of his successors to continue to speak for the free world as a whole. Anthony Eden's conduct of foreign affairs in the early 1950s appeared to demonstrate all the flair and confidence that Britain had exuded in greater times, emerging as the major broker in several important deals in Europe and between the superpowers. The visit to Britain of the Soviet leaders Bulganin and Kruschev in early 1956 was confirmation that Britain remained one of the wartime 'Big Three'. Britain's international status was brutally undermined, however, during the Suez crisis which dominated the rest of that year. To picture Gemal Abdul Nasser as 'the new Hitler', to determine that the Suez Canal was still a vital British concern which Egyptians were incapable of running efficiently and, above all, to engage in a shady conspiracy with the French and the Israelis to defeat Egyptian plans, might be said to have called into question Britain's right to be listened to at all. Nevertheless, so soon after the Second World War, the widespread international condemnation of Britain led to a closing of the ranks at home in support of British motives, if not her methods. Though the Labour Party called on the Conservatives to overthrow the Prime Minister, they were equally careful to point out that the fact that Eden was wrong did not make Nasser right. It cannot be denied that Suez was an unmitigated failure. Not only did it confirm Nasser's status in the Middle East, it also critically weakened Anglo-American co-operation at the time of the Soviet invasion of Hungary. It could well be argued that it was the Suez crisis which finally destroyed the mirage of Britain's great power-status: from this time on, Britain was a client of the United States, the most important and the most friendly client certainly, but still a client for all that.[12]

As Empire turned into Commonwealth, however, Britain could still claim that the role that she was playing as moral leader of so many emerging nations would mean that she would continue to count for a great deal. The development of her own independent nuclear deterrent, too, would mean that she would simply have to be listened to. At a time when British conventional defence commitments were eating up 8 per cent of GNP and threatening to rise alarmingly with the further development of NATO, a reliance on nuclear deterrence seemed to offer a cheaper way of maintaining great power status. The Defence White Paper of 1957 promised a large reduction in Britain's expensive conventional forces and their replacement by a nuclear deterrent in the form of the V-bombers. Even this major rethink left Britain dangerously overstretched in her defence commitments. The sheer cost and the rapid development of weapons technology soon made it clear that Britain simply could not hope to maintain full nuclear independence. The Americans were less interested in the British capacity for nuclear deterrence – their own nuclear umbrella, they felt, was ample for Europe – and rather more interested in Britain maintaining her conventional commitments in NATO. If NATO was ever to be fully integrated as a defence organisation, as was the Warsaw Pact, then the American attitude made a great deal of sense. Britain could never afford a nuclear umbrella that would rival that of either the Americans or the Soviets, so that British defence spending would best be concentrated on conventional weapons. Britain, on the other hand, did not want to be just another European power.

It was something of a coup on Macmillan's part to get President Kennedy to agree to sell Polaris to Britain, then, but it was mere pretence to argue that this maintained the independence of Britain's nuclear capacity. The submarines and the warheads were to be British but these would be useless without the American rockets. The doubts about the Nassau Agreement, and Britain's increasing reliance in defence on American technology, allowed the Labour party to begin to offer an alternative defence policy based on an increase in conventional weapons, which had the important subsidiary effect of backgrounding their internal differences on nuclear weapons. Labour, nevertheless, never managed to square their increasing emphasis on non-nuclear defence with the enormous cost it implied. The inescapable logic of Britain's desire to maintain great power status was that she would have to spend more than she could afford on armaments. Nuclear defence was cheaper but hideously dangerous, and of unproven military or diplomatic worth when weighed against the nuclear arsenals of the superpowers. Conventional weaponry was more expensive on the other hand, and might prove worthless if a new conflict developed quickly into a nuclear exchange.[13] The real question was not which form of armaments Britain should prioritise but whether she should try to maintain great-power status at all. Now that the Empire had indisputably gone, did spending on armaments have any more value than that of maintaining a nostalgic view of Britain's place in the world? Churchill's legacy had left Britain an unfortunate self-image which it was proving impossible to maintain. If the defence commitment continued, moreover, then it must seriously jeopardise the huge commitment to domestic expenditure which welfarism implied.

The Nassau Agreement, and the American connection more generally, also had the effect of confirming French hostility to Britain's application for entry to the Common Market. If Britain were to be frozen out of the movement towards European economic integration, then it was at least questionable whether the country could maintain the trade necessary to sustain the standard of living and the public services that her population now took for granted. In fact, Britain had supported ideas of European integration from the beginning but had been noticeably reticent about involving herself in any of the arrangements made, largely because she still did not consider herself a European country, as De Gaulle rightly commented. Macmillan regarded the British application for membership of the EEC as the first step not to the European federal state, but to an extended Atlantic alliance in which Britain would play the part of middleman between the US and Europe.[14] Once again, there was a broad bipartisanship at home on the question. The political divisions which the decision to apply for entry caused in Britain tended to be within the parties rather than between them. Many Conservatives could agree with the view of many in the Labour party that Britain should not sacrifice her responsibilities to the Commonwealth; there was equally strong cross-party support for the idea that membership would provide new markets for British goods, make British industry more competitive, and help finally to put an end to centuries of conflict within Europe. Indeed, it was to prove most difficult to enforce party discipline on this important issue during the next two decades, so thoroughly did it cut across party lines. In the process, many cross-party contacts were to be made which were to have real significance in the political realignment which was to take place as the consensus in domestic affairs came under fire. Having shared platforms with the Liberals in the campaign to gain popular support for the EEC, for instance, some on the Right of the Labour party were to find it easier to make the break that was finally to lead on to the development of a new party in the political centre.

International issues thus had a habit in this period of blowing back on the domestic consensus. The problem for the moment, however, was not a new centre party but an incipient extremism. The Left of the Conservative Party and the Right of the Labour party may have been only marginally divided on the major issues but the cost of consensus was that it left political space on the Right and on the Left. This was just as clear when the time came to consider the true nature of Britain's relationship with the Commonwealth, with the developing issue of immigration. R.A. Butler estimated that the establishment of the Commonwealth meant that a quarter of the population of the world was legally entitled to live in Britain. With bigger restrictions on immigration to countries which traditionally welcomed immigrants, such as the United States, Britain became a favourite destination. The development of the public services, moreover, meant that Britain was at first more than willing to take in this source of additional cheap labour. In a period in which planning had become all important, however, there were worries too that both central government and local authorities needed firmer estimates of the future needs in housing and social services than unrestricted and unpredictable immigration allowed. This rational political concern was vastly complicated, however, by the issue of racism.

The tendency of the new immigrants to congregate geographically underpinned the racist argument that working-class whites were being forced out of their traditional homes and being undercut for jobs by this new sub-class in British society which, it was further argued, refused to assimilate culturally. The Notting Hill riots of 1958 created real worries that racial tension would become part and parcel of British life unless some clear policy on immigration was formulated. The Immigration Act of 1962 fixed a quota for immigration, which came under immediate attack because of its racist implications; it was quite clearly designed to restrict the flow only of black immigrants. It remained true, however, that Labour in turn never managed to frame a restriction on immigration which did not have equally racist undertones.[15] Unfortunately, too, even to air the issue of immigration was to provoke the most unpleasant political repercussions. In the Smethwick election of 1964, the local Conservative candidate managed to reverse locally the national swing to Labour by mounting an implicitly racist campaign. In the emergency which arose in 1968, moreover, when the actions of the Kenyan government provoked a mass exodus of Asians to Britain, Enoch Powell provided a legitimisation of racism by demanding restrictions on Kenyan Asian entry – even though their very lives might be at risk – with his horrific predictions of bloody racial conflict in Britain. Rapid action by the Conservative leadership, however, was to ensure that this particular attempt to radicalise the party was effectively marginalised. Even so, it was soon to become clear that the predeliction for consensus inherent in the political machines was increasingly being allowed simply to disguise major unresolved problems.

THE LAST YEARS OF THE CONSENSUS

The last years of the Conservative ascendancy were clouded by a series of scandals which dominated the run-up to the 1964 general election. These scandals combined Cold War worries with renewed suspicions of the old boy network at home, and provided a kind of paradigm of the developing crisis in the postwar consensus. The uncovering of George Blake, along with the Vassall spy-case in October 1962, revived worries not fully allayed since the defection of Burgess and Maclean in 1951 about the competence as well as the loyalty of the British security services. The defection of Kim Philby in 1963 fed deeper fears that there was something rotten in the British establishment, concerns that were given full airing in the

Profumo scandal of June 1963. Not only did the Profumo scandal concern sex and spying once again but also the semi-gangster world of 'Rachmanism', involving the wholesale exploitation of tenants by private landlords. The clever new leader of the Labour Party, Harold Wilson, conjured up a conspiracy of traitorous, lecherous, exploitative establishment figures scratching each other's backs, protected by Tory incompetence. By this time, Macmillan was too ill to take him on, and the insensitive decision to replace him as Prime Minister by an hereditary earl only played into Wilson's hands. The 14th Earl of Home did not help his case by admitting laughingly in public that he knew nothing about economics: the self-styled '14th Mr Wilson', by contrast, was an academic economist promising that Labour would set about reforming the British economy with the 'white heat of technology'.

Having resigned with Bevan back in 1951, Wilson's appeal both to the Left and to the Right in the Labour Party combined with a superb television manner, at just the time when television was becoming the most important method of political image-building. He appeared to embody the classlessness of the 1945 revolution. He was young (the youngest cabinet minister and the youngest prime minister this century) at a time when youth culture was becoming respectable. In 1964 he seemed unbeatable, which makes it all the more surprising that Labour's election victory that year was so marginal. The fact is that, although the 1950s are often seen as gloomy years for Labour electorally, it was not a sudden turn-around that gave them electoral success in the 1960s. The overall shift in the vote to Labour in the 1960s was minimal. They won 43.8 per cent of the vote in 1959 and 44.1 per cent in 1964. They increased their share of the vote in 1966, when Wilson was still enjoying his honeymoon period with the electorate, but in 1970 Labour fell to 43 per cent, the lowest share of the vote the party had won since the war. On the other hand, the position of the Conservatives was not particularly rosey. By 1966, they were down to 41.9 per cent and only recovered to 46.4 per cent to win in 1970. Undoubtedly, the Liberal revival was already having some effect on both major parties' electoral prospects. Small though the total Liberal vote still was in the 1960s, it could have a dramatic effect in making and breaking governments when the votes for the two larger parties were so close. As dissatisfaction grew with the performance of governments of both persuasions during the 1960s and 1970s, the third force developed, adding fuel firstly to the Liberals' hopes that they could hold the balance of power, and later opening the prospect of an electoral breakthrough. The change in Liberal prospects was, in fact, both symptom and cause of new shifts both in political ideas and in voting patterns, as the impact of inflation began to eat away at the postwar consensus. As centrist politics failed, battles for control of the two major parties began, creating a situation in which continued centrism might need an alternative organisational home. This the Liberals were to provide.

Wilson's promise to introduce a new age of industrial expansion was undermined almost immediately by the problems of the economy. The much-vaunted 'white heat of technology' was duly applied to industry in the shape of a Ministry of Technology, a Science and Technology Act and an Industrial Expansion Act. It was clear within a few months of Labour taking office in 1964, however, that such measures were to be of simply cosmetic importance. British politics had entered a new and critical phase not simply because the government's majority was tiny, but also because the sense of approaching economic disaster was overwhelming. The Conservatives' attempt to engineer another boom had developed a major balance of payments crisis. The burden of what Wilson called 'thirteen years of Tory misrule' was a real one, but it was not helped by Labour's crisis management. Ruling out devaluation, the government decided on a deflationary budget, while fulfilling their election pledges to abolish prescription charges and raise sickness and unemployment benefits. The hope was that the concessions would tempt the TUC into an incomes policy, but the money markets interpreted the budget as complacency, in view of the balance of payments deficit. There followed an apparently uncontrollable run on sterling, requiring a $3 billion rescue operation by the Bank. A prices and incomes policy followed, voluntary in principle but with compulsory early warnings to allow government time to consider the likely effect of any increases. The Treasury hoped thereby to keep wage rises down to about 3.5 per cent, though in fact they were to rise by nearer 9 per cent in the year. Reinvigorated by Labour's handling of the sterling crisis and aware of the government's slender majority, the Conservatives ripped into James Callaghan's second budget; a third deflationary budget was to be necessary within the first year of the government, as the voluntary incomes policy showed no signs of taking effect.

Even with the increased confidence that came with the increased mandate in 1966, Labour proved unable to persuade the unions. A seamen's strike hit hard where it hurt most, at exports. Shortly afterwards the government's most important link with the unions, Frank Cousins, resigned from the cabinet over the incomes policy early warning scheme. Still the government refused to devalue, though the cabinet was deeply divided by the alternative – further massive deflation, and the introduction of a six-month wage freeze, followed by six months of severe wage restraint. A year later, moreover, the trade gap had narrowed but not closed and unemployment had gone up to half a million. The pound was sliding again and in November 1967 the government finally devalued and took an IMF loan. It is a remarkable testimony to the resilience of Wilson, and to the loyalty of his colleagues, that he survived not only this U-turn in policy but also the humiliating series of cuts in social spending that had to follow. These included the reintroduction of prescription charges, the issue on which he had resigned in 1950. It proved how much the party had matured since 1931 that the government did not collapse at this point. But the success of the Labour movement depended ultimately not just on the nerve of the political leadership but on maintaining the confidence and the co-operation of the industrial wing. This relationship was to be severely shaken at the end of the 1960s.[16]

With the relative failure of the voluntary incomes policy and the rash of unofficial strikes caused by the pay pause, the Prime Minister determined on bringing the unions to book. The result was 'In Place of Strife', a White Paper drafted by Barbara Castle which proposed a legally enforced cooling-off period and a ballot of all members before a strike. The

publication of the White paper led to an outcry from the
Labour back-benchers as well as from the TUC. It was clear,
too, that many senior ministers viewed the proposed legislation
with the gravest misgivings. Though Wilson persevered, it was
soon obvious that any legislation aimed at binding the unions
legally had no hope of getting through the House of Commons.
Wilson was forced into another policy U-turn when he
withdrew the proposals, in return for an undertaking from
the TUC that the unions would do their best to regulate
unofficial strikes. Nevertheless, the balance of payments moved
into the black in 1969 and Wilson recovered much of the clout
he had lost with the left of the party by looking forward to
further nationalisation, a national investment bank and new
wealth taxes. After five years in office, however, the Left was
wondering why Wilson had not thought of these things before.

At the same time, economic necessity drove huge spears into
the side of British defence policy, particularly as it was defence
spending which accounted for such a large proportion of
spending abroad. The axe was applied to defence expenditure
in 1965 by Denis Healey, particularly to the development of
expensive high-technology projects, which in turn was to have
severe effects on the British aircraft industry, as well as making
Britain ever more dependent on the US for weapons. Labour
found, as had the Conservatives, that the quickest way to cut
the defence bill, and yet retain at least a semblance of being a
great power, was to cut conventional arms. British international status suffered further setbacks, moreover, when a
second application for entry to the Common Market was
vetoed by the French. At the same time, the anti-marketeers'
alternative strategy of developing the Commonwealth
connection was undermined by the contortions into which
British diplomacy was thrown by increasing international
condemnation of South Africa, and then by the unilateral
declaration of independence by Rhodesia.

In the circumstances of so many dramatic and continuing
crises and reverses in both domestic and foreign politics, it was
in fact surprising that the government did not fare even worse
than it did in the 1970 election. The by-election reverses since
1966 had been staggering, as electors switched allegiance
directly from Labour to Conservative, missing out the

traditional Liberal half-way protest vote. Even though the party managers could still rely normally on the return of the party faithful at the time of a general election, a new volatility had developed in the electorate. The by-elections of the early 1970s were to show that it was not just the Labour party which was effected. Another element, though still immeasurable, was introduced into elections with the first successes of the revitalised nationalist movements in Wales and in Scotland. Here Labour seemed particularly vulnerable since, like the Liberals before them, they relied on the solid Celtic radical vote as bedrock support. The Conservatives, on the other hand, were also to be hit by the developing independent stance of Irish Unionism, and for a short period were even to look a little vulnerable to the extreme right English nationalists, the National Front. No doubt the fact that the new prosperity being enjoyed by so many in England did not reach much of Scotland, Northern Ireland or Wales had much to do with both the nationalist revivals and reactions to them. But nationalism was also a reaction to the culturally homogenising effects of the welfare revolution. Scotland, Northern Ireland and Wales retained strongly independent traditions, and the renewed interest in separatism throws into stronger relief what was going on in England at this time. In fact, in a number of different areas, below the surface details which election returns show us, there were clear signs that the consensus was under very serious threat. Nationalism played a small part in this but, paradoxically, the biggest threat to the postwar consensus was in large part its very success, which undermined the set of arguments which had created it in the first place.

In a seminal study in the 1950s, *The Uses of Literacy*, Richard Hoggart bemoaned the passing of traditional working-class culture and its replacement by a homogeneous, national popular culture.[17] As we have seen, this process had in fact been going on since the late nineteenth century, but there was an important new political truth at the core of Hoggart's concerns. The physical dismantling of the working-class ghettos bequeathed by the late nineteenth century helped to undermine that sense of community which was such an important element in working-class consciousness in Britain. Though there were to be new communities formed in the large exurban estates, the roots of a long tradition had been effectively cut. The extraordinary popularity of a television series such as *Coronation Street* into the late 1980s can only be put down to a nostalgia for a way of life, a context for working-class Englishness, which had disappeared since the end of the Second World War. Though many architectural and social catastrophes were produced during the housing revolution, for the most part the post-war housing boom had vastly improved the living conditions of the working class. At the same time it had removed much of that sense of identity, that non-combative solidarity that had been so typical of working-class reactions to the series of socio-economic pressures to which it had been exposed over a century. The results were complicated and often paradoxical. On the one hand, in combination with the rising standard of living, it increased the trend towards an apparent classlessness, which manifested itself not simply in superficialities like styles of dress and increased access to consumer durables, but also in 'classless' attitudes towards issues such as social policy or law and order, a 'politics of resentment' developing among the 'haves' against the cost of maintaining the 'have-nots'. Home ownership spread active and even eager participation in the structures of liberal capitalism through the social classes as never before.[18] The Labour party, by stressing the success of its 'social revolution by consensus', was ironically undermining the very basis of its continued support.

Perhaps the most obvious example of the apparent new classlessness of British society can be seen in the changes in education in the 1960s. It was in this decade that the high promises of the 1944 Education Act began to bear fruit. R.A. Butler had hoped to establish the three forms of secondary education – grammar, secondary modern and technical – as co-equal in status. In fact, the grammar schools had maintained their position at the top of the public-sector tree. Only with the beginning of the building of the comprehensive schools did the older divisions in education begin to break down. Though the comprehensive system was to develop its own problems, particularly in the larger schools in the inner-city areas, it did inaugurate an era of equality of opportunity in education. The expansion of higher education after the publication of the Robbins Report in 1963 also had potentially profound social consequences. Not only did the introduction of the Bachelor of Education degree lead to a fuller and much-needed professionalisation of school teaching, the wider access to higher education also built on the equality of opportunity which the comprehensive schools were promoting. University Colleges, founded in the interwar period to prepare student for the University of London external degree, were given independent status. Even more liberalising, the new universities were established from scratch, freed from the restricting traditions of the Oxbridge and London University syllabuses which had dominated higher education for so long. The number of full-time undergraduates in England and Wales rose from 56 000 in 1953/4 to 136 000 in 1967/8. Closer examination reveals, however, that the bulk of the new intake of home students was actually male, middle-class and white. The polytechnics, on the other hand, served a wider section of society, and some of them soon reached a standard of excellence both in teaching and research easily comparable with most universities. Almost immediately, however, reaction began. The publication of the Black Papers in 1969 and 1970 were the first warning shots across the bows of progressive educationalists, with their dire prophecy aimed at egalitarianism and equal opportunity: 'more means worse'. The eruption of student protest in 1968 was also to fix the attention of the New Right on the educational system as an example of the failures of collectivist politics.

On the other hand, there was as much evidence of resistance to the new classlessness as there was acceptance. Full employment meant even fuller union membership and an even more active campaign to secure greater rewards for working people than ever before. The beginnings of union-isation of the white-collar workers in the 1960s and 1970s, moreover, most spectacularly in the growth of the Association of Scientific, Technical and Managerial Staffs, suggested that the older confusions at the edges of the social classes might be giving way to a clearer divide between the owners of capital and workers of all kinds. The dislocation of the old communities also produced opportunities for the development of a more assertive and aggressive class feeling, particularly noticeable in the development of youth culture in the 1950s and 1960s. Yet much of youth culture was itself to develop in such a way as to overdetermine these new class divides, as middle-class youth appropriated successive fashions and stances or developed new ones of their own.[19] In this sense, youth developed as a new cross-current in the social formation, providing a vertical divide in the social hierarchy between young and old, rather than reinforcing the class divide. In the late 1960s and 1970s, too, the new feminism was to have a similar effect, emphasising the cross-class gender divisions which patriarchy had established.

Postwar feminism developed partly out of a frustration with the vagaries and the unforeseen consequences of apparently libertarian legislation. In the 1940s and 1950s, women moved massively into the permanent workforce of the nation and became a most important element in the development of the consumer economy, no longer simply as purchasers but now also as employees. Yet the traditional role of women as child-rearers continued to play a significant role in national ideology, reflected in concern with the problem of 'latch-key children', left alone at home after school while their mothers were working. The development of maternity and child welfare clinics made motherhood easier than it had been for the interwar generation, but in that they were aimed at mothers rather than fathers they also reinforced the role of women in the family. Major pieces of legislation on women's rights, in particular the Equal Pay Act and the Sexual Discrimination Act, did not fulfill the hopes that were placed in them as it became clear that legislation itself was not enough to reform deeply-engrained prejudices. Even the revolution in birth-control methods which, it was assumed, would not only free women from unwanted pregnancies but would also give them control over their sexuality for the first time, proved to be double-edged. The Brook Advisory Centres and the Family Planning Association developed the work that had been started by Marie Stopes after the Great War, and from the late 1960s the National Health Service provided its own free advice. The contraceptive pill, however, proved to be a potential health hazard and many couples returned to traditional male-controlled methods of birth control. Not only that but the

notion that women could control their own sexualities bred a
reaction to the era of 'permissiveness'. Abortion figures soared
and a bitter public debate arose on the right of women to
choose whether or not to terminate a pregnancy. Moreover,
the sexually-liberated woman allowed what Jeffrey Weeks has
called 'the eroticisation of modern culture' which, in
advertising and publishing, 'could focus on the female body
without most of the consequences which in earlier days had
been feared and expected'.[20] 'Permissiveness' itself, in short,
was soon rebalanced in favour of the male, thereby hastening
its destruction. New health fears – the growth in the incidence
of cervical cancer, for example – hastened the process. More
recently, the Aids crisis produced a rather less informed
backlash against another example of 1960s 'permissiveness',
the Sexual Offences Act, which had liberalised the laws on
homosexuality. Not that the Gay Liberation Movement felt
that the position of homosexuals had been adequately
protected by law, anyway, any more than did the feminists.

Just as older social frictions appeared to be squeezed out by
welfare politics, then, different ones appeared in different forms
to challenge the new alignment in sometimes spectacular
fashion, such as in 1968. But what happened in Britain in 1968
was nowhere near as significant as what happened in France or
in the United States. Much of the potential political impact of
these new frictions was to be neutralised as the new resistant
groupings failed to articulate their demands credibly or to
inter-react effectively or rapidly enough to meet the reaction.
In spite of wider working-class access to higher education, for
example, radical students failed to convince many working-
class activists in 1968 that they shared a common struggle, nor
did the doctrine of universal love appear to offer either an
immediate or a long-term solution to the balance of payments
problem and the pay pause. Feminism, moreover, was to
challenge the patriarchal terms in which so much of the new
radicalism was couched, demanding new forms of resistance
which did not simply reinforce and legitimise sexual
aggression.

LEFT AND RIGHT SINCE THE 1960S

From this rather diffused and disorganised basis, the New Left developed to reiterate the significance of socialist fundamentals in the new environment. Released from the thraldom produced by generations of unemployment, social deprivation and deferential politics, the New Left argued, a new radical fervour among sections of the electorate should galvanise Labour into a drive for socialism. The legislation of 1945 to 1951 was, for them, simply a foundation on which to build, the strength of which had already been seriously undermined not just by thirteen years of successful Tory realignment but by the wasted opportunities of six years of Labour rule in the 1960s.[21] Mainstream Labour thinkers such as Anthony Crosland and Richard Crossman, on the other hand, doubted the validity of what they saw as outdated nostrums. Clause IV of the Labour party constitution, for example, had been framed as long ago as 1918, before the possibility of a successful 'mixed economy' had even been conceived, and had nothing to do with the realities of life in postwar Britain. This argument developed a special vehemence after the defeat of Labour in 1970. The Left could legitimately argue that it had shown remarkable, almost unprecedented restraint in the 1960s, that it had not stabbed the party in the back, and that the Right had simply failed because it was misguided in its policies. It was perhaps only the tactical magic of Harold Wilson that was able to maintain Labour unity in the turbulent years of the governments of 1964 to 1970. Depending on one's political standpoint, the lesson of those years seemed to be either that the mixed economy did not give government enough power to direct the economy fully enough, or that it did not allow private industry the entrepreneurial initiative to make the best of market opportunities. Either way, the mixed economy could be considered a failure. A similar rethink was going on, though as usual less publicly, in the Conservative party. Shortly before the 1970 general election there were already signs that the New Right was gaining ground. At a strategy conference at the Selsdon Park Hotel, the party's leadership committed itself to large reductions in taxation and firm legislation aimed at the trades unions. The intention this time was not simply to create another vote-catching boom, rather, but to begin to roll back the process of state intervention that Keynes had inaugurated thirty years before.

Wilson ridiculed the proposals of 'Selsdon Man' for turning back the tide of history and, in fact, the monetarist right had to wait nearly ten years before it finally gained control of the Conservatives. The Heath government lost its nerve in the early 1970s. By 1972, it was clear that the government had underestimated how recessionary the effects of strict monetary policy could be. With unemployment reaching towards one million, politically such a damaging landmark redolent of 'the hungry thirties', inflation edged up noticeably. The effects of devaluation, forcing up both import prices and indirect taxation, and the rush of wage increases after the pay pause, were compounded by further deteriorations in the balance of payments. In the resultant sterling crisis, the pound was floated and inflation at home consequently increased. With a trade deficit of well over £1 billion, Britain had entered uncharted waters. It was understandable that the government became extremely jittery about the effectiveness of its new economic policy, retreating to the failed but politically more popular measures that had characterised all postwar governments.[22] 'Lame ducks' in industry were no longer to be allowed to collapse and increase unemployment. A statutory incomes and prices policy replaced the short new life of the market economy. The Industrial Relations Act, designed to deal with the spate of strikes which followed the incomes policy, only increased labour militancy.

As problems in the Middle East multiplied, moreover, the Arabs decided to attempt to force the hand of the West, firstly by limiting the supply of oil and then by jacking up the price. Part of the effect on the price of imports was to be offset by the more rapid development of Britain's own oil deposits in the North Sea (the new Middle Eastern oil prices actually made North Sea oil look much more commercially viable) but the short-term effect on the balance of payments was considerable. Since fuel prices were now likely to be the single most important factor in Britain's export drive, the government was even more determined to thwart the attempt by the mineworkers in 1974 to break their pay policy. Britain went on to a three-day week to conserve energy and to beat the miners' strike. Finally the Prime Minister, Edward Heath, called a general election, defining the strike as a straightforward challenge to the will of a democratically-elected government. What was on trial, however, was something by this time rather less durable than the parliamentary system, namely the decaying ethos of post-1945 economic policy. The miners' strike showed that the politics of confrontation were back, on a scale not known since the 1920s, and new political strategies were needed to deal with a new economic and social situation.

Another pointer to the depth of the change that was about to occur was the reorganisation of local government in 1974. Since the beginning of our period, it had been a partnership of central and local government which had administered Britain's peaceful revolution from individualism to collectivism. Local government had been the voice of regionalism to range against the harsher dictates of central state planning. Yet the more the state involved itself in social and economic planning, the more confined did the role of local government become. Though the period from the 1880s to the 1930s saw the state dependent on local expertise and bureaucracy, the period thereafter had seen a steady erosion of those responsibilities. The distinction between national and local services, necessary and possible in a diffused and decentralised society such as Britain still was to some extent between the wars, proved impossible to maintain in the era of Keynes and Beveridge. As the national community became more and more a single unit, it became more and more difficult for national politicians to maintain that there was a need for a strong tier of autonomous local government, particularly as much of the cost of financing local government switched inexorably from rates to government-provided rate support. The postwar legislation made inevitable a change in distribution of functions between central and local government, and between the larger units of local government and the smaller. At the same time, the growth in rate support inevitably led to demands that local government should be responsible to its paymasters as well as to the local electorate, particularly when governments found themselves stymied in their own electoral promises by the contrary promises of local councillors.

By the 1970s it was also becoming clear that many local authorities simply lacked the manpower and the resources to provide the level of service required in a technocratic age. Many of the Counties still reflected the social geography of pre-industrial Britain, and were too small or too large to be efficient. Neither did the boundaries between Counties and County Boroughs take much account of the new links between town and country which had been brought about by the better-off moving out of the towns to the rural hinterland, creating anomalies in the provision of services. At the same time, the many tiers of local government with their many different resonsiblities created real problems in planning, both for central government and for local authorities themselves. Unfortunately, these problems were not entirely solved by the restructuring of 1974. The new Non-Metropolitan Counties included many small towns within their boundaries, but the Metropolitan Counties rarely included their rural surroundings, an apparent concession to the electoral strength of the Tory shires. The two-tier system continued with the district councils within the new County administrations, moreover. The results were not to make rational planning any easier, nor to make for an obvious improvement in efficiency. At the same time, there was evidence that people felt alienated from the new, larger and more faceless bureaucracies of County Hall.

Of even greater consequence was to be the failure to contain local government spending. Through the 1960s and the 1970s rates support grants expanded, but it appeared that local authorities were using the grant to keep down rate increases rather than to provide expanded services. The large increases in rates in many areas in 1974, an inevitable consequence of inflation and government cutbacks as much as evidence of local government profligacy, unfortunately combined with the restructuring to give the impression that the whole system was deeply flawed. By the end of the 1970s, local government could be projected as the best evidence there was of the irresponsibility and the inefficiency of welfarism. For the New Right, too, the capture of some of the bigger Metropolitan Counties and the Greater London Council by the left of the Labour party confirmed local government as a major site of struggle between the forces of individualism and collectivism.

The new Labour government of 1974, with only just over 37 per cent of the vote, was Britain's first minority government since 1929. The shortest parliament for four hundred years was followed by another general election in which Labour, though winning a tiny overall majority, still won less than 40 per cent of the popular vote. The 'social contract' between the government and the unions failed to check inflation, which rose to 24 per cent by 1975. A wages policy followed, which was compulsory in effect, however much the government tried to fudge the issue. The government ploughed on through the second half of the 1970s, running to its bitter end in a 'winter of discontent' in 1978/9, which saw the Labour government confronted with a wave of strikes. Labour, indeed, only managed to survive so long in power by concluding a parliamentary pact with the Liberals, until they were finally forced to the polls when they were defeated on a vote of confidence in 1979.

Compared with the failure in the economy and in industrial relations, the domestic programme of the Labour governments of the 1970s seemed comparatively unimportant. The development of the National Investment Board, designed to give overall governmental direction to the development of investment, seemed to the Right to be only a covert method of nationalisation. With the continuing economic crisis, public ownership was to be further tarred with the brush of failure. Many of the newly nationalised industries were 'lame ducks', unlikely to survive without government money, and even the significant trend towards taking into public ownership concerns which could certainly make a profit was swamped by the dominating belief that 'socialism had made a mess of the economy'. After great soul-searching and internal divisions, Labour committed itself to a measure of devolution of power from London to Scotland and Wales, only to see the whole idea decisively rejected by the majority of Scots and Welsh. Labour had at least achieved a fair measure of national unity on the question of Britain's entry into the Common Market. Dubiously popular when Edward Heath had signed the

Treaty of Rome, and dubiously thorough though the renegotiation under Labour may have been, Wilson's refusal to make the Common Market a party matter secured a 2:1 majority in favour of staying in when the issue was put to the electorate in the form of a referendum.

In 1979, Labour went down to the biggest electoral swing since 1945. It was a suitably decisive end to forty-five years of British political history. This time the Conservatives believed that there could be no U-turns: there was, in the words of the new Prime Minister, Margaret Thatcher, 'no alternative' to strict monetary controls. There would have to be no loss of nerve, as there had been in the early 1970s. Fifteen years of lurching from one crisis to another had tested to destruction not just an economic idea but a theory of government.[23]

THE END OF THE POSTWAR ERA

Labour's naturally fissiparous tendencies had been disguised through most of the tumultuous years of the 1960s and 1970s by the undoubted political skills of Harold Wilson. The disguise, however, had never been a complete one and, once the pilot left the ship, the party underwent another of its periodic harrowing and very public self-analyses. But this time the damage was perhaps to be much more severe than the divisions which had characterised the 1930s or the 1950s. In the 1930s, the party could at least claim legitimately that it had not yet been given a full test in power with an overall majority. In the 1950s, Labour retained a large measure of credibility in the light of the work of the governments of 1945 to 1951; popular support remained relatively stable and relatively high, a mere couple of percentage points behind the Conservatives even in the direst periods of division between Bevanites and Gaitskellites. The divisions of the 1980s, however, took place against an already measurable medium-term decline in the party's popular support, the result of being in power for 12 of the 16 years before 1980, and of presiding over a demonstrably hopeless economic performance. In 1979, Labour dipped below 40 per cent of the popular vote for the first time since 1945 and, in 1983, they even dipped below 30 per cent, the worst result the party had suffered since 1918. Many, indeed, were forecasting the end of the Labour party altogether. The party's 1983 manifesto, committing Labour both to unilateral nuclear disarmament and to withdrawal from the Common Market, was dubbed by a dispirited Gerald Kaufman as 'the longest suicide note in history'.

The desertion of a small section of the right wing of the party to form the Social Democratic party, and then to ally with the Liberals, was a blow much more serious than mere numbers might suggest. In many ways, the desertion was as damaging to Labour in the 1980s as was the desertion of the Unionists from the Liberal party a century previously. Support for a third party made it difficult to defeat the Conservatives in those key marginals which were essential to an overall victory in a general election. In some ways, the desertion of the SDP left Labour worse off than the desertion of the Unionists had left the Liberals, for at least the Liberals were left ideologically less ambivalent when the whigs departed. The Labour Party of Michael Foot and Neil Kinnock, however, was still dominated by Keynesian retreads, and the Left – at the time of writing at least – has failed to win decisively the battle for an alternative economic strategy. The result was to leave the Labour Party in the 1980s perilously exposed as a factional grouping, wondering what went wrong and what hit it.

What had hit it was a right-wing strategy prepared, for the first time since the emergence of Labour as a significant political grouping, to take the party on. Before 1914, the Liberals had moved to the Left in an attempt to neutralise the Labour challenge. In spite of some right-wing support, during and just after the Great War for Lord Birkenhead's plea to 'resist socialism or perish', the Conservative party between the wars had largely maintained both a centrist approach and a concessionary attitude to the Left. When Labour's great moment came, in 1940 and the war years, the Conservatives offered no great resistance and quickly fell in behind the Labour bandwagon in the 1950s. There was a stutter of resistance at the beginning of the Heath government of 1970 to 1974, but it was only when Margaret Thatcher assumed the leadership of the Conservatives that the Right was prepared to launch a sustained and head-on assault on the gradualist encroachment of leftist theory into the 'common sense' of British politics. It was a strategy Labour had never encountered before and which clearly shook the party to its foundations. It was also a successful strategy because Labour had nailed its colours to the mast, gone for broke with Keynes in the 1940s, and signally failed to offer a new panacea when those ideas ran out of time. Though they had cut back on the astronomical sums being spent in maintaining defence, the decades of massive overspending in this area had taken their toll. The turning-point, however, was the late 1960s, when Labour failed to shape and to give a lead to new radical pressures, as the party had done in the 1940s. All the analyses of voting patterns seemed to show that the radical vote of the 1960s which, flawed though it was in so many of its ideas, might have provided a spearhead for a revival of the Left in the 1970s, had instead grown disenchanted with Labour. The new youth vote, meanwhile, was growing up in the gloomy Wilson–Heath years with a cynically contemptuous attitude towards centrism as a whole, which was to be shaped and directed by the New Right. It was beginning to look, by the mid-1980s, as though the only way out for the British Left was to forget nearly a century of evolutionary development, to go back to basics and to build a mass party from scratch.

Clearly, Keynes and Beveridge themselves should not take the blame. Beveridge had proposed a thoroughly humane, wholly unexceptionable list of priorities for conducting decent social relationships. What he had underestimated was the cost of providing what became the new basics. The cost of maintaining an acceptable standard of living among the poorer sections of society was to increase disproportionately as expectations naturally rose as a result of the improved standard of living of the majority. The right to good health was also to become very expensive to maintain, as improved health facilities kept more people alive longer and as ever more sophisticated medical technology made it possible to transform the very understanding of what was curable, and which sick people therefore had a human right to expect in terms of treatment. Keynes had never suggested that the budgetary techniques he recommended could maintain indefinitely a broken-backed economy; the notion of counter-cyclical investment was no excuse for politicians', industrialists' or unionists' unwillingness or inability to deal with problems of competitiveness. Keynes had also foreseen the possibility that the new techniques would only have a finite life. Pushed in argument once on the likely inflationary effects of his ideas, he had admitted that, 'in the long run' this was a fair criticism but, 'in the long run, we are all dead'. By the 1970s, Keynes was indeed dead, though the Keynesians were not.[24]

The fact was that Labour's 'respectable alternative' had produced its revolution but, fundamentally, nothing had changed. Everyone was richer but everyone expected to get richer still: inflation threatened those expectations. By the 1970s the 'locust years' of mass unemployment, so important in underpinning the political ideas of the post-1945 generation, had faded from the popular memory. The welfarism which had sprung from that faded popular memory had simply expunged from British political culture the old worries about the excesses of unrestrained private enterprise. Ironically, in the process, it had created the ideal basis for a new popular capitalism. And in the Falklands War the New Right was given the opportunity to re-focus the process of British history, just as Labour had been able to do in 1940. The international emergency provided the opportunity for a breathtakingly basic attack on the assumptions that had dominated consensually for so long. It had been the first sustained shift to the Right this century and there were signs, after three successive victories at the polls, that Thatcherism itself might have become consensual. Certainly, there was no evidence of a sustained alternative philosophy developing: on the contrary, both Labour and Alliance and their successors in the SLD themselves shifted to the Right in an attempt to maintain a place for themselves in the new political framework. Already it was becoming clear that the direction of British politics in the twenty-first century would be radically different from that of the twentieth century.

Conclusion

The general election of 1979 saw the beginning of the 'Thatcher revolution'. Ten years later, there was no clear sign that that revolution was finished, even if the government's popularity might have been on the wane. In fact, there is clearly a long way to go if Thatcherism is really to reverse the process that has taken almost one hundred years to develop in Britain. Not even such a radical group of politicians would dare, as yet at least, attack openly the whole concept of the National Health Service. Kenneth Clark's reforms in medicine have allowed Labour some valuable propaganda, sowing doubts even among Conservatives about Mrs Thatcher's declaration that 'the health service is safe with us.' There are still some relics from the age of welfare politics which remain sacred. Certainly, however, the radical implications of Conservative rule through the 1980s should not be under-estimated. There have been fundamental reverses in economic and social policy which would have seemed politically impossible just twenty years ago. Winning three general elections in a row, and refusing to be turned from their fundamentalist approach, the Conservatives have producd a wholly different set of assumptions about the role of the state in the national life. In the 1960s, anyone would safely assume that a failing large industrial concern would be saved by government money, but by the late 1980s anyone would safely assume that it would not. Twenty years ago, electors could naturally assume that personal taxation would inevitably remain high to allow the state to perform its many duties in social engineering; now, people probably expect that taxation will remain relatively low, as the state 'frees the individual'. Asked what a fourth Thatcher government should do, Nicholas Ridley recently replied: 'Nothing. That is the proper role of government'. The comment is a useful measure to judge the changes in political attitudes in the 1980s.

Even on the political Left, many find these new basic assumptions no longer shocking. The British have already got used to the new political facts of life. What had seemed to be the inevitable course of British history suddenly seems old hat. U-turns were confidently predicted, particularly with the unpopularity of the first Thatcher government before the Falklands War, but they never happened. The Labour party, meanwhile, was paralysed by internal dissensions, by an inability to produce a credible alternative strategy, and by the apparently inevitable slippage in its vote. A solid phalanx of Tory seats in the South East and in the Midlands looked impervious through the 1980s. While in previous periods of the history of the Labour party in opposition this had been simply frustrating, it may be terminally damaging this time. No one has taken on the Labour party and attacked its basic philosophy of politics so straightforwardly before. The result is that the collectivist cause looks no longer like the progressive, radical philosophy it had seemed for nearly ninety years; it looks like something that was tried and which needed to be replaced. Labour has been forced to move to the right as a result. Though it is dangerous to predict the future on the basis of historical experience, it is difficult to believe that a return to Keynesianism, even the moderated form currently being put forward by the Labour party, would have any more success than it did in the 1960s.

If history cannot be used to predict the future of Thatcherism, it can at least explain how it happened. The very success of generations of welfare politics has broken down much of the dynamic of the 'them' and 'us' spirit which Labour exploited, and to which the Conservatives conceded for so long. All the preconditions of contemporary popular capitalism have their roots in the development of the Welfare State: the attack on the slums gave birth to a housing policy which eventually produced the property-owning democracy; the democratisation of education made every schoolchild a potential yuppie; large-scale nationalisation provided the opportunity for mass participation in share ownership when the industries were privatised; Social Security and the National

Health Service provided the decent basic standard of living and of health to contrast with the traditional assumption that capitalism produced poverty and misery.

Collectivism led not to socialism, then, as the Labour party (and, indeed, its opponents) had always assumed it would, and it would be a savage irony if the historic mission of the British socialist tradition proved to be only to provide the basis of a rejuvenated capitalism. Such a conclusion, however, was always conceivable, given the complicated process through which collectivism and state intervention operated in Britain from the late nineteenth century. It was the perceived potential for class conflict which governed the decision to begin the process of state intervention in the first place, and it was the relative success of state intervention which prevented class consciousness ever fully emerging as the be-all and end-all of British politics. The British working class was never given the opportunity to develop to full class consciousness, or to organise accordingly, because of the rapid and continuous process of adaptation which went on at the level of the state, and in which working-class leaders themselves became heavily involved. This hegemonic adaptation began as soon as the possibility of renewed class friction had reared its ugly head in the period of the Great Price Fall. The New Liberals led the way and, though stymied by the Irish issue, had at least held the Labour challenge at bay before 1914. Labour had consequently moved rapidly from the left to the centre, the Lib-Labism of the core of its membership demanding a more moderate approach than that offered by radical groups like the Social Democratic Federation.

This capture of Labour politics by the moderate-minded Labour Aristocrats effectively froze the development of working-class consciousness before it became an acute problem. In effect, what it offered was a working-class leadership of liberalism, a watchful and caring eye on capitalism, which appeared to make a fully-blown socialist alternative redundant. Such a notion was given persuasive theoretical form by the Fabians, with their commitment to the evolutionary path to socialism through the ballot box. It was given an added dimension of practicality, too, when the Liberal party collapsed in the Great War and Labour was given its opportunity. In the interwar period, the development of the Russian Revolution seemed to confirm all the worst fears about revolutionary socialism, while the development of fascism also suggested that overhasty commitments to change might provoke a devastating right-wing backlash.

By the beginning of the interwar period, Conservatism was also to see that there were dangers in simply resisting socialism, particularly socialism of the moderate kind peddled by such as Ramsay MacDonald and Philip Snowden. Baldwin's brand of pragmatic interventionism may have had none of the proselytising zeal for undermining socialism by concession that had characterised the New Liberals, but its effect was the same. The working class was divided by the regional effects of the Great Depression, as it had previously been divided between Labour Aristocrats and unskilled workers, and the General Strike only confirmed what was evident from a quick look at the parliamentary leaders of the Labour movement, that there was no sign even of a nascent revolutionary vanguard. But the General Strike was dangerous enough in its implications to confirm Baldwin's instinctive belief that concession was better than confrontation. Just as the minority union militants had unwittingly strengthened the hand of the moderate-minded TUC leaders in their dealings with government in the Great War, so the General Strike confirmed the belief of the mainstream moderate right that the Labour party should be accepted as the respectable voice of the working class. Labour's politics might be questionable, but they were certainly better than the communists, and they were an essential brake on militancy in an inherently dangerous economic and social context. Meanwhile, experiments in the development of social policy and economic rationalisation could offset some of the worst social consequences of a global, if temporary, failure of capitalism.

By the end of the interwar period, Britain had developed most of the practical basics of a Welfare State, though not the theory. Piecemeal additions to the social security framework laid out by the prewar Liberals had widened enormously the scope of state responsibilities in this area, while the first intrusions into the industrial structure had confirmed what the Great War had hinted, that in an emergency government had a duty to intervene for the benefit of society as a whole. Yet Baldwin's consensus was to prove flawed, just as the consensus that Lloyd George had tried to engineer was flawed, by the pressures on compromise produced by war. The commitment of the Conservatives to appeasement was to leave the party in 1940 in the hands of a man who was a great war leader but a political incompetent, creating a vaccuum in domestic philosophy into which Labour rushed to find waiting for them in government, as it were, the ideas of Keynes and then of Beveridge.

Thus armed, Labour used the opportunity of 'the People's War' to turn the evolution of state intervention from a pragmatic strategy, which it had largely been for Liberals and Conservatives, into a crusade. The creation of the Welfare State was Britain's revolution, as far as Labour was concerned. Yet still the problem of relative economic decline continued and the new techniques of budgetary manipulation proved incapable of dealing with problems in the balance of trade and with inflation. A set of policies designed to avoid social friction had themselves provoked bitter industrial unrest and political crisis by the late 1960s. 'Permissive' legislation, moreover, designed to protect women, blacks and gays as underprivileged individuals in a collectivist society, had neither succeeded in satisfying those groups nor in preventing a backlash of resentment from Britain's 'silent majority'. Below the surface of politics, an undertow of popular opinion constructed a conspiracy of militant trade unionists, black activists and ultra-Left councillors holding the majority to ransom with their constant demands for more protective legislation, and more tax- and rate-payers' money. It was this undertow which swept the New Right into power after the 'winter of discontent' in 1979. The general elections of 1979, 1983 and 1987 proved that a revolution is only a revolution as long as a majority accepts it. Revolution from the top does not necessarily lead to that sea-change in cultural values in the social formation that is necessary to make revolution permanent.

By the 1980s, indeed, Labour and Conservative consensual politicians of the postwar period had become the new 'Guilty Men'. Victorian values were back in fashion, and British capitalism was given the chance to exploit the relatively stable and frictionless social structure that three generations of politicians had engineered. State intervention was designed to avoid class friction, and it remains to be seen whether the new notions of popular capitalism will be able to do the same, or whether one last blast from the heirs of Adam Smith and David Ricardo will finally dispel the notion that Britain is an inherently stable country. Britain has been stable because politicians helped to make it so and, whatever failures may be laid at the doors of the people who have governed the country for the last hundred years, they at least deserve credit for that.

NOTES

1 The Crisis of Liberalism

1. See D. Fraser, *The Evolution of the Welfare State* (London, 1984).
2. See P. F. Clarke, *Liberals and Social Democrats* (Cambridge, 1978); *Lancashire and the New Liberalism* (Cambridge, 1971); S. Collini, *Liberalism and Sociology* (Cambridge, 1978); M. Freeden, *The New Liberalism: An Ideology of Social Reform* (London, 1978); H. V. Emy, *Liberals, Radicals and Socialist Politics* (Cambridge, 1973); I. Bradley, *The Optimists: Themes in Victorian Liberalism* (London, 1980).
3. S. Saul, *The Myth of the Great Depression* (London, 1969).
4. S. Payne, 'The Emergence of the Large Scale Company in Britain', *Economic History Review*, (1967); D. McLoskey, 'Did Victorian Britain Fail?', *Economic History Review*, (1970).
5. R. Malcolmson, *Popular Recreations in English Society* (Cambridge, 1973). See also, P. Johnson, *Saving and Spending: The Working Class Economy* (London, 1985); S. Meacham, *A Life Apart: The English Working Class, 1880–1914*, London (1977); D. C. Moore, *The Politics of Deference* (Brighton, 1976).
6. H. Cunningham, *Leisure in the Industrial Revolution* (London, 1980).
7. See G. Stedman Jones 'Working Class Culture and Working Class Politics', *Journal of Social History* (1974).
8. J. Camplin, *The Rise of the Plutocrats: Wealth and Power in Edwardian England* (London, 1978).
9. G. Crossick, *The Lower Middle Class in Britain* (London, 1980).
10. H. J. Dyos, *Victorian Suburb* (London, 1966); A. A. Jackson, *Semi-Detached London* (London, 1975); D. Thorne, *Suburbia* (London, 1972); A. Briggs, *Victorian Cities* (London, 1968).
11. Quoted in P. Thompson, *The Edwardians* (London, 1975), p. 11.
12. For the best work on the Labour Aristocracy, see R. Gray, *The Aristocracy of Labour in Britain* (London and Basingstoke, 1981); 'The Labour Aristocracy', *British Society for the Study of Labour History* (1980); *The Labour Aristocracy in Victorian Edinburgh* (London, 1986); E. J. Hobsbawm, 'The Labour Aristocracy Twenty Five Years On', *British Society for the Study of Labour History* (1980).

13. See P. Keating, *In Darkest England* (Glasgow, 1976).
14. B. Rowntree, *Poverty* (London, 1901).
15. J. Harris, *William Beveridge* (London, 1977).
16. A. Soffer, 'The Revolution in English Social Thought', *American Historical Review* (1970).
17. R. Shannon, *The Crisis of Imperialism* (London, 1974) p. 271.
18. P. Magnus, *Gladstone* (London, 1954).
19. See R.F. Foster, *Lord Randolph Churchill* (London, 1982); R. Rhodes James, *Lord Randolph Churchill* (London, 1959).
20. See M. Kinnear, *The British Voter* (New York, 1968).
21. H. Heyck, 'Home Rule, Radicalism and the Liberal Party, *Journal of British Studies* (1974); see also W.C. Lubenow, 'Irish Home Rule and the Social Basis of the Great Divide in the Liberal Party', *Historical Journal* (1985).
22. See M.E. Rose, *The Relief of Poverty, 1832–1914* (London, 1972).
23. See J. Lovell, *British Trade Unions 1875–1933* (London, 1972); H. Pelling, *A History of British Trade Unions* (Harmondsworth, 1981).
24. See P. Thompson, 'Liberals, Radicals and Labour in London', *Past and Present* (1964); *Socialists, Liberals and Labour: The Struggle for London* (London, 1967).
25. See E. Hobsbawm, *Labouring Men* (London, 1968).
26. H. Pelling, *Origins of the Labour Party* (London, 1965) and *Popular Politics and Society in Late Victorian Britain* (London, 1968); R. Moore, *The Emergence of the Labour Party* (London, 1978); P. Adelman, *The Rise of the Labour Party* (London, 1972); K. Burgess, *The Challenge of Labour* (London, 1980); J. Hinton, *Labour and Socialism* (Brighton, 1983); D. Howell, *A Lost Left* (Manchester, 1986); E.M. Hunt, *British Labour History, 1815–1914* (London, 1981); R. McKibbin, 'Why was there no Marxism in Britain?', *English Historical Review* (1984); K.O. Morgan, *Keir Hardie* (London, 1975); A. Wright (ed.) *British Socialism and Socialist Thought* (London, 1983).
27. R. Robinson and G. Gallagher, *Africa and the Victorians* (Basingstoke, 1981).
28. A.P. Thornton, *The Imperial Idea and its Enemies* (London, 1966). See also G.L. Bernstein, 'Sir Henry Campbell Bannerman and the Liberal Imperialists', *Journal of British Studies* (1983); R. Jay, *Joseph Chamberlain* (London, 1981); D. Judd, *Radical Joe* (London, 1977).
29. Thornton, *The Imperial Idea*, p. 86.
30. See J.M. Mackenzie (ed.) *Imperialism and Popular Culture* (Manchester, 1986).
31. R. Blake, *Bonar Law* (London, 1955).
32. See A. Russell, *Liberal Landslide: The General Election of 1906* (Newton Abbot, 1973); M. Bentley, *The Climax of Liberal Politics* (London, 1987).

33. C. Cook, *A Short History of the Liberal Party* (London and Basingstoke, 1977).

34. Quoted in Fraser, *Evolution of the Welfare State*, p. 129.

35. See P. Thane, *Origins of British Social Policy* (London, 1978); M. A. Crowther, 'Family and State Responsibility in Britain', *Historical Journal* (1982); H. Pelling, 'State Intervention and Social Legislation before 1914', *Historical Journal* (1967); R. Birch, *The Shaping of the Welfare State* (London, 1976); B. K. Murray, *The People's Budget* (London, 1980).

36. R. Davidson, *Whitehall and the Labour Problem in Late Victorian and Edwardian England* (London, 1984).

37. R. McKibbin, *The Evolution of the Labour Party* (London, 1974); P. F. Clarke, 'The Electoral Positions of the Liberal and Labour Parties', *English Historical Review* (1975); D. Powell, 'The New Liberalism and the Rise of Labour', *Historical Journal* (1986); G. L. Bernstein, 'Liberalism and the Progressive Alliance', *Historical Journal* (1983); R. Murphy, 'Faction and the Home Rule Crisis', *History* (1986).

2 The Impact of the Great War

1. A. Marwick, *War and Social Change in the Twentieth Century* (London, 1974).

2. A. Marwick, *The Deluge* (Harmondsworth, 1965); A. S. Milward, *The Economic Effects of the World Wars on Britain* (London, 1970).

3. See K. Burt (ed.) *War and the State: The Transformation of British Government, 1914–1919* (London, 1982).

4. A. Marwick, *Britain in the Century of Total War* (London, 1968).

5. P. E. Dewey, 'Military Recruiting and the British Labour Force', *Historical Journal* (1984).

6. See T. Wilson, *Britain and the Great War* (Oxford, 1986); J. M. Winter, *The Great War and the British People* (London, 1987).

7. See I. F. Becket and K. Simpson (eds), *A Nation in Arms* (Manchester, 1985).

8. See the archive of the Great War letters held by the Imperial War Museum, some of which have been published in M. Moynihan (ed.) *Letters from Armageddon* (Newton Abbot, 1973).

9. See, for example, H. Macmillan, *Winds of Change* (London, 1966).

10. A. John, *By the Sweat of their Brow* (London, 1978).

11. J. Liddington, 'Women Cotton Workers and the Suffrage Campaign', in S. Burman (ed.) *Fit Work for Women* (London, 1979).

12. P. Branca, *Silent Sisterhood* (London, 1975).

13. A. Rosen, *Rise Up, Women!* (London, 1974); C. Rover, *Women's Suffrage and Party Politics* (London, 1967); M. Pugh, *Electoral Reform in Peace and War* (London, 1978); S. S. Holton, *Feminism and Democracy* (Cambridge, 1986); D. Morgan, *Suffragists and Liberals* (Oxford, 1975); S. Pankhurst, *The Suffragette Movement* (London, 1977); B. Harrison, *Separate Spheres: The Opposition to Women's Votes in Britain* (London, 1978).

14. A. Marwick, *Women at War* (London, 1977).

15. G. Braybon, *Women Workers in the First World War* (London, 1981); L. Middleton, *Women in the Labour Movement* (London, 1978).

16. M. Stopes, *Married Love* (London, 1918); C. Rover, *Love, Morals and the Feminists* (London, 1970).

17. See the archive of interviews with women workers in the Great War held by the Imperial War Museum.

18. See *Oral History*, Special Issue on Women (1977).

19. H. Pelling, *A History of British Trade Unionism* (Harmondsworth, 1975).

20. J. Hinton, *The First Shop Stewards Movement* (London, 1973); H. Pelling, *A History of British Trade Unionism* (Harmondsworth, 1981).

21. H. Clegg, *A History of British Trade Unionism since 1889, vol. 11, 1911–1933* (Oxford, 1985).

22. B. Waites, *A Class Society at War* (Leamington Spa, 1987).

23. B. Waites, 'The Government of the Home Front and the "Moral Economy" of the Working Class', in P. Liddle (ed.) *Home Fires and Foreign Fields* (London, 1985); B. Waites, 'The Effects of the First World War on Class and Status in Britain, *Journal of Contemporary History* (1976); A. Marwick, 'The Impact of the Great War on British Society', *Journal of Contemporary History* (1968).

24. J. Winter, *Socialism and the Challenge of War* (London, 1974); S. White, *Britain and the Bolshevik Revolution* (London, 1979).

25. R. McKibbin, *The Evolution of the Labour Party* (London, 1974).

26. D. Marquand, *Ramsay MacDonald* (London, 1977).

27. Winter, *Socialism and the Challenge of War*.

28. G. D. H. Cole, *A History of the Labour Party* (London, 1948).

29. R. McKibbin, *Evolution of the Labour Party* (London, 1977).

30. M. Bentley, *The Climax of Liberal Politics* (London, 1987); M. Freeden, *Liberalism Divided* (Oxford, 1986); J. Grigg, 'Liberals on Trial', in A. Sked and C. Cook (eds) *Crisis and Controversy* (London, 1976); J. Grigg *Lloyd George: From Peace to War* (London, 1985); C. Hazelhurst, *Politicians at War* (London, 1971); S. Koss, 'The Destruction of Britain's Last Liberal Government', *Journal of Modern History* (1968); K.O. Morgan, *Consensus and Disunity: The Lloyd George Government* (Oxford, 1979); P. Rowland, *Lloyd George* (London, 1975); J. Turner, *Lloyd George's Secretariat* (Cambridge, 1980).

31. T. Wilson, *The Myriad Faces of War* (Oxford, 1986).

32. R. Douglas, 'The Background to the Coupon Election', *English Historical Review* (1971); R. J. Scally, *Origins of the Lloyd George Coalition* (Princeton, 1975); T. Wilson, *The Downfall of the Liberal Party* (London, 1966); C. Wrigley, *David Lloyd George and the Labour Movement* (Brighton, 1977).

33. M. Kinnear, *The Fall of Lloyd George* (London, 1973).

3 The Impact of the Depression

1.   P. Fearon, *The Origins and Nature of the Great Slump, 1919–1932* (London, 1979); A. Booth and M. Pack, *Employment, Capital and Economic Policy in Great Britain, 1918–1939* (Oxford, 1985); J. K. Galbraith, *The Great Crash, 1929* (Harmondsworth, 1969); A. S. Milward, *The Economic Effects of the World Wars on Britain* (London, 1970).

2.   K. G. P. Matthews, 'Was Sterling Overvalued in 1925?', *Economic History Review* (1986); W. Garside and T. Hatton, 'Keynesian Policy and British Unemployment in the 1930s', *Economic History Review* (1985).

3.   M. Stewart, *Keynes and After* (Harmondsworth, 1983); D. Moggridge, *Keynes* (London, 1977).

4.   D. Aldcroft and H. W. Richardson, *The British Economy, 1870–1939* (London, 1969).

5.   D. Hancock, 'The Reduction of Unemployment as a Problem of Government Policy', *Economic History Review* (1962/3); R. C. Self, *The Tories and Tariffs* (London, 1986).

6.   A. Booth, 'Britain in the 1930s: A Managed Economy?', *Economic History Review* (1970).

7.   G. C. Peden, *British Rearmament and the Treasury* (Edinburgh, 1979); R. P. Shay, *British Rearmament in the Thirties* (Princeton, 1977).

8.   D. H. Aldcroft, *The British Economy*, vol. 1, *1920–1951* (Brighton, 1986).

9.   S. Glynn and J. Oxborrow, *Interwar Britain: A Social and Economic History* (London, 1976); C. Cook and J. Stevenson, *The Slump: Society and Politics During the Depression* (London, 1978); C. L. Mowat, *Britain between the Wars* (London, 1968).

10. B. Disraeli, *Sybil* (Harmondsworth, 1980).

11. K. Hancock, 'The Reduction of Unemployment', *Economic History Review* (1962/3).

12. Pilgrim Trust, *Men Without Work* (Cambridge, 1938).

13. E. Wilkinson, *The Town that was Murdered* (London, 1934).

14. R. Hayburn, 'The National Unemployed Workers' Movement', *International Review of Social History* (1983).

15. C. Webster, 'Health, Welfare and Unemployment during the Depression', *Past and Present* (1985).

16. N. F. R. Crafts, 'Long-Term Unemployment in Britain in the 1930s', *Economic History Review* (1987).

17. B. Gilbert, *British Social Policy, 1914–1939* (London, 1973).

18. S.B. Rowntree, *Progress and Poverty* (London, 1941).

19. Rowntree, p. 56.

20. *Oral History*, Special Issue on Women *(1977)*.

21. M. Swenarton, *Homes Fit for Heroes* (London, 1981); A. S. Wohl, *The Eternal Slum* (London, 1977).

22. H. Clegg, *A History of British Trade Unions since 1889*, vol. 11, *1911–1933* (Oxford, 1985).

23. G. A. Phillips, 'The Triple Alliance in 1914', *Economic History Review* (1971).

24. See W. Ashworth and M. Pegg, *The History of the British Coal Industry*, vol. 5 (Oxford, 1986).

25. See K. Middlemas and J. Barnes, *Baldwin: A Biography* (London, 1969).

26. P. Renshaw, *The General Strike* (London, 1975).

27. A. Bullock, *The Life and Times of Ernest Bevin*, vol. 1 (London, 1960); N. Branson, *Britain in the 1920s* (London, 1975); A. Clinton, *The Trade Union Rank and File* (Manchester, 1977); J. Lovell, *British Trade Unions* (London, 1979).

28. R. Challinor, *The Origins of British Bolshevism* (London, 1977); S. MacIntyre, *Little Moscows: Communism and Working Class Militancy* (London, 1980); H. Pelling, *History of the British Communist Party* (London, 1975).

29. M. Cowling, *The Impact of Labour, 1920–1924* (Cambridge, 1973); K. Burgess, *The Challenge of Labour: Shaping British Society* (London, 1980); C. Cook, *The Age of Alignment* (London, 1975).

30. C. Cross, *The Fascists in Britain* (London, 1961); K. Lunn and C. Thurlow, *British Fascism* (London, 1980).

31. C. Bell, *Times Reports 1931* (London, 1975); R. Skidelsky, *Politicans and the Slump* (London, 1967).

32. R. Barker, 'Political Myth: Ramsay MacDonald and the Labour Party', *History* (1975); R. Bassett, *1931: Political Crisis* (London, 1958); H. Berkeley, *The Myth that Will Not Die: The Formation of the National Government, 1931* (London, 1978); D. Marquand, *Ramsay MacDonald* (London, 1977); D. Butler (ed.) *Coalitions in British Politics* (London, 1978); D. H. Close, 'The Re-alignemnt of the Electorate in 1931', *History* (1982).

33. B. Pimlott, *Labour and the Left in the 1930s* (Cambridge, 1977); R. Dare, 'Intellectuals and British Labour after 1931', *Historical Journal* (1983); R. Eatwell and R. Wright, 'Labour and the Lessons of 1931', *History* (1978).

34. P. Adelman, *British Politics in the 1930s and 1940s* (Cambridge, 1987); N. Branson and M. Heinemann, *Britain in the 1930s* (St. Albans, 1973).

35. *Gaumont British*, 'Munich' (October 1983); see also N. Pronay, 'British Newsreels in the 1930s', *History* (1971 and 1972); J. Curran *et al.* (eds) *Mass Communications and Society* (Penguin, Harmondsworth, 1979); P. Miles and M. Smith, *Cinema, Literature and Society: Elite and Mass Culture in Britain between the Wars* (London, 1987).

36. D. Southgate, *The Conservative Leadership* (London, 1974); R. Jenkins, *Baldwin* (London, 1987); M. Pugh, *The Tories and the People* (Oxford, 1985); J. Ramsden, *The Conservative Party: The Age of Balfour and Baldwin* (London, 1978); G. C. Webber, *The Ideology of the British Right* (London, 1986).

37. M. Smith, *British Air Strategy between the Wars* (Oxford, 1984).

38. W. Rock, *British Appeasement in the Thirties* (London, 1972); R. Douglas, *In the Year of Munich* (London, 1977); G. C. Peden, 'The Economic Background of Appeasement', *History* (1984.

39. R. Rhodes James, *Churchill: A Study in Failure, 1900–1939* (London 1970); M. Cowling, *The Impact of Hitler* (Cambridge, 1975); R. Douglas, *The Advent of War* (Basingstoke, 1978).

40. A. Marwick, 'Middle Opinion in the 1930s', *English Historical Review* (1964) pp. 285–98.

4 The Impact of the Second World War

1. 'Cato', *Guilty Men* (London, 1940).

2. Mass Observation, *War Begins at Home* (London, 1940).

3. See P. Miles and M. Smith, *Cinema, Literature and Society: Elite and Mass Culture in Britain Between the Wars* (London, 1987).

4. *The Times*, London, 25 October 1940.

5. J. B. Priestley, *Postscripts* (London, 1940).

6. G. Orwell, 'Poetry and the Microphone', *Collected Essays, Journals and Letters*, vol. 2 (Harmondsworth, 1968).

7. T. H. O'Brien, *Civil Defence* (London, 1950).

8. R. Titmuss, *Problems of Social Policy* (London, 1950).

9. A. Calder, *The People's War: Britain, 1939–1945* (London, 1969); T. Harrisson, *Living through the Blitz* (London, 1976).

10. R. Inman, *Labour in the Munitions Industries* (London, 1957).

11. J. Macnicol, 'The Effect of Evacuation' in H. A. L. Smith (ed.) *War and Social Change* (Manchester, 1986).

12. N. Longmate, *The GIs* (London, 1975).

13. J. Ellis, *The Sharp End of War (London, 1982)*.

14. Mass Observation, *The Journey Home* (London, 1945); G. Braybon and P. Summerfield, *Out of the Cage: Women's Experiences in Two World Wars*

(London, 1987); M. R. Higgonet, *Behind the Lines: Gender in the Two World Wars* (New Haven, 1987); P. Summerfield, *Women Workers in the Second World War* (London, 1984).

15.   P. Addison, *The Road to 1945* (London, 1975); P. Adelman, *British Politics in the 1930s and 1940s* (Cambridge, 1987); R. Douglas, *New Alliances* (London, 1982).

16.   E. Bevin, *The Job to be Done* (London, 1942).

17.   M. Gowing. 'The Organisation of Manpower during the Second World War', *Journal of Contemporary History* (1976); Mass Observation, *War Factory,* (London, 1945).

18.   A. Bullock, *The Life and Times of Ernest Bevin*, vol. 2 (London, 1967).

19.   T. Carpenter, 'Corporatism in Britain, 1930–1945', *Journal of Contemporary History* (1976). 20. Herbert Morrisson, *The State and Industry* (London, 1944); A. Horne, *Harold Macmillan* (London, 1989) 21. J. M. Keynes, *How to Pay for the War* (London, 1940). 22. Cmd 6527, *Employment Policy* (London, 1944); see also A. Booth, 'Economic advice at the Centre of British government, 1939–1941', *Historical Journal* (1986); M. Stewart, *Keynes and After* (Harmondsworth, 1983).

23.   Cmd 6404, *Social Insurance and Allied Services* (London, 1942).

24.   Calder, p. 526; see also T. Cutler *et al.*, *Keynes, Beveridge and Beyond* (London, 1986); K. Jefferys, 'British Politics and Social Policy during the Second World War', *Historical Journal* (1987); H. L. Smith, *War and Social Change: British Society in the Second World War* (Manchester, 1986).

25.   See J. Harris, *William Beveridge* (Oxford, 1977); D. E. Ashford, *The Emergence of the Welfare State* (Oxford, 1986); R.C. Birch, *The Shaping of the Welfare State* (London, 1976); J. Macnicol, *The Movement for Family Allowances* (London, 1980).

26.   *Social Insurance*, p. 4.

27.   K. Jeffereys, 'R. A. Butler, the Board of Education and the 1944 Education Act', *History* (1984).

28.   M. Gilbert, *Winston Churchill*, vols. 6 and 7 (London, 1984, 1986); R. Rhodes James, *Churchill: A Study in Failure, 1900–1939* (London, 1970); D. Kavanagh, *Crisis, Charisma and the British Political Leadership* (London, 1974); R. Thompson, *Generalissimo Churchill* (London, 1973).

29.   J. Colville, *The Fringes of Power* (London, 1985). 30. M. E. Howard, *The Mediterranean Strategy in World War* (London, 1968); M. Kitchen, 'Winston Churchill and the Soviet Union during the Second World War', *Historical Journal* (1987).

5   The Postwar Consensus and its Demise

1.   See G. McCulloch, 'Labour, the Left and the British General Election of 1945', *Journal of British Studies* (1985); T. Burridge, *Clement Attlee*

230 NOTES

(London, 1985); R. Butterworth, *The British Labour Government, 1945–1951* (Buckland, 1970); K. Harris, *Attlee* (London, 1982); H. Pelling, *The Labour Governments, 1945–1951* (London, 1984); J. Schneer, 'Hopes Shattered or Deferred . . . ', *Journal of Modern History* (1984).

2. D. H. Aldcroft, *The British Economy*, vol. 1 (Brighton, 1986); A. Cairncross, *Years of Recovery: British Economic Policy, 1945–1951* (London, 1985); N. Rollings, 'British Budgetary Policy, 1945–54', *Economic History Review* (1988).

3. R. Eatwell, *The 1945–1951 Labour Governments* (London, 1979); A. S. Milward, *The Economic Effects of the World Wars on Britain* (London, 1970).

4. A. Sked and C. Cook, *Postwar Britain* (Harmonsdworth, 1984) p. 28.

5. E. Durbin, *New Jerusalems: The Labour Party and the Economics of Democratic Socialism* (London, 1985); W. Ashworth and M. Pegg, *The History of the British Coal Industry*, vol. 5 (Oxford, 1986).

6. R. Kelf Cohen, *Twenty Years of Nationalisation* (London, 1969); T. Carpenter, 'Corporatism in Britain, 1930–1945', *Journal of Contemporary History* (1976).

7. M. Foot, *Aneurin Bevan*, vol. 2 (London, 1973); J. Campbell, 'Demythologising Nye Bevan', *History Today* (1987).

8. K. O. Morgan, *Labour in Power* (Oxford, 1984); D. E. Ashford, *The Emergence of the Welfare State* (Oxford, 1986); C. J. Bartlett, *History of Postwar Britain* (Oxford, 1978); S. Haseler, *The Gaitskellites* (London, 1969).

9. Foot, *Bevan*, 2.

10. S. Pollard, *The Wasting of the British Economy* (London, 1984); A. Gamble and A. Walkland, *The British Party System and Economic Planning* (Oxford, 1984); P. Hare, *Planning the British Economy* (London, 1985).

11. F. T. Blackaby, *British Economic Management, 1960–1974* (Cambridge, 1979); F. Boyd, *British Politics in Transition* (London, 1964); R. Rhodes James, *Ambitions and Realities, British Politics, 1964–70* (London, 1972).

12. D. C. Watt, *Succeeding John Bull: America in Britain's Place* (Cambridge, 1984); R. Lamb, *The Failure of the Eden Government* (London, 1987).

13. J. Bayliss, *Anglo-American Defence Relations* (London, 1984).

14. See J. W. Young, 'Churchill's "No" to Europe', *Historical Journal* (1985).

15. P. Foot, *Immigration and Race in British Politics* (London, 1965).

16. A. Sked and C. Cook, *Postwar Britain* (Harmondsworth, 1979); S. Beer, *Modern British Politics* (London, 1965); C. Cook and J. Ramsden, *Trends in British Government since 1945* (London, 1978); P. Hennessy and A. Seldon, *Ruling Performance: British Governments from Attlee to Thatcher* (Oxford, 1987).

17.   R. Hoggart, *The Uses of Literacy* (London, 1957).
18.   M. J. Daunton, *Property Owning Democracy* (London, 1987); A. T. Marwick, *British Society since 1945* (Harmondsworth, 1982).
19.   D. Hebdige, *Subculture: The Meaning of Style* (Methuen, 1979).
20.   J. Weeks, *Sex, Politics and Society* (London, 1981); *Coming Out* (London, 1977); J. Lewis, *Women in England* (Brighton, 1986).
21.   See R. Blackburn and A. Cockburn, *Student Power* (Harmondsworth, 1969).
22.   B. Elbaum and B. Lagowick, *The Decline of the British Economy* (Oxford, 1986); C. Feinstein, *The Managed Economy* (London, 1983).
23.   S. Brittan, *Steering the Economy* (Harmondsworth, 1971); M. Holmes, *The Labour Government, 1974–1979* (London, 1985).
24.   M. Stewart, *Keynes and Afen* (Harmondsworth, 1973); T. Cutler et al., *Keynes, Beveridge and Beyond* (London, 1986); P. Jenkins, *Mrs. Thatcher's Revolution: The Ending of the Socialist Era* (London, 1987); D. Kavanagh, *Thatcherism and British Politics* (Oxford, 1987).

BIBLIOGRAPHY

Addison, P., *The Road to 1945* (London, Cape, 1975).
Adelman, P., *Gladstone, Disraeli and Later Victorian Politics* (London, Longman, 1970).
——, *The Rise of the Labour Party* (London, Longman, 1972).
——, *British Politics in the 1930s and 1940s* (Cambridge University Press, 1987).
Aldcroft, D., and Richardson D. H., *The British Economy, 1870–1939* (London, Macmillan, 1969).
——, (ed.) *The Development of British Industry and Foreign Competition* (London, Allen & Unwin, 1968).
Aldcroft, D. H., *The British Economy*, vol. 1, *1920–1951* (Brighton, Harvester, 1986).
Ashford, D. E., *The Emergence of the Welfare State* (Oxford, Blackwell, 1986).
Ashworth, W. and Pegg, M., *The History of the British Coal Industry*, vol. 5 (Oxford, Clarendon Press, 1986).
Ausubel, H., *The Late Victorians* (Toronto and London, Van Nostrand, 1955).
Balfour, M., *Britain and Joseph Chamberlain* (London, Allen & Unwin, 1985).
Ball, A. R., *British Political Parties* (London, Macmillan, 1981).
Banks, O., *Becoming a Feminist* (Brighton, Wheatsheaf, 1986).
Barker, R., 'Political Myth: Ramsay MacDonald and the Labour Party', *History* (1975).
——, *Political Ideas in Modern Britain* (London, Methuen, 1978).
Barker, T., and Drake, M., *Population and Society in Britain, 1850–90* (London, Batsford, 1982).
Bartlett, C. J., *A History of Post-War Britain* (Bodley Head, Oxford, 1978).
Bassett, R., *1931 Political Crisis* (London, Macmillan, 1958).
Baylis, J., *Anglo-American Defence Relations* (London, Macmillan, 1981).
Bean, J. M. W. (ed.) *The Political Culture of Modern Britain* (London, Hamish Hamilton, 1987).
Beaverbrook, Lord, *Men and Power, 1917–1918* (London, Heinemann, 1956).
——, *The Decline and Fall of Lloyd George* (London, Collins, 1966).
Bebbington, D. W., *The Nonconformist Conscience: Chapel and Politics* (London, Allen & Unwin, 1981).
Beckett, I. F. W., and Simpson, K., *A Nation in Arms* (Manchester, Manchester University Press, 1985).
Bell, C., *Times Reports 1931* (London, Times Publications , 1975).

Bentley, M., *The Climax of Liberal Politics* (London, Edward Arnold, 1987).

Berkeley, H., *The Myth that Will Not Die* (London, Croom Helm, 1978).

Bernstein, G. L., 'Liberalism and the Progressive Alliance, 1910–1914', *Historical Journal* (1983).

——, 'Sir Henry Campbell Bannerman and the Liberal Imperialists', *Journal of British Studies* (1983).

Beveridge, W., *Social Insurance and Allied Services* (London, HMSO, 1942).

Bevin, E., *The Job to be Done* (London, Heinemann, 1942).

Birch, R. C., *The Shaping of the Welfare State* (London, Longman, 1976).

Blackaby, F. T., *British Economic Management, 1960–1974* (Cambridge University Press, 1979).

Blackburn, R. and Cockburn, A. (eds) *Student Power* (Harmondsworth, Penguin, 1969).

Blake, R., *The Unknown Prime Minister: Andrew Bonar Law* (London, Eyre & Spottiswoode, 1955).

——, *Disraeli* (Oxford University Press, 1966).

——, *The Conservative Party from Peel to Churchill* (London, Eyre & Spottiswoode, 1970).

—— and Cecil, H.(eds) *Salisbury* (London, Macmillan, 1987).

Bond, B., *British Military Policy Between the Wars* (Oxford University Press, 1980).

Booth, A. and Pack, M., *Employment, Capital and Economic Policy in Great Britain (Oxford, Blackwell, 1985)*.

——, 'Economic Advice at the Centre of British Government, 1939–1941', *Historical Journal* (1986).

——, 'Britain in the 1930s: A Managed Economy?', *Economic History Review* (1987).

Booth, W., *In Darkest England, and The Way Out* (London, Salvation Army, 1890).

Boyd, F., *British Politics in Transition* (London and Dunmow, Pall Mall, 1964).

Bradley, I., *The Optimists: Themes and Personalities in Victorian Liberalism*(London, Faber , 1980).

Branson, N., *Britain in the 1920s* (London, Weidenfeld and Nicolson,1975).

—— and Heinemann, M., *Britain in the 1930s* (St Albans, Panther, 1973).

Braybon, G., *Women Workers in the First World War* (London, Croom Helm, 1981).

—— and Summerfield, P., *Out of the Cage: Women's Experiences in Two World Wars* (London, Pandora, 1987).

Briggs, A., *Victorian Cities* (Harmondsworth, Penguin, 1968).

Brittan, S., *Steering the Economy: The Role of the Treasury* (Harmondsworth, Pelican, 1971).

Broadberry, S., *The British Economy between the Wars*(Oxford, Blackwell, 1986).

Browne, H., *Joseph Chamberlain – Radicalism and Empire* (London, Longman, 1974).

Bruce, M., *The Coming of the Welfare State* (London, Batsford, 1965).

——, *The Rise of the Welfare State* (London, Weidenfeld and Nicolson, 1973).

Bullock, A., *The Life and Times of Ernest Bevin*, 3 vols (London, Heinemann, 1960–84).

Burgess, K., *The Challenge of Labour: Shaping British Society* (London, Croom Helm, 1980).

Burk, K. (ed.), *War and the State: The Transformation of British Government* (London, Allen & Unwin, 1982).

Burridge, T., *British Labour and Hitler's War* (London, Deutsch, 1976).

——, *Clement Attlee: A Political Biography* (London, Cape, 1985).

Butler, D. (ed.) *Coalitions in British Politics* (London, Macmillan, 1978).

—— and Butler, G. , *British Political Facts, 1900–1985* (London, Macmillan, 6th edn, 1986).

Butler, Lord, *The Conservatives: A History* (London, Allen & Unwin, 1977).

Butterworth, R., *The British Labour Government, 1945–1951* (London, Heinemann, 1970).

Cairncross, A., *Years of Recovery: British Economic Policy, 1945–51* (London, Methuen, 1985).

Calder, A., *The People's War* (London, Cape, 1969).

Campbell, J., 'Demythologising Nye Bevan', *History Today*, 37/4 (1987).

Camplin, J., *The Rise of the Plutocrats* (London, Constable, 1978).

Carpenter, L., *G.D.H. Cole: An Intellectual Biography* (Cambridge University Press, 1973).

Carpenter, T., 'Corporatism in Britain, 1930–1945', *Journal of Contemporary History* (1976).

Cato, *Guilty Men* (London, Gollancz, 1940).

Challinor, R., *Origins of British Bolshevism* (London, Croom Helm, 1977).

Clarke, P. F., *Lancashire and the New Liberalism* (Cambridge University Press, 1971).

——, 'Review of McKibbin's "Evolution of the Labour Party"', *English Historical Review* (1976).

——, *Liberals and Social Democrats* (Cambridge University Press, 1978).

——, 'The Electoral Position of the Liberal and Labour Parties', *English Historical Review* (1975).

Clegg, H., *History of British Trade Unionism*, vol. 2 (Oxford University Press, 1985).

Clinton, A., *The Trade Union Rank and File: Trades Councils* (Manchester University Press, 1977).

Close, D. H., 'Conservatives and Coalition after the War', *Journal of Modern History* (1973).

———, 'The Realignment of the British Electorate in 1931', *History* (1982).

Cole, G. D. H., *History of the Labour Party* (London, Routledge, 1948).

Collini, S., *Liberalism and Sociology: L.T. Hobhouse and Political Argument* (Cambridge University Press, 1978).

Colville, J., *The Fringes of Power* (London, Norton, 1985).

Constantine, S., *Social Conditions in Britain between the Wars* (London, Methuen, 1983).

Cook, C., *A Short History of the Liberal Party* (London & Basingstoke, Macmillan, 1977).

—— and Ramsden, J., *Trends in British Politics since 1945* (London, Macmillan, 1978).

—— and Stevenson, J., *The Slump: Society and Politics during the Depression* (London, Cape, 1978).

———, *Longman's Atlas of Modern British History* (London, Longman, 1978).

———, *The Age of Alignment: Electoral Politics, 1922–31* (London, Macmillan, 1975).

Cowling, M., *The Impact of Labour: 1920–1924* (Cambridge University Press, 1971).

———, *The Impact of Hitler* (Cambridge University Press, 1975).

Crafts, N. F. R., 'Long-term Unemployment in Britain in the 1930s', *Economic History Review* (1987).

Cronin, J. E., *Labour and Society in Britain, 1918–79* (London, Batsford, 1984).

Cross, C. , *The Fascists in Britain* (London, Barrie & Rockcliffe, 1961).

———, *The Liberals in Power, 1905–1914* (London, Barrie and Rockcliffe, 1963).

Cross, M. and Mallen, D., *Local Government and Politics* (London, Longman, 1978).

Crossick, G. *The Lower Middle Class in Britain* (London, Croom Helm, 1977).

———, 'Classes and Masses in Victorian England', *History Today*, 37/3 (1987).

Crow, D., *The Edwardian Woman* (London, Allen & Unwin, 1978).

Crowther, M.A., 'Family and State Responsibility in Britain', *Historical Journal* (1982).

Curran, J. *et al.* (eds) *Mass Communications and Society* (Harmondsworth, Penguin, 1979).

Cutler, T., *et al.*, *Keynes, Beveridge and Beyond* (London, Routledge, 1986).

Dangerfield, G. *The Strange Death of Liberal England* (London, Constable, 1936).

Dare, R., 'Intellectuals and British Labour after 1931', *Historical Journal* (1983).

Darwin, J. G., 'The Chanak Crisis and the British Cabinet', *History* (1980).

———, 'The Fear of Falling: British Politics and Imperial Decline', *Transactions of the Royal Historical Society* (1986).

Daunton, M. J., *A Property-Owning Democracy* (London, Faber, 1987).

Davidson, R., *Whitehall and the Labour Problem* (London, Croom Helm, 1984).

Desmarais, R. H., 'The Government's Strike-Breaking Organisation', *Journal of Contemporary History* (1970).

Dewey, P. E., 'Military Recruiting and the British Labour Force', *Historical Journal* (1984).

Dilks, D. (ed.) *Retreat from Power*, vol. 1, *1906–1939*; vol. 2, *After 1939* (London, Macmillan, 1981).

Disraeli, B., *Sybil* (Harmondsworth, Penguin, 1980).

Douglas, R., 'Background to the Coupon Election . . . ', *English Historical Review* (1971).

——, *In the Year of Munich* (London, Macmillan, 1977).

——, *The Advent of War* (London, Macmillan, 1978).

——, *New Alliances* (London, Macmillan, 1982).

Durbin, E., *New Jerusalems: the Labour Party and Economics* (London, Routledge, 1985).

Dyhouse, C., *Girls Growing Up in Late Victorian and Edwardian England* (London, Routledge, 1981).

Dyos, H. J., *Victorian Suburb* (Leicester University Press, 1966).

Eatwell, R., *The 1945–51 Labour Government* (London, Batsford, 1979).

Eatwell, R. and Wright, A., 'Labour and the Lessons of 1931', *History* (1978).

Edwards, J., *The British Government and the Spanish Civil War* (London, Macmillan, 1979).

Elbaum, B. and Lagowick, D., *The Decline of the British Economy* (Oxford, Clarendon Press, 1986).

Eldridge, C. C. (ed.) *Late Victorian Imperialism* (London, Macmillan, 1978).

Eldridge, C. C. (ed.) *British Imperialism in the Nineteenth Century* (London, Macmillan, 1984).

Ellis, J., *The Sharp End of War* (London, Corgi, 1982).

Emy, H., *Liberals, Radicals and Socialist Politics, 1892–19* (Cambridge University Press, 1973).

Ensor, R. C. K., 'Some Political and Economic Inter-Reactions in Late Victorian Britain', *Transactions of the Royal Historical Society* (1949).

Fearon, P., *The Origins and Nature of the Great Slump, 1929–32* (London, Macmillan, 1979).

Feinstein, C., *The Managed Economy* (London, Heinemann, 1983).

Fleay, C. and Saunders, M., 'Labour Party Policy and the Spanish Civil War', *Historical Journal* (1985).

Foot, M., *Aneurin Bevan*, 2 vols. (London, New English Library, 1967, 1973).

Foot, P., *Immigration and Race in British Politics* (Harmondsworth, Penguin, 1965).

Foote, G., *The Labour Party's Political Thought* (London, Croom Helm, 1985).

Foster, R. F. *Lord Randolph Churchill* (Oxford, Clarendon Press, 1982).

Francis, H., 'Welsh Miners and the Spanish Civil War', *Journal of Contemporary History* (1970).

Fraser, D., 'The Unionist Debacle of 1911 . . . ', *Journal of Modern History* (1963).

——, *Urban Politics in Victorian England* (Leicester University Press, 1976).

——, *Power and Authority in the Victorian City* (Oxford, Blackwell, 1979).

——, *Evolution of the Welfare State* (London, Macmillan, 1984).

——, (ed.) *The New Poor Law in the Nineteenth Century* (London, Macmillan, 1976).

Freeden, M., *The New Liberalism: An Ideology of Social Reform* (Oxford University Press, 1978).

——, *Liberalism Divided* (Oxford, Clarendon Press, 1986).

Galbraith, J. K., *The Great Crash, 1929* (Harmondsworth, Penguin, 1969).

Gallup Polls, *Britain, 1937–1975* 2 vols (New York, Garland, 1977).

Gamble, A., *Britain in Decline* (London, Macmillan, 1985).

—— and Walkland, S.A., *The British Party System and Economic Planning* (Oxford, Clarendon Press, 1984).

Garside, W. R. and Hatton, T. J., 'Keynesian Policy and British Unemployment in the 1930s', *Economic History Review* (1985).

George, H., *Progress and Poverty* (New York, Appleton, 1880).

Gilbert, B., *British Social Policy, 1914-1939* (London, Batsford, 1969).

Gilbert, B. B., 'David Lloyd George in 1911 and 1914', *Historical Journal* (1985).

Gilbert, M., *Finest Hour: Winston Churchill, 1939–41* (London, Heinemann, 1984).

——, *Winston Churchill, 7: Road to Victory, 1941–1945* (London, Heinemann, 1986).

Glynn, S. and Oxborrow, J., *Interwar Britain – A Social and Economic History* (London, Allen & Unwin, 1976).

Golby, J. M., and; Purdue, W., *The Civilisation of the Crowd* (London, Batsford, 1984).

Gowing, M., 'The Organisation of Manpower during the Second World War', *Journal of Contemporary History* (1976).

Gray, R., *The Aristocracy of Labour in Nineteenth Century Britain* (London, Macmillan, 1981).

——, 'The Deconstructing of the Working Class' *Social History* (1986).

Gray, R. Q., *The Labour Aristocracy in Victorian Edinburgh* (Oxford University ——, 'The Labour Aristocracy', *Bulletin of the Society for the Study of Labour History* (1980).

Green, E. E. H, 'Radical Conservatism: The Genesis of Tariff Reform' *Historical Journal* (1985).

Grigg, J., 'Liberals on Trial', in A. Sked and C.Cook, *Crisis and Controversy* (London, Macmillan, 1976).

———, *Lloyd George: from Peace to War, 1912–26* (London, Methuen, 1985).

Hancock, K. J., 'The Reduction of Unemployment . . . ', *Economic History Review* (1962/3).

Hare, P., *Planning the British Economy* (London, Macmillan, 1985).

Harris, J., *William Beveridge* (Oxford University Press, 1977).

Harrison, B., *Separate Spheres: The Opposition to Women's Suffrage* (London, Croom Helm, 1978).

———, 'Women in a Man's House: The Women MPs, 1919–45', *Historical Journal* (1986).

Harrisson, T., *Living Through the Blitz* (Harmondsworth, Penguin, 1976).

Haseler, S., *The Gaitskellites* (London, Macmillan, 1969).

Hay, J. R., *Origins of the Liberal Social Reforms* (London, Macmillan, 1975).

Hayburn, R., 'The National Unemployed Workers' Movement', *International Review of Social History* (1983).

Hayes, P., *Modern British Foreign Policy: The Twentieth Century* (London, A. and C. Black, 1978).

Hazelhurst, C., 'Asquith as Prime Minister', *English Historical Review* (1970).

———, *Politicians at War, July 1914 to May 1915* (London, Cape, 1971).

———., 'The Baldwinite Conspiracy', *Historical Studies* (1974).

Hennessy, P. and Seldon, A., *Ruling Performance: British Governments from Attlee to Thatcher* (Oxford, Polity Press, 1987).

Hewison, R., *The Heritage Industry* (London, Methuen, 1987).

Heyck, H., 'Home Rule, Radicalism and the Liberal Party', *Journal of British Studies* (1974).

Higgonet, M. R. *et al.*, *Behind the Lines: Gender in the Two World Wars* (New Haven, Yale, 1987).

Hinsley, F. H. (ed.) *British Foreign Policy under Sir Edward Grey* (Cambridge University Press, 1977).

Hinton, J., *The First Shop Steward's Movement* (London, Weidenfeld & Nicolson, 1973).

———, *Labour and Socialism* (Brighton, Harvester, 1983).

Hobsbawm, E. J., *Labouring Men* (London, Weidenfeld & Nicolson, 1964).

———, 'The Labour Aristocracy 25 Years On', *Bulletin of the Society for the Study of Labour History* (1980).

Hollis, P. (ed.) *Women in Public, 1850–1900* (London, Allen & Unwin, 1979).

Holmes, M., *The Labour Government, 1974–9* (London, Macmillan, 1985).

Holton, S. S., *Feminism and Democracy* (Cambridge University Press, 1986).

Horne, A., *Harold Macmillan* (London, Viking, 1989).

Howell, D., *A Lost Left* (Manchester University Press, 1986).

Humphries, J., 'Interwar house building...', *Business History* (1987).

Hunt, E. H., *British Labour History, 1815–1914* (London, Weidenfeld & Nicolson, 1981).

Hurt, J. S., *Elementary Schooling and the Working Classes* (London, Routledge, 1979).

Hutton, W., *The Revolution that Never Was: An Assessment of Keynesian Economics* (London, Longman, 1986).

Hyam, R., *Britain's Imperial Century, 1815–1914* (London, Batsford, 1976).

Jackson, A. A., *Semi-Detached London* (London, Allen & Unwin, 1975).

James, R. Rhodes, *Lord Randolph Churchill* (London, Weidenfeld & Nicolson, 1959).

——, *Churchill A Study in Failure, 1900–1939* (London, Weidenfeld & Nicolson, 1970).

——, *Ambitions and Realities; British Politics, 1964–70* (London, Weidenfeld & Nicolson, 1972).

——, *The British Revolution, 1880–1939*, 2 vols, (London, Hamish Hamilton, 1976, 1977).

Jay, R., *Joseph Chamberlain: A Political Study* (Oxford University Press, 1981).

Jefferys, K., 'British Politics and Social Policy during the Second World War', *Historical Journal* (1987).

——, 'R. A. Butler, the Board of Education and the 1944 Education Act', *History* (1984).

Jeffrey, K., 'The Army and Internal Security', *Bulletin of the Society for the Study of Labour History* (1981).

Jenkins, P., *Mrs Thatcher's Revolution: The Ending of the Socialist Era* (London, Cape, 1987).

Jenkins, R., *Baldwin* (London, Collins, 1987).

John, A., *By the Sweat of their Brow* (London, Croom Helm, 1978).

Johnson, P., *'Saving and Spending': The Working Class Economy* (Oxford University Press, 1985).

Jones, D. K., *The Making of the Education System, 1851–1881* (London, Routledge, 1977).

Judd, D., *Radical Joe: A Life of Joseph Chamberlain* (London, Hamish Hamilton, 1977).

Kavanagh, D., *Crisis, Charisma and the British Political Leadership* (London & Beverly Hills, Sage, 1974).

——, *Thatcherism and British Politics: The End of Consensus?* (Oxford, Clarendon, 1987).

Keating, P., *Into Darkest England* (London, Macmillan, 1976).

Kennedy, P. M., *The Rise of the Anglo-German Antagonism, 1860–1914* (London, Allen & Unwin, 1980).

——, *The Realities Behind Diplomacy* (London, Allen & Unwin, 1982).

Keynes, J. M., *How to Pay for the War* (London, Macmillan, 1940).

Kinnear, M., *The British Voter (Ithaca, Cornell University Press, 1969)*.

——, *The Fall of Lloyd George* (London, Macmillan, 1973).

Kirby, M. W., *The British Coalmining Industry, 1870–1946* (London, Macmillan, 1977).

Kitchen, M., 'Winston Churchill and the Soviet Union during the Second World War', *Historical Journal* (1987).

Koss, S., 'The Destruction of Britain's Last Liberal Government', *Journal of Modern History* (1968).

Koss, S., *The Rise and Fall of the Political Press in Britain* (London, Hamish Hamilton, 1984).

Kunz, D. B., *The Battle for Britain's Gold Standard in 1931* (London, Croom Helm, 1987).

Lamb, R., *The Failure of the Eden Government* (London, Sidgwick and Jackson, 1987).

Lee, A. J., *The Origins of the Popular Press in England* (London, Croom Helm, 1976).

Lewis, J., *Women in England, 1870–1950* (Brighton, Wheatsheaf, 1986).

Liddington, J. 'Women Cotton Workers and the Suffrage Campaign', in S. Buirman, (ed.) *Fit Work for Women* (London, Croom Helm, 1979).

Liddle P. H. (ed.) *Home Fires and Foreign Fields* (London, Brasseys, 1985).

Longmate, N., *The GIs* (London, Hutchinson, 1975).

Lovell, J., *British Trade Unions, 1875-1933* (London, Macmillan, 1979).

Lowe, R., 'Welfare Legislation and the Unions . . . ', *Historical Journal* (1982).

Lubenow, W. C., 'Irish Home Rule and ... the Liberals', *Historical Journal* (1985).

Lunn, K. and Thurlow, R.C, *British Fascism* (London, Croom Helm, 1980).

MacIntyre, S., *Little Moscows: Communism and Working Class Militancy* (London, Croom Helm, 1980).

Mackenzie, J. M. (ed.) *Imperialism and Popular Culture* (Manchester University Press, 1986).

Maclaine, I., *Ministry of Morale* (London, Allen & Unwin, 1979).

Macmillan, H., *Winds of Change, 1914–1939* (London, Macmillan, 1966).

Macnicol, J., *The Movement for Family Allowances* (London, Heinemann, 1980).

Magnus, P., *Gladstone* (London, John Muray, 1954).

Marquand, D., *Ramsay MacDonald* (London, Cape, 1977).

Marsh, D. C., *The Changing Social Structure of England and Wales* (London & New York, Routledge and Kegan Paul, 1965).

Marsh, P., *Lord Salisbury's Domestic Statecraft* (Brighton, Harvester, 1978).

Marwick, A., *The Deluge* (Harmondsworth, Penguin, 1965).

——, *War and Social Change in the Twentieth Century* (London, Macmillan, 1974).

——, 'Middle Opinion in the 1930s', *English Historical Review* (1964).

——, 'The Labour Party and the Welfare State', *American Historical Review* (1967).

——, 'The Impact of the Great War on British Society', *Journal of Contemporary History* (1968).

——, *Britain in the Century of Total War* (Harmondsworth, Penguin, 1968).

——, *Women at War* (London, Fontana, 1975).

——, *British Society Since 1945* (Harmondsworth, Penguin, 1982).

Mass Observation, *War Begins at Home* (Harmondsworth, Penguin, 1940).

——, *The Journey Home* (London, Publishing Guild, 1945).

——, *War Factory* (London, Century Hutchinson, 1987).

Matthews, K. G. P., 'Was Sterling Overvalued in 1925?', *Economic History Review* (1986).

Matthews, R. C. O. and Feinstein, C. H., *British Economic Growth, 1856–1973* (Oxford University Press, 1983).

McCloskey, D., 'Did Victorian Britain Fail?', *Economic History Review* (1970).

McCulloch, G., 'Labour, the Left and the . . . Election of 1945', *Journal of British Studies* (1985).

McKibbin, R., *The Evolution of the Labour Party, 1910–1924* (Oxford University Press, 1974).

——, 'Working Class Gambling in Britain, 1880–1939', *Past & Present* (1979).

——, 'Why Was There No Marxism in Great Britain?', *English Historical Review* (1984).

McLaren, A., *Birth Control in Nineteenth Century England* (London, Croom Helm, 1978).

Meacham, S., *A Life Apart: The English Working Class, 1880–1914* (London, Thames & Hudson, 1977).

Meller, H. E., *Leisure and the Changing City, 1870–1914* (London, Routledge, 1976).

Middlemas, K., and Barnes, J., *Baldwin – A Biography* (London, Weidenfeld & Nicolson, 1969).

Middleton, L., *Women in the Labour Movement* (London, Croom Helm, 1978).

Middleton, R., *Towards the Managed Economy: Keynes and the Treasury* (London, Methuen, 1985).

Miles, P. and Smith, M.S., *Cinema, Literature & Society: Elite & Mass Culture* (London, Croom Helm, 1987).

Milward, A. S., *The Economic Effects of the World Wars on Britain* (London, Macmillan, 1970).

Mitchison, R., *British Population Change Since 1860* (London, Macmillan, 1977).

Mommsen, W. J. (ed.) *The Emergence of the Welfare State in Britain and Germany* (London, Croom Helm, 1981).

Moore, D. C., *The Politics of Deference* (Brighton, Harvester, 1976).

Moore, R., *The Emergence of the Labour Party* (London, Hodder & Stoughton, 1978).

Morgan, A., *J. Ramsay MacDonald* (Manchester University Press, 1987).

Morgan, D., *Suffragists and Liberals* (Oxford University Press, 1975).

Morgan, K.O., 'Lloyd George's Premiership', *Journal of Modern History* (1964).

——, *Keir Hardie* (Oxford University Press, 1975).

——, *Consensus and Disunity: The Lloyd George Government* (Oxford University Press, 1979).

——, *Labour in Power* (Oxford University Press, 1984).

Morisson, H., *The State and Industry* (London, Fabian Society, 1944).

Mowat, C.L., 'Baldwin Restored', *Journal of Modern History* (1955).

——, *Britain Between the Wars* (London, Methuen, 1968).

Moynihan, M. (ed.) *Letters from Armageddon* (Newton Abbot, David & Charles, 1973).

Murphy, R., 'Faction and the Home Rule Crisis, 1912–14', *History* (1986).

Murray, B.K., 'Politics of the People's Budget', *Historical Journal* (1973).

——, *The People's Budget, 1909–10* (Oxford University Press, 1980).

Musgrave, P.W., *Society and Education in England since 1800* (London, Methuen, 1968).

O'Brien, P.K., 'Britain's Economy between the Wars', *Past and Present* (1987).

O'Brien, T., *Civil Defence* (London, HMSO, 1950).

O'Day, A., *The Edwardian Age: Conflict and Stability, 1900–19* (London, Macmillan, 1979).

Oral History, 1977, Special Issue on Women.

Orwell, G., *Collected Essays, Journalism and Letters*, 4 vols (Harmondsworth, Penguin, 1968).

Ovendale, R. (ed.) *The Foreign Policy of the Labour Governments, 1945–51* (Leicester University Press, 1984).

Pankhurst, S., *The Suffragette Movement* (London, Virago reprint, 1977).

Payne, P.L., 'Emergence of the Large-Scale Company in Britain', *Economic History Review* (1967).

Peden, G.C., 'The Economic Background of Appeasement', *History* (1984).

——, *Keynes, the Treasury and British Economic Policy* (London, Macmillan, 1987).

Pelling, H., *Origins of the Labour Party* (Oxford University Press, 1965).

——, 'State Intervention and Social Legislation before 1914', *Historical Journal* (1967).

——, *Popular Politics and Society in Late Victorian Britain* (London, Macmillan, 1968).

——, *History of the British Communist Party* (Harmondsworth, Penguin, 1975).

——, *History of British Trade Unionism* (Harmondsworth, Penguin, 1981).

——, 'The Politics of the Osborne Judgement', *Historical Journal* (1982).

——, *The Labour Governments, 1945–51* (London, Macmillan, 1984).

Perkin, H., *Origins of Modern English Society* (London, Routledge, 1969).

Phillips, G., 'The Triple Alliance in 1914', *Economic History Review* (1971).

Phillips, G. D., *The Diehards: Aristocratic Society and Politics* (London, Harvard University Press, 1979).

Pilgrim Trust, *Men Without Work* (Cambridge University Press, 1938).

Pimlott, B., *Labour and the Left in the 1930s* (Cambridge University Press, 1977).

Pollard, S. *The Gold Standard and Employment Policies Between the Wars* (London, Methuen, 1970).

——, *The Wasting of the British Economy* (London, Croom Helm, 1984).

Pope, R. and Boyle, B., *British Economic Performance, 1880–1980* (London, Croom Helm, 1984).

Powell, D., 'The Liberal Ministries and Labour, 1892–5', *History* (1983).

——, 'The New Liberalism and the Rise of Labour', *Historical Journal* (1986).

Price, R., *An Imperial War and the British Working Class* (London, Routledge, 1972).

Pugh, M., *Electoral Reform in Peace and War, 1906–18* (London, Routledge, 1978).

——, *The Tories and the People* (Oxford, Blackwell, 1985).

——, *The Making of Modern British Politics, 1867–1939* (Oxford, Blackwell, 1982).

Pugh, P., *100 Years of Fabian Socialism* (London, Methuen, 1984).

Quinault, R., 'John Bright and Joseph Chamberlain', *Historical Journal* (1985).

Ramsden J., *The Conservative Party: The Age of Balfour and Baldwin* (London, Longman, 1978).

Rempel, R. A., *Unionists Divided* (Newton Abbot, David & Charles, 1972).

Rendall, J., *Equal or Different: Women's Politics 1880–1914* (Oxford, Blackwell, 1987).

Richards, J. and Sheridan, D., *Mass Observation at the Movies* (London, Routledge, 1987).

Robbins, K., *The Eclipse of a Great Power: Modern Britain* (London, Longman, 1983).

Robinson, R. and Gallagher, J., *Africa and the Victorians* (London, Macmillan, 1981).

Rock, W. R., *British Appeasement in the Thirties* (London, Edward Arnold, 1972).

Rollings, N., 'British Budgetary Policy, 1945–1954', *Economic History Review* (1988).

Rose, M. E., *The Relief of Poverty, 1832–1914* (London, Macmillan, 1972).

Rosen, A., *Rise Up, Women!* (London, Routledge, 1974).

Rover, C., *Women's Suffrage and Party Politics* (London, Routledge, 1967).

Rowland, P., *The Last Liberal Governments* (London, Barrie & Richards, 1968).

——, *Lloyd George* (London, Barrie & Jenkins, 1975).

Rowntree, S. B., *Progress and Poverty* (London, Longman, 1941).

——, *Poverty: A Study in Town Life* (London, Longman, 1901).

——, *Poverty and the Welfare State* (London, Longman, 1951).

Rubin, G., *The Munitions Act, State Regulations and the Unions* (Oxford, Clarendon Press, 1987).

Rubinstein, W.D., *Before the Suffragettes* (Brighton, Harvester, 1986).

Russell, A., *Liberal Landslide* (Newton Abbot, David & Charles, 1973).

Saul, S. B., *The Myth of the Great Depression* (London, Macmillan, 1978).

Scally, R.J., *Origins of the Lloyd George Coalition* (Princeton University Press, 1975).

Schmidt, G., *The Politics and Economics of Appeasement* (Leamington Spa, Berg, 1986).

Schneer, J., 'Hopes Deferred or Shattered . . .', *Journal of Modern History* (1984).

Self, R. C., *Tories and Tariffs* (London, Garland, 1986).

Shannon, R., *Crisis of Imperialism* (London, Paladin, 1974).

Shay, R. P., *British Rearmament in the Thirties* (Princeton University Press, 1977).

Sked, A., *Britain's Decline: Problems and Perspectives* (Oxford, Blackwell, 1986).

—— and Cook, C., *Postwar Britain: A Political History* (Harmondsworth, Pelican, 1979).

Skidelsky, R., *Politicians and the Slump* (London, Macmillan, 1967).

Smellie, K. B., *A History of Local Government* (London, Allen & Unwin, 1957,

Smith, D., *Conflict and Compromise: Class Formation in English Society* (London, Routledge, 1983).

Smith, H., 'Sex vs. Class: British Feminists and the Labour Movement', *The Historian* (1984/5).

Smith, H. L., *War and Social Change: British Society in the Second World War* (Manchester University Press, 1986).

Smith, M. S., 'Rearmament and Deterrence in Britain . . .', *Journal of Strategic Studies* (1979).

——, *British Air Strategy between the Wars* (Oxford, Clarendon Press, 1984).

Soffer, 'The Revolution in English Social Thought . . .', *American Historical Review* (1970).

Southgate, D., *The Conservative Leadership* (London, Macmillan, 1974).

Stannage, T., *Baldwin Thwarts the Opposition: The Election of 1935* (London, Croom Helm, 1980).

Stewart, M., *Keynes and After* (Harmondsworth, Penguin, 1983).

Storch, R. D. (ed.) *Popular Culture and Custom in Nineteenth Century England* (London, Croom Helm, 1982).

Summerfield, P., *Women Workers in the Second World War* (London, Croom Helm, 1984).

Supple, B., *History of the British Coal Industry*, vol. 1, *1914–46* (Oxford, Clarendon Press, 1987).

Swenarton, M., *Homes Fit for Heroes* (London, Heinemann, 1981).

Sykes, A., *Tariff Reform in British Politics* (London, Oxford University Press, 1979).

——, 'The Radical Right and the Crisis of Conservatism', *Historical Journal* (1983).

Taylor, A.J.P., *English History, 1914–1945* (Oxford University Press, 1965).

——, *Origins of the Second World War* (Harmondsworth, Penguin, 1973).

Taylor, R., *Salisbury* (London, Allen Lane, 1975).

Terrins, D. and Whitehead, D., *100 Years of Fabianism* (London, Fabian Society, 1984).

Thane, P., *The Origins of British Social Policy* (London, Croom Helm, 1978).

——, 'The Working Class and State Welfare in Britain', *Historical Journal* (1984) pp. 877–90.

Thompson, P., 'Liberals, Radicals and Labour in London', *Past and Present* (1964).

——, *Socialists, Liberals and Labour: The Struggle for London* (London, Weidenfeld & Nicolson, 1967).

——, *The Edwardians* (London, Paladin, 1975).

Thompson, R., *Generalissimo Churchill* (London, Hodder & Stoughton, 1973).

Thornton, A.P., *The Imperial Idea and Its Enemies* (London, Macmillan, 1966).

Thorpe, A., 'Arthur Henderson and the British Political Crisis of 1931', *Historical Journal* (1988).

Tickner, L., *The Spectacle of Women: Imagery of the Suffrage Campaign* (London, Chatto & Windus, 1987).

Titmuss, R. M., *Essays on the Welfare State* (London, Allen & Unwin, 1969).

——, *Problems of Social Policy* (London, HMSO, 1950).

Turner, J., *Lloyd George's Secretariat* (Cambridge University Press, 1980).

Vellacott, J., 'Feminist Consciousness and the First World War', *History Workshop* (1987).

Waites, B., 'Effects of the Great War on Class and Status in Britain', *Journal of Contemporary History* (1976).

——, *A Class Society at War: England, 1914–18* (Leamington Spa, Berg, 1987).

Walder, D., *The Chanak Crisis* (London, Hutchinson, 1969).

Walkland, S. A. (ed.) *The House of Commons in the Twentieth Century* (Cambridge University Press, 1979).

Waller, J and V.-R., *Women in Wartime: Women's Magazines, 1939–45* (London, Macdonald, 1987).

Wardle, D., *English Popular Education, 1780–1970* (Cambridge University Press, 1970).

Watt, D. C., *Succeeding John Bull: America in Britain's Place* (Cambridge University Press, 1984).

Webb, R. K., *Modern England* (London, Allen & Unwin, 1969).

Webber, G. C., *The Ideology of the British Right, 1918–1939* (London, Croom Helm, 1986).

Webster, C., 'Health, Welfare and Unemployment during the Depression', *Past & Present* (1985).

Weeks, J., *Coming Out: Homosexual Politics in Britain* (London, Quartet, 1979).

——, *Sex, Politics and Society (London, Longman, 1981)*.

Weiler, P., 'British Labour and the Cold War', *Journal of British Studies* (1987).

Weston, C. C., 'Salisbury and the Lords', *Historical Journal* (1982).

White, S., *Britain and the Bolshevik Revolution* (London, Macmillan, 1979).

Wilkinson, E., *The Town that was Murdered* (London, Left Book Club, 1935).

Williams, P., *Hugh Gaitskell: A Political Biography* (London, Johnathan Cape, 1979).

Williamson, P., 'Baldwin . . . and the 1929 General Election', *Historical Journal* (1982).

Wilson, T., 'The Liberals and the Coupon Election of 1918', *Journal of Modern History* (1964).

——, *The Downfall of the Liberal Party* (London, Collins, 1966).

——, 'Britain's "Moral Commitment" to France in 1914', *History* (1979).

——, *The Myriad Faces of War: Britain and the Great War* (Oxford, Polity Press, 1986).

Winter, J. M., *Socialism and the Challenge of War* (London, Routledge, 1974).

——, *The Great War and the British People* (London, Macmillan, 1987).

Wohl, A. S., *The Eternal Slum* (London, Edward Arnold, 1977).

Wright, A., 'A Century of Fabianism, 1884–1984', *Historical Journal* (1984).

—— (ed.) *British Socialism and Socialist Thought* (London, Longman, 1983).

Wright, A. W., *G. D. H. Cole and Socialist Democracy* (Oxford University Press, 1979).

Wrigley, C., *David Lloyd George and the Labour Movement* (Brighton, Harvester, 1977).

——, *Lloyd George and the Challenge of Labour* (Brighton, Harvester, 1986).

—— (ed.) *History of British Industrial Relations*, vol. 2 (Brighton, Harvester, 1986).

Young, J. W., 'Churchill's "No" to Europe', *Historical Journal* (1985).

Youngson, A. J., *Britain's Economic Growth, 1920–1966* (London, Allen & Unwin, 1968).

INDEX

250 INDEX